CRITICAL RACE CONSCIOUSNESS

CRITICAL RACE CONSCIOUSNESS
RECONSIDERING AMERICAN IDEOLOGIES OF RACIAL JUSTICE

GARY PELLER

Paradigm Publishers
Boulder • London

Copyright © 2012 by Paradigm Publishers

Published in the United States by Paradigm Publishers, 2845 Wilderness Place, Boulder, Colorado 80301 USA.

Paradigm Publishers is the trade name of Birkenkamp & Company, LLC, Dean Birkenkamp, President and Publisher.

Library of Congress Cataloging-in-Publication Data

Peller, Gary.
  Critical race consciousness : reconsidering American ideologies of racial justice / Gary Peller.
      p. cm.
  Includes bibliographical references and index.
  ISBN 978-1-59451-905-5 (pbk. : alk. paper)
    1. United States—Race relations—History—20th century. 2. Civil rights movements—United States—History—20th century. 3. Black nationalism—United States—History—20th century. 4. Multiculturalism—United States—History—20th century. I. Title.
  E185.61.P455 2011
  305.800973—dc22

                                                                    2011008504

Printed and bound in the United States of America on acid-free paper that meets the standards of the American National Standard for Permanence of Paper for Printed Library Materials.

Designed and Typeset by Straight Creek Bookmakers.

16 15 14 13 12   5 4 3 2 1

For my mother

CONTENTS

ACKNOWLEDGMENTS

I am grateful to many friends and allies who provided criticism, feedback, and encouragement for this project.

In particular, many of the ideas contained in this book were developed in the midst of my intellectual and political engagement with Duncan Kennedy, Kimberlé Crenshaw, and Peter Gabel over the course of two decades. Daniel Hornal and Christopher Clark provided excellent research assistance, and Betsy Kuhn gave her time generously to help edit and prepare the manuscript.

Part of Chapters 1 through 4 originally appeared in *Duke Law Journal*. Parts of Chapter 6 originally appeared in *Race, Law, and Culture: Reflections on* Brown v. Board of Education (Oxford Univ. Press 1997). Part of Chapter 7 originally appeared in *Tikkun* magazine.

Gary Peller
March 3, 2011
Washington D.C.

INTRODUCTION

> The entire civil rights struggle needs a new interpretation, a broader
> interpretation. We need to look at this civil rights thing from another
> angle—from the inside as well as from the outside. To those of us whose
> philosophy is Black nationalism, the only way you can get involved in the
> civil rights struggle is to give it a new interpretation. The old interpreta-
> tion excluded us. It kept us out.[1]
>
> Malcolm X, 1963

This book presents a critical analysis of dominant American ideologies about
racial justice over the past 50 years or so.[2]

Despite the racial progress reflected in the 2008 election of Barack Obama
as president of the United States, the Black community in America is in crisis
on a variety of fronts: economic, educational, cultural, and spiritual.[3] At the
very moment that an African American man leads the American government,
the Black community itself lacks leadership, strategies, and a compelling vision
for the future. The Black middle class, integrated into mainstream workplaces,
schools, and suburbs, and often insecure about its own racial identity, has mostly
abandoned its traditional role as a bridge between poor and working-class Blacks
and the white (now somewhat integrated) mainstream.[4] Progressive whites, once
allies of Black progress, are wary of intervening and have for several decades
adopted an implicit posture of "benign neglect."[5] My goal here is to trace the
particularly *ideological* roots of this contemporary situation.

In contrast to the celebratory manner in which the conventional narratives of
America's racial progress treat the Supreme Court's decision in *Brown v. Board*

of Education and the subsequent development of civil rights law in the 1960s, I offer a critical analysis of the role "integrationist" ideology has played in *limiting* race reform over the last several decades.

The conventional treatment of the history of American racial "enlightenment" presents the struggle for civil rights and against white supremacy as the defining racial conflict of the 1960s. For this narrative, the election of Barack Obama represents the symbolic completion of the struggle against the exclusion of Blacks from positions of power and prestige (although most would add the qualification, "There is still much work to be done.").

However, the important struggles over race in the 1960s and 1970s were not solely between the proponents of civil rights and those of white supremacy. The meanings of racial subordination and Black liberation (of "civil rights") were themselves contested. Critical elements of the structure of contemporary racial discourse were set in the conflict *within* the so-called civil rights community over the meaning of racial justice.

My thesis is that today's conventional wisdom about race was forged in the ideological confrontation between liberal integrationism and Black nationalism during the 1960s and 1970s, and in the resulting marginalization of Black nationalists like Malcolm X and the Black Panthers, accomplished by identifying their race consciousness with that of white supremacists. Instead of a nationalist frame, race has been understood through a set of beliefs—what I call "integrationism"—that locates racial oppression in the social structure of prejudice and stereotype based on skin color and that identifies progress with the transcendence of a racial consciousness about the world.

As I describe it, Black nationalism—at least as articulated in the late 1960s—was a sophisticated theoretical alternative to this liberal view of race and not a Black version of white supremacy ideology, as integrationists insist. In its articulations by Malcolm X, Eldridge Cleaver, the Black Panthers, Harold Cruse, and other leftist nationalists, Black nationalism embodied a deep, historicist critique of the universalist assumptions of the "civil rights" conception of racial progress.

However, Malcolm X did identify the basic racial compromise that the incorporation of "the civil rights struggle" into mainstream American culture would eventually embody: Along with the suppression of white racism that was the widely celebrated aim of civil rights reform, the dominant conception of racial justice was framed to require that Black nationalism be equated with white supremacy and that race consciousness on the part of either whites or Blacks be marginalized as beyond the good sense of "enlightened" American culture.

To understand the dynamics that produced this particular cultural bargain, it is important to comprehend the different meaning that race consciousness historically represented for whites and Blacks in America. Among whites, the conflict over race has traditionally been structured around an opposition between white supremacists supporting segregation and white liberals and progressives committed to integration and civil rights reform. To the latter, looking through the prism of integrationist ideology, a nationalist conception of racial identity distinguished backward, ignorant whites from cosmopolitan, educated whites. Whites who took race as central to their self-identity thereby expressed a commitment to racial supremacy; whites who opposed racism understood that opposition to require the transcendence of racial identity in favor of integration and colorblindness. Progressive whites, largely ignorant of the nationalist tradition in African American thought and history, largely sided with white liberals and the Black middle class in rejecting nationalist approaches to race relations. Projecting themselves as the enlightened *avant-garde* of the white community, liberals and progressives reflexively associated race nationalism with the repressive history of white supremacy and failed to develop either a consciousness or political practice that comprehended racial identity and power as centrally formative factors in American social relations.[6]

In contrast, within at least a faction of the African American community, Black nationalists (on both the right and left) have historically opposed an integrationist understanding of racial progress. Instead, they have asserted a positive and liberating role for race consciousness, as a source of community, culture, and solidarity, and as something to build upon, rather than transcend. They developed a thorough critique of integrationism as inevitably, or at least historically, linked to assimilation. Within the white community, the issue of race consciousness symbolically divided whites committed to racial justice from whites committed to racial domination. Within the Black community, however, the issue of race consciousness historically divided Blacks committed to norms of racial solidarity from two groups: from Black assimilationists who found white culture more attractive, and from Blacks who found integration preferable if the price of Black racial identity was the continuation of white racial identity in its traditional, repressive form.

The conflict between nationalists and integrationists in the late 1960s and early 1970s represented a critical juncture in American race relations. By then, Black nationalism arguably had overtaken integrationism as the dominant ideology of racial liberation among African Americans, while virtually all liberal and progressive whites had embraced a vision of integration as the ultimate definition of racial justice. Although there has been some refinement since this historical moment—particularly the development of progressive and, to a more limited extent, national commitments to a limited form of "multiculturalism"—the basic boundaries of contemporary mainstream thinking about race were set in the early 1970s, when a loose coalition of "moderate" African Americans joined liberal and progressive whites to resist and equate Black nationalists and white supremacists. In 1964, when Malcolm X asserted that this conventional interpretation of civil rights excluded Black nationalists, he could not have foreseen that nationalist activism would revitalize and transform the struggle against racial oppression in the late 1960s and early 1970s, only to be relegated once more to the cultural margins and urban street corners by the 1980s.

I argue that the ideology of integrationism that prevailed in the conflict of the late 1960s and early 1970s was ultimately conservative and apologetic. The dominance of this integrationist ideology helped establish the particular and narrow manner in which racial power would be understood, and thereby helped to legitimate and perpetuate the existing racial distribution of power and prestige, even as it recommended marginal reform. Put bluntly, it provided the ideological basis for leaving in place a set of social and institutional practices within which African Americans would continue to lose out to whites.

It is true that ending formal policies of racial exclusion and expanding and empowering the Black middle class were important achievements of the civil rights movement. However, the exercise of American racial power was not limited to the exclusion of Blacks from mainstream institutions. The construction of a discourse, of an entire set of cultural practices, within which the open and explicit subordination of African Americans could seem normal was instead broadly inscribed into the everyday institutional culture of schools, offices, legislatures, streets, and neighborhoods, and possibly into the very meaning of what constitutes the rational and the civilized. In retrospect, and without ignoring the real gains made in ending overt white supremacist practices, it is remarkable how little change liberal reformists demanded before they heralded the end of American apartheid.

The civil rights–era consensus among the "enlightened" over how to effect racial progress has ended. In our times, conservatives utilize the "progressive" rhetoric of tolerance, colorblindness, and equal opportunity that once characterized transformative discourse to mark the limits of reform or even reverse it.[7] However, it would be a mistake to think that today's conservative discourse is simply a bad-faith distortion of a progressive worldview. Serious limits to the integrationist vision existed from the beginning. The fact that support for substantively reformist programs such as affirmative action has typically been articulated in the defensive rhetoric of "remedy" or "diversity"—posed as counterbalancing factors to "lack of merit"—is only one manifestation of deeper ways that civil rights reformism often worked to legitimate the very social practices that originally were to be reformed.

To comprehend the historical frame within which contemporary race-reform discourse operates, it is necessary to review the dynamics that led to the installation of integrationism as the dominant and enlightened way to understand race, and to the rejection of Black nationalism as an extremist and backward doctrine. This is a complex story. In the first part of this book, I set out simply to describe this cultural development in broad outline form: Chapter 1 summarizes the central analytics and assumptions of the integrationist worldview in roughly the form that it was understood in the 1960s and 1970s. Chapter 2 contrasts integrationism with Black nationalism as Malcolm X and others articulated it in the 1960s.

My purpose in these first two chapters is to depict integrationism and nationalism as starkly contrasting discourses of racial justice. I do this in part to identify integrationism as a particular racial ideology—depending for its persuasiveness on certain background images of social life that are controversial, rather than self-evident—and in part to present Black nationalism in a systematic, theoretical frame to counter the deep-seated image in conventional discourse that Black nationalism merely embodies an emotional, angry reaction to oppression, rather than an alternative, coherent, and reasoned analysis of the meaning of racial domination.

In Chapter 3, I discuss the different ways that integrationism and nationalism can manifest themselves, suggesting that the two worldviews do not necessarily need to take the pure and bipolar forms that I describe. Integrationism can be deeply collectivist and critical of existing social practices, as the Martin Luther King, Jr.–led civil rights movement demonstrated. Further, as the Nation of Islam has dramatically demonstrated throughout its history, Black nationalism can be deeply conservative and authoritarian in how it identifies and polices the boundaries of Black authenticity.

Nevertheless, I argue in Chapter 4 that the contemporary image of racial justice in terms of transcending race consciousness was embraced in part to resolve the particular "threat" that Black nationalism represented in the late 1960s and early 1970s. In the background of today's dominant discourse about race, there are the traces of profound cultural anxiety rooted in the broad-ranging critique that militant nationalists lodged against the assumptions of everyday life in American institutions.

In Chapter 5, I turn to the more localized struggle over the meaning of racial justice in American constitutional law and consider how a conservative, integrationist approach to race frames American race discrimination doctrine. I trace the development through an analysis of the racial and legal mindset of *Brown* and its effect on the ways that the constitutional issues of racial justice influenced, and were influenced by, the perceived crisis of legitimacy that American law faced more generally.

In Chapter 6, I analyze the emergence of multiculturalism as the dominant racial discourse of progressive whites and middle-class Blacks in the 1980s and 1990s. In particular, I criticize the manner in which the multicultural stance embraced by most liberals and progressives has helped to immobilize whites from virtually any engagement with the Black community, resulting in the kind of "benign neglect" I referred to earlier. I connect this phenomenon to a *laissez-faire* conception of multiculturalism that mistakenly treats cultural groups as independent, pre-existing objects of perception, rather than hybrid, multiple, and dialectically and historically constituted *effects* of power. This essentializing is necessary to project the clear, clean borders that principled multiculturalists are committed to respecting.

I conclude in Chapter 7 by arguing that the kind of "identity politics" implicit in concern for the well-being of the Black community need not take the essentializing form of the "vulgar Black nationalism"[8] of the Nation of Islam or the quixotic quest for purity that is characteristic of Afro-centric and multicultural projects. I develop this point through a response to self-described "postmodern" critics of identity frames like those asserted by Black nationalists. I argue these critics confuse the fact that categories of social identity such as "the Black community" have no "essence" with the conclusion that they are therefore not a meaningful way to comprehend our social field. In my presentation, a postmodern nationalism is opposed to *fundamentalist* claims that identity categories like "the Black community" have an essential, ahistorical, necessary core, but that is not to deny the very social existence of such categories. In my view, a progressive understanding of the terms of community solidarity and recognition—of "identity"—should see identity "borders" as contested, inessential, multiple, porous, and effects of social power ... but no less real for all that.

CHAPTER 1
THE STRUCTURE OF INTEGRATIONIST IDEOLOGY

A segregated school system isn't necessarily the same situation that exists in an all-white neighborhood. A school system in an all-white neighborhood is not a segregated school system. The only time it's segregated is when it is in a community other than white, but at the same time is controlled by the whites. So my understanding of a segregated school system, or a segregated community, or a segregated school, is a school that's controlled by people other than those that go there.... On the other hand, if we can get an all-Black school, that we can control, staff it ourselves with the type of teachers that have our good at heart, with the type of books that have in them many of the missing ingredients that have produced this inferiority complex in our people, then we don't feel that an all-Black school is necessarily a segregated school. It's only segregated when it's controlled by someone from outside. I hope I'm making my point. I just can't see where if white people can go to a white classroom and there are no Negroes present and it doesn't affect the academic diet they're receiving, then I don't see where an all-Black classroom can be affected by the absence of white children.... So, what the integrationists, in my opinion, are saying, when they say that whites and Blacks must go to school together, is that the whites are so much superior that just their presence in a Black classroom balances it out. I can't go along with that.[1]

Malcolm X, 1963

Today, the story of the civil rights struggle commonly is told in linear fashion, as if progress in race relations followed a teleological evolution—from an ignorant time, when racial status was taken to signify real and meaningful differences between people, to the present, enlightened time, when race is properly understood in mainstream culture not to make a difference except as a vestige of unfortunate historical oppression or in terms of a vague and largely privatized "cultural heritage."

This sense of linear evolution has lent an aura of inevitability to the story, as if the progression from the racial caste system of American slavery to the widespread acceptance of integration and the transcendence of race consciousness as the unquestioned goals of social progress were historically determined. But the process has been neither linear nor inevitable. The institution of racial integration as a social norm results from a cultural struggle, played out in various theaters of social power, over the meaning of racial domination and racial justice in America. The sense of integrationism as the inevitable means to achieve racial enlightenment reflects both the institutionalization of a particular understanding of what racism means and the marginalization of not only white supremacists, but also the opposing analysis represented in the 1960s by Malcolm X and other Black nationalists.

It is no longer controversial within mainstream American legal culture that the goal of racial justice consists of something called "integration." The disagreements today revolve around how widely to enforce integrationist norms. In legal and public-policy circles, conservatives and liberals distinguish themselves according to their positions on affirmative action[2] or whether intent must exist for a determination of discrimination.[3] These are important issues, and often the choice between a narrow and wide interpretation of the integrationist vision makes a real, even material, difference. But the constant and repetitive struggle over the proper way to implement integrationist norms suppresses from consideration the fact that disagreements occur only within the confines of a shared set of beliefs that comprehend racism as a form of "discrimination."

I want to discuss here how integrationism came to officially define racial enlightenment less than a decade after racial integration was part of a wider program of broad demands for radical reform of American society. I argue that integrationism achieved mainstream, institutionalized status in part because it was domesticated. Rather than constituting a broad-ranging indictment of the reigning social structure, as it once did, the goal of civil rights was itself "integrated" into the dominant cultural rhetoric. Seen through the universalizing lenses of the liberal American ideology of progress and enlightenment, racial integration appears as part of a general societal discourse that comprehends legitimacy in terms of policing borders between rationality and objectivity on one hand and prejudice and bias on the other. The American mainstream successfully contained the potentially radical struggle of racial liberation within the frame of "civil rights" and thereby rendered it conventional and conservative.

First, I describe the analytic components of integrationism as it has been understood in mainstream American culture. Second, I relate the integrationist categories of prejudice, discrimination, and segregation to background images of rationality and universality in liberal and enlightenment thought. Then, I suggest that this way of thinking about race can serve not only to criticize, but also to legitimize various social practices. This analysis concludes with a discussion of how the integrationist reform of public schools reflects at a practical, institutional level the features I describe at an ideological one.

The point of discussing integrationism in this way is to show that the currently dominant vision of racial justice is not inevitable or self-evident, but rather is situated within the confines of a particular set of social, cultural, and philosophical assumptions about the world. Its dominance presupposes a set of political and social choices that could have been, and can be, made differently. After describing integrationism, I contrast it with the opposing Black nationalist analysis of race.

The Analytic Components of Integrationism

The goal of racial integration has taken many forms and has been supported by various worldviews. At one time, the idea of racial integration represented a powerful, spiritually rooted social resistance movement that threatened to destabilize the status quo of American institutional life in profound ways. Under the banner of integrationism, hundreds of thousands of people mobilized to challenge political, economic, and cultural power relations in cities and towns across the country, employing tactics that included mass protest, economic boycotts, civil disobedience, sit-ins, and strikes.[4] Therefore, there is nothing intrinsic to the concept of racial integration that demands that it be understood in the way I am about to describe it. What I want to capture here is the general cultural sense that became dominant in the late 1960s and 1970s of what racism consists of and how to overcome it.

From this perspective, integrationism should be understood to comprise a set of attitudes and beliefs for perceiving the meaning of racist domination and for identifying the goals of racial justice. The concepts of prejudice, discrimination, and segregation are the key structural elements of this ideology. Each idea embodies a different manifestation of what is seen as the central aspect of racism: the distortion of reason through the prism of myth and ignorance.

In the integrationist perspective, racism is rooted in consciousness, in the cognitive process that attributes social significance to the arbitrary trait of skin color. The mental side of racism is accordingly represented as either "prejudice," the prejudging of a person according to mythological stereotypes, or "bias," the process of being influenced by subjective factors. The key image here is irrationalism. The problem with prejudice is that it obscures the work of reason by clouding perception with beliefs rooted in superstition.[5] The paradigmatic manifestation is the white supremacist myth structure that asserts natural, biological differences between Blacks and whites—the familiar identification of whites with intelligence, industriousness, and piousness, and the corresponding association of Blacks with dullness, laziness, and lustfulness.[6] The opposite of the ignorance that appears as racism is knowledge, truth gleaned from actual interracial experience, rather than mythologies of stereotype.

In the integrationist ideology, racism achieves social form when the distortion of prejudice in consciousness subsequently translates into practice. Here, racism manifests itself in the practice of "discrimination," in the disparate treatment of whites and Blacks that the irrational attribution of difference is supposed to justify. After slavery, the paradigmatic practice of racism in its systematic, social form was the Jim Crow system of *de jure* (legally imposed) segregation, which institutionalized racial apartheid on the basis of an ideology of white supremacy.[7] And just as "prejudice" is implicitly contrasted with knowledge, discrimination is contrasted with neutrality—the social practice of equal treatment.

The solution to segregation, then, is integration, understood as a social vision opposed to racism, in each realm in which racism manifests itself. Within popular consciousness, integration means overcoming prejudice based on skin color. Therefore, reflecting one dimension of integrationist ideology, "enlightened" liberals began to understand themselves as possible racists to the extent that they believed in irrational images of people based on skin-color stereotypes. The ideal was to transcend stereotypes in favor of treating people as individuals, free from racial-group identification.[8]

At the level of practice, the integrationist cure for discrimination is equal treatment according to neutral norms. At the institutional level, integrationism obviously means an end to the social system of racial segregation. In sum, the cure for racism would be equal treatment on an individual level and integration on an institutional level. Integrationists believed the two would go hand in hand. Once neutrality replaced discrimination, equal opportunity would lead to integrated institutions.[9] Experience in integrated institutions would in turn replace the ignorance of racism with the knowledge that actual contact provides. This deep link between racism and ignorance on one hand and integration and knowledge on the other helps explain the initial focus of integrationists on public education: children who attend integrated schools would learn the truth about each other's unique individuality before they came to believe stereotypes rooted in ignorance. By attending the same schools, children would in turn have equal opportunity at the various roles in American social life.[10]

The integrationists' diagnosis of the distortions of the white supremacy ideology focuses on the failure of white supremacists to recognize the universal characteristics shared by whites and Blacks. According to the integrationists, white racists perceive the world through a false structure of "same" and "other" that utilizes a concept of Blacks as "other" and denies that the attributes that characterize the white racists exist in the "others." Thus, the rationality and piousness that supposedly characterize whites are, within racist ideology, denied to Blacks. The integrationist proposes to correct this situation by demonstrating an even distribution of these characteristics across race lines; Blacks can be rational and pious, and whites can be emotional and lustful. In other words, according to integrationist ideology, racists make the mistake of "essentializing" racial categories and believing that there is some necessary, intrinsic relationship between race and particular social characteristics. Integrationists are committed to the view that race makes no real difference between people, except as unfortunate historical vestiges of irrational discrimination.[11] In an extreme form of the integrationist picture, the hope is that when contact occurs between different groups in society, not only race, but *all* "ethnic identity will become a thing of the past."[12]

Race, Universal Reason, and Liberal Progress

Of course, this is a highly abstracted model of what I mean by the "ideology of integrationism." I assume these general ideas about race are so familiar that simply evoking them calls to mind the fuller meaning of integrationism in mainstream American culture. But at the same time, it is important to grasp the integrationist worldview at this level of generality. Integrationists comprehend racism at a high level of abstraction in part because they wish to transcend the bias of particularity that they see as the root of racist consciousness. Integrationism, in short, links with a broader set of liberal images—images that connect truth, universalism, and progress.

A commitment to universalism and an association of universalism with truth and particularism with ignorance form the substructure of American integrationist consciousness.[13] This universalism is the common theme that connects the integrationist analytic distinctions between reason and prejudice, objectivity and bias, neutrality and discrimination, and integration and segregation. Each dichotomy envisions a realm of impersonality, understood as the transcendence of subjective bias and contrasted with an image of a realm of distortion where particularity and stereotype reign. Integrationist beliefs are organized around the familiar enlightenment story of progress as the movement from mere belief and superstition to knowledge and reason, from the particular (and therefore parochial) to the universal (and therefore enlightened).[14]

Within this frame for organizing social perception, controversy revolves around how to categorize particular social practices as either rational and neutral, or irrational and biased. Liberals and conservatives can be distinguished by how far they believe the realms of either bias or neutrality extend. But conservatives' and liberals' basic comprehension of racial justice has the same underlying structure: to universalize institutional practices to efface the distortions of irrational factors like race, and thereby make social life neutral to racial identity. To both liberals and conservatives, racism consists of a form of distortion that could be superseded by an aracial arena of social understanding. Once we remove prejudice, reason will take its place; once we remove discrimination, neutrality will take its place; once we remove segregation, integration will take its place.[15]

One way this universalizing character of integrationism manifests itself in perception is that diverse social phenomena begin to appear the same because they are all viewed through the same analytic lens. From within this structure for cataloguing and organizing thinking about social life, racism becomes equivalent to other forms of prejudice and discrimination based on irrational stereotypes. Social domination based on race, gender, sexual preference, religion, age, national origin, language, and physical disability or appearance can all be categorized as the same phenomena because they all represent bias—deviation from a neutral, rational standard. Similarly, the fact that relations between whites and African, Asian, and Latin Americans are all perceived as presenting the issues of "discrimination against racial minorities" in legal and political discourse reflects the same structure of abstraction. From this structure, it begins to appear that the social subordination of various groups does not have a complex, particular, and historical context, but rather is a formal, numeric problem of the relations of majorities to minorities, unified under the concept "discrimination."

Consequently, given the universalist dimension to integrationist thinking, it is plausible to conceive of a category of "reverse racism," which is really not "reverse" at all. Because racism means a deviation from a universal norm of objectivity, it can be practiced by anyone—and anyone can be its victim—regardless of particular historical circumstances or power relations. Thus, within the integrationist ideology, a Black person who stereotypes whites is racist in the same way as a white person who harbors prejudice against Blacks. And Blacks who discriminate against whites are guilty of the same kind of racism as whites who discriminate against Blacks. Anyone can engage in racism because we can identify racism from a vantage point of race neutrality, of not making someone's race count for anything. The symmetry of the integrationist picture is rooted in the idea that racism consists of possessing a race consciousness about the world, in thinking that race should make a difference in social relations.

Finally, given the idea of immutability common to categories of "discrimination," the story of the struggle against racism can be related in a way that follows the basic script of liberal progress more generally. Race consciousness is associated with status-based social coercion, where individuals are treated in a particular way because of the arbitrary fact of membership in a social group they did not choose. The transcendence of race consciousness represents a social movement toward the freedom of the individual to choose group identification. Like classical images of the common law, the vision underlying integrationist ideology is of American culture working itself pure by overcoming the distortions of various kinds of prejudice in favor of the increasing rationalization of institutional forms, which in turn provides greater individual liberty to choose, free of coercive social power. Freedom from racial discrimination is but one instance of the historical move from status to contract, from caste to individual liberty.[16] Individualism and universalism are thereby linked.[17]

The aims of racial integration seem self-evident because they are one part of a web of meaning that constitutes the dominant ideology of the nature of social progress itself. The meaning of race has been grafted onto other central cultural images of progress, so that the transition from segregation to integration and from race consciousness to race neutrality mirrors the movements from myth to enlightenment, ignorance to knowledge, superstition to reason, primitive culture to civilization, religion to secularism,[18] and most importantly, the historical self-understanding of liberal society as representing the movement from status to individual liberty. In other words, integrationist ideology comprehends the issue of racial domination by viewing race relations through stock images about the nature of progress in liberal society and through the prism of a qualitative difference between liberal enlightenment and feudal hierarchy. The struggle against racism, having become the struggle against "race," thus appears natural and inevitable, as simply another part of the teleological progression toward the liberation of social life.[19]

Integration and Legitimation

This liberal integrationist approach to race has some real allure. The image of universality and its correlate aim of transcending racial consciousness form a large part of the deep appeal that the integrationist vision has for many of us. This vision seems to reflect, at the ideological level, the occasional glimpses we attain in personal experience of a deeply shared identity as fellow human be- ings in what are often the best moments of social life. The aspiration for racial integration confirms our sense of the possibility of true and authentic relations that transcend race and other forms of cultural distance, difference, and status. And integrationism appeals to the utopian ideal that these moments could be translated into organized institutional practices because, at the core, we are all the same, "regardless of race."

But this universalism also marks the narrowing limits of integrationist ideol- ogy. Understanding this aspect of integrationism helps one to comprehend how people could view the manner in which racial integration has actually proceeded in American life as an unquestionably progressive reform of race relations.

As I have described it, integrationism is organized around an image of reason and neutrality that claims the transcendence of bias and prejudice. The liberal discourse of race represented by integrationism actually contains within itself two distinct ways to perceive social practices. On one hand, the possibility of bias and prejudice constitutes a language of critique and reform that provides a framework to articulate necessary changes in society. On the other hand, this liberal discourse constitutes a narrative of legitimation, a language for concluding that particular social practices are fair because they are objective and unbiased. This second aspect of liberal discourse represents a conception of a realm of social life outside the influence of racial history and politics.

Take, for example, the debate about affirmative action. In this context, those interested in progressive reform employ race consciousness. The familiar "dilemma" that surrounds affirmative action is that it requires the use of race as a socially significant category, although the deepest aims of integrationist ideology point toward the transcendence of race consciousness.

The dominant discourse about affirmative action reflects the core categories of the liberal theory of race I described. The issues in the affirmative action debate are organized around the same structural opposition between reason and bias. Here, the category of "merit" represents the universal, impersonal side of integrationist perception. The use of race-conscious means to distribute social goods is problematic because it represents a deviation from the impersonality of merit. Thus, liberal support of affirmative action has always been defensive because its proponents themselves experience it, at least in part, as dissonant with their most fundamental convictions. Affirmative action has been characterized as an exceptional remedy for past injustice, rather than an affirmative right rooted in present social circumstances. It has been characterized as temporary and only necessary to achieve integration, at which time equal opportunity can take over. Affirmative action has been defended on the grounds that its beneficiaries have suffered from a "deprived" background, so that putting a thumb on the scales of social decision-making on the side of minorities helps even out the otherwise rational competition for social goods.[20]

Alternatively, affirmative action has been defended on the basis of promoting diversity, an approach that challenges the notion of merit as the sole basis on which to distribute social opportunities. According to this justification, merit is only one value to be vindicated in determining admission to various institutions. Alongside merit is the value of having a racially diversified society (or institution), a justification that can be used to counterbalance merit as a criterion.[21]

Whether articulated in terms of remedy or diversity, this discourse assumes that minority applicants are less qualified on neutral, impersonal, and objective criteria. Thus, to integrate institutions, we must compromise meritocratic standards either temporarily (to break the cycles of institutional life that racial domination entailed) or permanently (by diffusing merit with other ends such as diversity). Today, conservative integrationists preach a principled commitment to colorblindness in institutional practices, even if it results in segregated institutions, and liberal integrationists advocate limited, effects-oriented race consciousness to ensure that some integration actually takes place. But from within the discourse through which they perceive the issues, both commit to the premise that the category of merit itself is neutral, impersonal, and somehow developed outside the economy of social power, with its significant currency of race, class, and gender that marks American social life.[22]

Given their view of the pervasive nature of American racism, at least in the recent past, it is conceivable that integrationists might have demanded a radical transformation of social practices before they assumed the existence of merit-based decision-making. Instead, integrationists assumed that fair, impersonal criteria would simply be what remained once the distortion of race consciousness was removed. One manifestation of this assumption was that the purportedly broad social transformation reflected in the national struggle against racism resulted in hardly any change in administrative personnel. The transformation from a Jim Crow racial regime to an integrationist one was thought to require only a change in the rules of social decision-making. The same whites who once carried out the formal program of American apartheid actually kept their jobs as decision-makers charged with evaluating merit in the employment offices of companies and the admissions offices of schools in the postsegregation world. In institution after institution, progressive reformists have found themselves struggling over the implementation of racial integration with the former administrators of racial segregation, many of whom soon constituted an old guard "concerned" about the deterioration of "standards."

American law schools, where I have spent most of my professional life, provide a straightforward example. I started teaching in 1982 at the University of Virginia School of Law. Like all other public universities in the South, the school had been segregated by law and refused to admit Black students until ordered to do so by federal courts.[23] The Commonwealth of Virginia's leaders conceived and executed a coordinated and temporarily successful "massive resistance" to integration throughout the 1950s, going so far as to close entire school systems across the state, rather than comply with the school integration orders of the federal courts.[24] A segregationist president led the University of Virginia in resisting integration after *Brown*. It was not until the late 1960s and early 1970s that the law school and the rest of the university stopped systematically excluding Blacks from study or segregating them from white students when enrolled.[25] Nevertheless, by the early 1980s, Blacks represented less than 7% of the university's law school enrollment, despite the fact that the state as a whole was approximately 19% Black.[26] The faculty was then all white, although a Black tax professor had taught there for several years in the 1970s.

I was assigned to the admissions committee, and in turn to the subcommittee responsible for evaluating minority applicants. Whether it was explicit or not, I understood that the goal was to admit all "qualified" minority applicants. The school's public position was that it wished to increase minority enrollment. The school was also committed to affirmative action, if covertly. There is no doubt that minority students were commonly admitted with lower test scores and grades than white students, although the degree of exception to ordinary standards was kept secret. I agreed with the policies (although not necessarily with the secrecy part). I had the sense that other "selective" law schools did the same thing, but I wondered why more Black students were not enrolled in light of these policies.

At our first meeting, the other committee members introduced me to how they evaluated the applicants. Like admissions decisions at other elite law schools, the virtually exclusive criteria were the applicant's Law School Admission Test (LSAT) score and undergraduate grades, weighed by the relative competitiveness of the undergraduate school (itself determined by average scores on the LSAT). One of my colleagues, a senior member of the faculty, announced that he would deny admission to any candidate from a historically Black college, no matter how high the grades they earned there, unless the applicant also had exceptionally high LSAT scores, on the ground that graduation from an all-Black undergraduate college did not demonstrate the student's preparedness for studying law at a rigorous institution like the University of Virginia School of Law. Conversely, good grades at a predominantly white college would make up for a relatively low LSAT score. The long-time admissions director emphasized to me that it would be unfair to the applicant to admit him for a course of study that he would be unable to complete.[27] There was more to the ongoing, case-by-case discussion of qualifications, but I think this is enough description to begin the discussion.

I have the sense that the moment in time I am describing—the deliberation of the University of Virginia School of Law minority admissions subcommittee in a conference room in Charlottesville, Virginia, in the fall of 1984, say—is representative of meetings, decisions, and practices at other institutions, around other conference tables, all over the nation at the time. It partly suggests, in microcosm, the manner in which power (here, the power to permit or prohibit law study at the school) is constructed, exercised, and reproduced *ideologically* in institutions, and more specifically the narrowness of reform associated with the move from racial apartheid toward racial equality in the late part of the 20th century.

First, it is notable that the decisions on which applicants to admit were still being made exclusively by whites. Not only was the Virginia law faculty all white, it (and perhaps the minority admissions subcommittee itself) was composed of many of the very same professors who had taught when the school resisted the integration of Black students (or at least were teachers hired by that group). Likewise, any long-serving admissions director would likely have administered the segregative policies that the school had only recently abandoned. In other words, the same people who managed the segregated institution were left with authority over the integrated one, including the power to determine the extent of integration by defining what would constitute qualifications required to attend (or teach at) the school.

The second notable feature is the assumption that, except for the inclusion of Black students, everything else about the school and study there would remain the same after the school stopped outright racial exclusion. Accordingly, the school continued to use the same selection criteria used during segregation, save the overt racial exclusion. The heavy reliance on the standardized LSAT, despite the fact that it is widely known to have a racially disproportionate impact, was justified by the statistically significant correlation between scores and first-year law school performance.

The problem with that justification, however, was that law was itself implicated in racial subordination. The duly enacted laws of the states mandated Jim Crow–style racial segregation and subordination, and until *Brown*, the Supreme Court declared "separate but equal" consistent with the Constitution's guarantee of equal protection. Even in the years since chattel slavery was abolished, a virtually all-white legal profession had enjoyed more than a century to fashion legal doctrines and arguments that justified and legitimized racial subordination in society in general and in the legal profession in particular. All-white law faculties taught these doctrines to white law students, defending the rationality and justness of the doctrines and of the legal regime that included them.

White race ideology helped structure and taint not only the content of what law schools taught, but also the institutional culture within which it was taught. Like other segregated places, the everyday experience at the law school—in classrooms, faculty offices, hallways, and the institution as a whole—was constituted, at least in part, by the manner in which racial subordination was normalized into the everyday and the mundane. Only a few years before, Blacks had been (in)visible only as maids, janitors, food service and maintenance workers, and the occasional receptionist. The patterns of deference and authority inscribed into the everyday interactions (or lack thereof) between faculty and students and those beneath them in the social hierarchy—in elevators, in line at the cafeteria, or at a committee meeting while the trash was removed—were at least partly racial, to the extent that from inside the white group, for example, seeing a Black person would lead to an immediate assumption of inferiority on the socioeconomic and cultural hierarchy ("Do you work here?"). Conversely, a Black student entering the environment would also face these existing patterns and would be forced to negotiate an immediate response. The culture of the classrooms, styles of teaching, content of arguments, tenor of teacher/student relations, and the rest of institutional life were the arguable residue of generations of white lawyers constructing a profession and society in which the subordination of African Americans was rationalized, legalized, and (more generally) normalized.[28]

Now, to return to the context of the minority admissions subcommittee, the University of Virginia School of Law context, with its history of explicitly embracing racial segregation and the open bias that my colleague expressed against traditionally Black schools, provides a particularly vivid example of the limits of integrationist reform. "Integration" left institutional power intact in the hands of the very same personnel who had earlier run the institution on a segregated basis. Differences at other predominantly white law schools without the same history or personnel were, I think, merely of degree. As I suggested earlier, by the 1980s, the University of Virginia School of Law wanted desperately to enroll more Blacks, if for no other reason than because no law school aspiring to national recognition could fail to do so.

From this more critical perspective, even the most objective-seeming selection criteria—performance on the standardized LSAT—is open to question, and the problem cannot be resolved by reliance on correlation between LSAT scores and performance in the first year of law school. Proponents of the test accept "the first year of law school" as if it were an objective, aracial standard; in fact, the first-year experience had been constructed by institutions that had long embraced the very same doctrines that excluded Black students and faculty in the first place. It assumed, in other words, that nothing about law schools would change with integration except the racial composition of the student body and eventually the faculty.

In this way, the integrationism that emerged from the 1960s and 1970s reproduced and legitimized many of the institutional practices that had been created during the period of open white supremacy ideology. One can imagine how racial integration could have been part of a dramatic, critical remaking of

American institutions, particularly institutions (like law schools) that had been directly implicated in enforcing and rationalizing segregation. Instead, integrationist ideology justified a narrow interpretation of what would be required to end the racial apartheid of the American legal profession.

I do not mean to suggest that everyone who had run segregated institutions should have been purged, or that everything about law or legal education was necessarily racially tainted. I am simply suggesting that the very opposite assumption clearly was not warranted. Taking seriously the manner in which racial power had been exercised and rationalized at least required a more critical examination of the existing practices of formerly segregated institutions.

Even more dramatic than the continuity of personnel (because the particular people in power eventually age, retire, and die) is the fact that the same criteria that defined the "standards" during the period of explicit racism continue to be used, as long as they are not linked "directly" to racial factors. Within liberal integrationism, racism, defined as a deviation from neutral, impersonal norms, focused on the exclusion of people of color. With the abolition of racism, the idea was that all the rest of the cultural practices of formerly segregated institutions would stay the same. From within the integrationist ideology of neutral standards, no conceptual base existed from which integrationists could question whether "standards," definitions of "merit," and the other myriad features of the day-to-day aspects of institutional life constructed or maintained during segregation might have reflected deeper aspects of a culture within which the explicit exclusion of Blacks seemed uncontroversial. Integrationists, organizing their perception of racial justice around images of objectivity, rationality, and neutrality, never considered whether this language for distinguishing the worthy from the unworthy itself might serve to help justify racial domination—if not to its victims, then at least to white beneficiaries who need to believe their social positions are the result of something more than brute social power and racial domination.

Liberal integrationist ideology is structured so that some social practices are taken out of the economy of race relations and understood to be undistorted by racial power. To be sure, no analytically necessary point from within the terms of the integrationist view of race exists at which the line between racial discrimination and neutral meritocracy must be drawn. One can imagine that the very definition of what constitutes qualifications to attend law school, work as a police officer, own a home, live in a particular neighborhood, or have a particular income could be challenged as either directly rooted in the distortions of white supremacy or more indirectly dependent on a rhetoric through which the powerful generally justify their share of the distribution of social benefits. And, in some contexts, reform within the integrationist tradition followed this path.

However, integrationism also labels the distribution of social goods "impersonal" and "neutral" once we remove "distortions" like race consciousness. Integrationists tend to understand racism as a particular, identifiable deviation from an otherwise rational decision-making process that is not based in the history of social struggle between groups and worldviews. This narrow image of the domain of racial power characterizes the tendency of liberal integrationism to become part of a self-justifying ideology of privilege and status. The realm of "neutral" social practices from which to identify bias and deviation constitutes a whole set of institutional characteristics removed from critical view as themselves historical, contingent, and culturally specific—a realm that is itself a manifestation of group power, of politics. This obscures the possibility that the very core values of liberal integrationists—the ideals of objectivity, rationality, and neutrality—were historically constructed from particular perspectives and as responses to specific historical situations, rather than representing the transcendence of perspective itself.

Integrationism in Social Form: Public Schools

To this point, I have described integrationism as a set of ideas that forms a recognizable worldview about race. But the ideology I am evoking does not simply exist in people's heads as a group of concepts. That is, although these beliefs do characterize recognizable social and legal philosophies, integrationist ideology and the liberal dualities that provide its context are more diffuse and in the background of our social world than the popular image of a philosophy suggests. I think that we should see integrationism as one part of a more general cultural meaning system, as a consciousness, rather than a worked-out theory. Integrationist assumptions do not manifest themselves solely in self-conscious legal and political argument about race, but instead provide the filter for how we experience, perceive, and construct a broad range of social relations and institutional practices. Seeing integrationism as the "race" component of a wider cultural ideology reflects the sense that a wide array of social practices and programs for reform hang together—not necessarily logically entailed, but nevertheless recognizable as a particular discourse in our culture.

Consider the program for reform of Southern public schools in which integrationism played a central part in the 1960s. Public education, at least in the South, embodied the most realized attempt to institutionalize cultural assumptions of the liberal, enlightenment ideology underlying integrationism. Integrationists put tremendous energy and effort into the struggle over Southern schools. Here, the universalism of liberal race ideology appeared as a commitment to centralism in institutional culture and a corresponding opposition to local control, and the terms of the cultural compromise reflected in the national embrace of integrationism were clearest. In liberal education reform, the definition of what constitutes enlightened good sense was drawn in negative contrast to an image of the "backward" and ignorant whites who opposed racial integration of Southern public schools and whose lack of enlightenment was further symbolized by their embrace of the "mythologies" of fundamentalist religion. Liberal integrationism entailed a trade-off of this "redneck" culture with African American culture. In consideration for the suppression of white Southern working-class culture in schools, Blacks were expected to accede to the suppression of African American culture as well. Instead, school life would be characterized by the particular culture of technocracy and professionalism, presented as the aracial, neutral face of "quality" in education and as the transcendence of localism and particularity.

Racial integration of Southern schools represented only one aspect of the liberal reform of public education. Roughly simultaneous with the constitutional prohibition of racial segregation in public education, school prayer was also declared an unconstitutional violation of the norm of state neutrality.[29] There was a deep link between these two major reforms. The logic of the joint rejection of school segregation and school prayer was contained in the sense that each reform reflected a progressive move from ignorance and parochialism to enlightenment and equality, from the particular and biased to the universal and objective.[30] Just as school segregation represented the bias of primitive racial beliefs of white supremacists, school prayer represented the bias of local, primitive religious beliefs. Just as school segregation formed one manifestation of the social face of racial discrimination, compulsory school prayer was the social face of religious intolerance, of discrimination according to theology. And just as school integration substituted universal and neutral norms for the particularities of white supremacist myth, the ban on school prayer substituted a neutral, secular discourse for the particularities of religious belief.[31]

The similarity in the way segregation and prayer were understood is one manifestation of the deep connections between integrationism as an ideology and centralism as an institutional norm. Today's culture of public education is marked by a commitment in institutional life to the same kind of universalizing that integrationism reflects in ideological form. Along with the banning of the perceived local biases of segregationism and religion, a great centralization of curriculum and administration has occurred. The advanced degrees of administrators, prevalent professional status of school board members, implementation of standardized tests on a widespread basis, exclusion of religion from schools, and near-universal replacement of corporal punishment ("paddling," in the Southern vernacular) with therapeutic or contractual counseling approaches to student discipline all reflect the attempt to substitute a standardized national culture of public school administration for the perceived repression, rooted in parochialism, of the former institutional culture of Southern schools.

There is no analytic reason to account for the simultaneous occurrence of all these changes in the culture of the public schools. Racial integration has been just one part of a more general "sanitization" of Southern public education. The formerly maternal relationship between teacher and student has been replaced by cool, professional distance. Graduate schools teaching expertly tested methods of instruction replaced the traditional training of teachers through contact with older faculty. The decentralization of curriculum now exists only as a formality because public education has, for all practical purposes except funding, been nationalized. The standardized test and cultural commitment to the No. 2 pencil are the lived, institutionalized rituals that reflect the commitment to impersonality and objectivity at the ideological level.[32]

In educational discourse, professionalism plays the same symbolic role that merit plays in the affirmative action debates—a neutral alternative to irrational bias. Liberal reformers of public education in the late 1950s and 1960s associated professionalism with centralism and understood that both provide a way to oppose local parochialism: "The public interest is almost invariably better served by leaving professional questions to the professionals."[33] Likewise, "local control results in the same kind of intellectual parochialism that characterizes schools in totalitarian countries."[34] Professionalism became the legitimizing rhetoric of public school administration.

The embrace of images of centralism and professionalism responded to the liberal perception of the previous problems with public education, that localism and parochialism compromised neutrality and objectivity. And the underlying assumption was that once public education eradicated the influences of locality and bias, it would achieve a neutral, acultural form that, precisely because of its impersonality, would treat everyone alike. Localism, like race consciousness, had to be resisted because it threatened the connection of universalism, individualism, and truth with the particularism of culture, community, and politics. Myron Lieberman, a leading liberal commentator of the time, argued that "[n]ational survival now requires educational policies which are not subject to local veto.... It is becoming increasingly clear that local control cannot in practice be reconciled with the ideals of a democratic society.... Local control is a major cause of the dull parochialism and attenuated totalitarianism that characterizes public education in operation."[35]

Which brings us back to the Malcolm X quote that introduces this chapter. In his view, the problem with school "segregation" was not the failure to integrate Black and white children, but rather the dynamics of power and control that formed the historical context of racial separation. Whereas liberals experienced integrationism as a progressive rejection of the bias and parochialism of the local in favor of the impersonality of centralized authority, Malcolm X asserted that the very goal of the struggle against racism was to achieve local control, to liberate community institutions from "outside, colonial" rule. While the dominant culture translated the demand for local control as the "states' rights" discourse of Southern racism and the religious dogma of Southern fundamentalists, Malcolm X associated local control with racial liberation; while integrationists understood public school integration to be the institutional synonym for racial justice, Malcolm X asserted that integration was a manifestation of white supremacist ideology. To grasp how he could understand racial liberation in terms so diametrically opposed to the mainstream discourse of liberal integrationism, it makes sense to turn in the next chapter to the alternative ideology of race developed by Malcolm X and other Black nationalists.

CHAPTER 2
THE BLACK NATIONALIST CRITIQUE

Thus, within the Black community there are two separate challenges to the traditional integration policy which long has constituted the major objective of established Negro leadership. There is the general skepticism that the Negro, even after having transformed himself into a white Black-man, will enjoy full acceptance in American society; and there is the longer-range doubt that even should complete integration somehow be achieved, it would prove to be really desirable, for its price may be the total absorption and disappearance of the race—a sort of painless genocide. Understandably, it is the Black masses who have most vociferously articulated these dangers of assimilation, for they have watched with alarm as the more fortunate among their ranks have gradually risen to the top only to be promptly "integrated" off into the white community—absorbed into another culture, often with undisguised contempt for all that had previously constituted their racial and cultural heritage. Also, it was the Black masses who first perceived that integration actually increases the white community's control over the Black one by destroying institutions, and by absorbing Black leadership and coinciding its interests with those of the white community.... Such injurious, if unintended, side effects of integration have been felt in almost every layer of the Black community.[1]

Robert S. Browne, 1968

Like integrationism, nationalism among African Americans has taken various forms and has been associated with divergent worldviews.[2] The long tradition dates back to antebellum proposals by Martin Delany and others to colonize parts of Africa as a homeland for American Blacks.[3] Some form of nationalism was manifest in Booker T. Washington's self-help and separatist ideas of Black advancement.[4] Black nationalism in its modern, urban form can be traced among the poor to the organizing efforts of Marcus Garvey in the 1930s[5] and the Black Muslims since,[6] and among the middle class to W. E. B. Du Bois' critique of the National Association for the Advancement of Colored People's (NAACP's) policy of integrationism in the 1930s.[7] There is little doubt, however, that Black nationalism had its most complete and sophisticated theoretical development, as well as its greatest mass appeal, during the 1960s and early 1970s, when it was articulated as an alternative worldview to integrationism and as part of a program of radical social transformation by (among others) Malcolm X,[8] Eldridge Cleaver,[9] Kwame Ture,[10] Amiri Baraka,[11] Harold Cruse,[12] the Black Panthers,[13] and quickly expanding factions of the Student Nonviolent Coordinating Committee (SNCC) and the Congress of Racial Equality (CORE).[14]

I will discuss Black nationalism with specific reference to the ways in which it was articulated in the late 1960s and early 1970s. My goal is not to provide a complete social history or philosophical account, but instead to sketch out, in general form, the ways in which nationalists opposed the understanding of race embodied by integrationist ideology.

The controversy in the mid-1960s over the slogan "Black Power" exemplifies the contrast between integrationists and Black nationalists. I begin the introduction to nationalism with a brief analysis of the issues at stake in the Black Power idea. I then discuss the nationalist critique of integration at an institutional level, focusing on public schools and the movement for community control. In the third section, I describe ways in which nationalist intellectuals contested more general and abstract epistemological assumptions of liberal integrationism. I conclude this chapter with a discussion of the systematic differences between integrationist and nationalist analyses of the meaning of racial domination and reform.

Black Power

The Black nationalist position received its first modern wave of sustained mass exposure in 1966 when Willie Ricks and Kwame Ture (then known as Stokely Carmichael) began using the term "Black Power" during the March Against Fear in Mississippi.[15] Tension between integrationist and nationalist approaches had already erupted within and between various civil rights organizations, but the high-profile and polarized controversy over the term "Black Power" transformed what had been largely an underground conflict into a full-scale, highly charged public debate over the fundamental direction and conception of the civil rights movement.

The term "Black Power" first gained publicity when Richard Wright so entitled his autobiographical reflections on Africa.[16] In 1966, U.S. Representative Adam Clayton Powell, Jr., used it as a political slogan, without much notoriety, during Howard University commencement exercises.[17] But it was not until Ricks and Carmichael began using the slogan during the March Against Fear that it gained mass appeal.

The slogan originated as part of the competition between the Dr. Martin Luther King, Jr./Southern Christian Leadership Conference (SCLC) faction and the SNCC faction of the march's organizers. Tension between the civil rights groups dated back at least to the 1961 Albany campaign, where SNCC organizers attempted to mobilize the Black community *en masse* to resist the racial structure of the city as a whole, and where disagreements arose between SNCC organizers and the SCLC as to the militancy of nonviolent tactics—whether to violate federal court orders against marches, and more generally, whether the civil rights campaign should be focused on building community strength or persuading the federal government to grant civil rights.[18] By the 1963 March on Washington, the ideology of the groups had substantially diverged, with the SCLC leadership supporting the passage of the Civil Rights Act and cooperation with the Kennedy administration, and John Lewis of SNCC prepared to deliver a scathing attack on the government and the slow pace of race reform, including opposition to the Civil Rights Act as "too little, too late."[19]

At the March Against Fear, the rift opened around the question of nonviolence and, reflecting the beginnings of nationalist sentiment among the SNCC/CORE organizers, around the issue of whether to permit white participation in the march. Symbolically, the positions were represented by competing crowd chants, with SCLC organizers trying to get the crowd to chant "Freedom Now" and SNCC organizers challenging with "Black Power."[20]

To be sure, the slogan "Black Power" did not itself have a necessarily nationalist meaning; in fact, a virtual cottage industry was created around attempts to define its meaning, and many of its exponents were clearly integrationist.[21] The Black Power Conference called by Powell and held in Newark in 1967 reflected the broad disagreements among those characterizing themselves as Black Power activists.[22] Nevertheless, it is clear that, for most, the "Black Power" slogan represented the beginning of repudiation of integrationist/civil rights ideology in favor of some form of nationalism.[23]

Mainstream reactions to the idea of comprehending the civil rights movement as a struggle for Black Power reflect the discourse associated with the marginalization of nationalist race consciousness in the dominant cultural rhetoric. Both Black and white integrationists equated Black Power with white supremacy.[24] Hubert Humphrey responded by "rejecting calls for racism, whether they come from a throat that is white or one that is Black."[25] Roy Wilkins charged that "no matter how endlessly they try to explain it, the term 'Black Power' means anti-white power." He characterized Black Power as "a reverse Mississippi, a reverse Hitler, a reverse Ku Klux Klan."[26] *Time* and Kenneth Clark each referred to Black Power as a "racist philosophy,"[27] and *The Crisis,* the publication of the NAACP, called Black Power advocates "Black neo-segregationists" and "advocates of apartheid."[28] In fact, the virulent and extreme denunciation of Black Power symbolized the unity of what would quickly become the new center of American consciousness about race.[29]

The integrationists saw two problems with Black Power. First, the concept assumed that power should be distributed on a racial basis, thereby assuming that American society should be thought of in terms of separate white and Black communities. Thus, Black Power violated both the integrationist principle to transcend race consciousness at the ideological level and the integrationist program to end the segregation of whites and Blacks at the institutional and community levels.

Second, the Black Power concept troubled integrationists because it assumed that *power* determined the distribution of social resources and opportunities, rather than reason or merit. It was not simply the theory of Black Power that engendered the charged reaction, but resistance to the reigning liberal idea of progress through reasoned discussion and deliberation that the Black Power movement, for a time, embodied. The clenched fist of the Black Power salute and the militaristic affectation of many Black nationalist groups were the overt physical manifestations of this dimension of the movement.

Through the ideological filters of integrationism, Black nationalism and white supremacy appear essentially the same because both are rooted in race consciousness, in the idea that race matters to one's perception and experience of the world. Integrationists saw nationalists as regressive because, in the integrationist view, progress meant transcending race as a basis of social decision-making, and in the long term, replacing power with reason as the basis for the distribution of resources. With the centering of integrationism as the mainstream ideology of American good sense, nationalism became marginalized as an extremist and backward worldview, the irrational correlate in the Black community to the never-say-die segregationists of the white community.

The equation of Black nationalists and white supremacists assumes a neutral standard from which to identify race consciousness as a deviation and link race inherently to prejudice and domination. When viewed in terms of the actual context of history and power relations between racial groups in America, however, white supremacy and Black nationalism embody very different understandings of race.

The mainstream reactions to Black nationalism were so vociferous not because the Black Power movement presented any real threat of racial domination by Blacks, but rather, I think, because Black nationalism embodied a profound rejection of the reigning ideology for understanding the distribution of power and privilege in American society. Just as integrationism became the mainstream discourse for racial justice—to the extent it could be articulated in the terms of a deep, cultural self-identity of enlightenment, through evolution toward rationality and objectivity—the nationalist analysis of racial justice became threatening in part because it challenged the universalist assumptions underlying these images of progress. These images were challenged as elements of a particular ideology of power and of the particular culture of whites.

Nationalism as a Critique of Universalism

For the most part, integrationists never comprehended the analysis of racial domination presented by Black nationalists. From their universalist view of racism as a distortion of an otherwise aracial rationality, integrationists interpreted the race consciousness of Black nationalists as the mark of racism and never considered the nationalist position as a competing, alternative, and systematic analysis of the meaning of racial domination. Thus, when Black nationalists declared integration "a subterfuge for white supremacy"[30] representing "a form of painless genocide,"[31] integrationists could not comprehend what they were talking about. The nationalist worldview was based on a fundamentally different set of beliefs and perceptual categories through which reforms that looked progressive to integrationists looked regressive to nationalists.

The contrast between the integrationist commitment to centralization and expertise in public education and Malcolm X's discourse of local, community control was only one manifestation of the deep and thorough opposition between integrationists and nationalists on the more basic issue of the meaning of race in America. Where integrationists understood race through the prism of universalism, through which race consciousness appeared arbitrary, irrational, and symmetrically evil (whether practiced by whites or Blacks), nationalists viewed race in the particular context of American history, where racial identity was seen as a central basis for comprehending the significance of various social relations as they are actually lived and experienced, and within which the meaning of race was anything but symmetrical. The opposition between centralism and local control that distinguished integrationist and nationalist rhetoric about schools had its philosophical correlates in the opposition between timeless (as opposed to historicist) views about identity and group consciousness, between the discourses of impersonal professionalism and ideas of organic community, and most generally between the assumptions of "universalism" and the assertions of qualitative cultural differences encompassed in the idea of "nationalism."

These basic differences are reflected in the very idea that African Americans compose a "nation." This starting point is commonly associated with separatism in general and with the demand for a separate nation as a homeland for American Blacks in particular. But while at least some geographic separation has often characterized nationalist programs,[32] and while several nationalist groups have advocated the idea of a formal nation-state,[33] there is, as I see it, no necessary relation between nationalism as a way to understand race relations and a formal demand for geographic separation.[34]

Instead, the image of African Americans as a "nation within a nation"[35] should be understood as a symbol of the core assertion that race consciousness constitutes African Americans as a distinct social community, in much the same way that national self-identity operates to establish the terms of recognition and identity in "regular" nations.[36] In contrast to the integrationist premise that Blacks and whites are essentially the same, the idea of race as the organizing basis for group consciousness asserts that Blacks and whites are different, in the sense of coming from different communities, neighborhoods, churches, families, and histories, and of being in various ways foreigners to each other.[37] And in contrast to the white supremacist ideology of natural, essential racial characteristics, the image of nationhood locates differences between whites and Blacks in social history, in the temporal context in which all national identity must come into being. As Clarence Munford put it:

> It is different from other emergent nations only in that it consists of forcibly transplanted colonial subjects who have acquired cohesive identity in the course of centuries of struggle against enslavement, cultural alienation, and the spiritual cannibalism of white racism. This common history which the Black people of America share is manifested in a concrete national culture with a peculiar 'spiritual complexion,' or psychological temperament. Though the Black nation expresses its thoughts, emotions, and aspirations in the same tongue as American whites, the different conditions of existence … have, from generation to generation, welded the bonds of a national experience as different from that of white existence as day is from night. And what differentiates nations from one another are dissimilar conditions of life.[38]

The depth of identification of self and recognition of others implicit in the idea of nationhood based on generations of "dissimilar conditions of life" marks a vision of community that cannot be captured in the liberal dichotomies of either liberty and coercion, or reason and myth. The public assertion of spiritual cohesion represented by Black nationhood contested the liberal border between public objectivity and private sentiment underlying the link between universality and individualism.[39] Nationhood, understood as a historically created community, assumes that social bonds of identity, recognition, and solidarity can be liberating and fulfilling outside the family.

In this way, nationalists articulated what might be seen as a "historicized" view of social relations. In opposition to the universal vantage point used by integrationists to identify bias and prejudice, nationalists presented the time-bound, messy, and inherently particular social relations between nations as the central ground from which to perceive race. In opposition to the essentializing of race engaged in by white supremacists, nationalists located the meaning of race in history, in the social structures that people, rather than God or some objectified nature, have created.

Again, the commitment to a historical view means there is no objective or natural necessity to the way groups, identities, and social meanings have been structured. Because the structure of race relations is a social creation, it could have been constructed differently in the past and could still be changed in the future. But the nationalist view contrasts with the liberal image of group identity as either an irrational status or a matter of choice, a voluntary, willed association. The idea of a nationalist base for social identity is, instead, a form of existentialist collectivism—the idea that we are, in a sense, thrown into history, with aspects of social reality already structured to limit some possibilities, while making other ones available.

Rather than imagining that people simply exist as autonomous individuals who create social relations out of acts of private will, Clarence Munford, for example, saw African Americans in the collectivist terms of traditions and communities that provide the historical context for individual identity. From a nationalist perspective, the fact that African Americans compose a socially created community, in terms of a contingent history, does not mean the community that exists should be rejected because it represents either a distortion that must be transcended or the result of domination that must be erased. Against the liberal image that group identity and status are opposed to the possibility of individual freedom, the nationalist perspective sees in historical structures the very basis for social meaning.[40]

The Nationalist Interpretation of School Integration

> "Integration" as a goal speaks to the problem of Blackness not only in an unrealistic way but also in a despicable way. It is based on complete acceptance of the fact that in order to have a decent house or education, Black people must move into a white neighborhood, or send their children to a white school. This reinforces, among both Black and white, the idea that "white" is automatically superior and "Black" is by definition inferior. For this reason, "integration" is a subterfuge for the maintenance of white supremacy.... The goal is not to take Black children out of the Black community and expose them to white middle-class values; the goal is to build and strengthen the Black community.... "Integration" also means that Black people must give up their identity, deny their heritage.... The fact is that integration, as traditionally articulated, would abolish the Black community. The fact is that what must be abolished is not the Black community but the dependent colonial status that has been inflicted on it.[41]
>
> Kwame Ture (then Stokely Carmichael), 1967

The conception that African Americans created "a concrete national culture" and constitute an integral, historically created, national community within the structure of American social relations is crucial to understanding the divergent ways nationalists and integrationists understand racial domination. Compare, for example, the different ways that nationalists and integrationists interpreted public school integration.

Nationalists believed that school integration was undesirable for two main reasons. First, integration of Black and white schools entailed the abolition of one of the few organized institutions in the Black community. Therefore, school integration contributed an even greater loss of social power: Blacks lost the ability to control and shape their children's education. As Malcolm X described community control, it was necessary to create the curriculum, textbooks, and general content of educational life in a way that would respond to the needs and wishes of the Black community. By conceiving of African Americans in national-ist terms, Black nationalists focused attention on the impact of race reform on the community as a whole and evaluated integration according to whether the Black community was made stronger or weaker.[42] As Ture and Charles Hamilton stated, "[t]he racial and cultural personality of the Black community must be preserved and the community must win its freedom while preserving its cultural integrity.... This is the essential difference between integration as it is currently practiced and the concept of Black Power."[43]

Second, nationalists asserted that school integration meant the adaptation of Blacks to white norms. To quote Ture and Hamilton again, integration entailed "taking Black children out of the Black community and exposing them to white middle-class values." Of course, there was no analytically intrinsic content to the idea of integration mandating that school integration proceed on the basis of white cultural norms, just as there was nothing intrinsic to the concept of integration that entailed Robert Browne's image of "the Negro ... transform[ing] himself into a white Black-man."[44] Carmichael and Browne highlighted an aspect of American racial integration buried in the mainstream ideology of neutrality and universalism, but central to the Black nationalists' analysis—a consideration of the cultural terms on which integration in social institutions would proceed. According to Cruse, the commitment to integration embodied absorption into white culture through the failure to recognize the integrity of the Black culture created in conditions of domination:

> [T]he Negro working class has been roped in and tied to the chariot of racial integration driven by the Negro middle class. In this drive for integration the Negro working class is being told in a thousand ways that it must give up its ethnicity and become human, universal, full fledged American. Within the

context of this forced alliance of class claims there can be no room for Negro art ... or art institutions ... because all of this is self-segregation which hangs up 'our' drive for integration.[45] In fact, "[t]he integrationist philosophy sees Negro ghettos as products of racial segregation that should not even exist. Hence, nothing in the traditions of ghettos is worth preserving even when the ghettoes do exist in actuality. This is typical integrationist logic on all things social."[46]

In more general terms, this understanding of integrationism as based on a vision of a "universal, full-fledged American" underlies the sense expressed by Ture, Hamilton, and Browne that integration entailed the abolition of the Black community. Because integrationists had no conceptual category with which to comprehend African Americans as a separate national group, they largely ignored the possibility of understanding racial justice in terms of the transfer of resources and power to the Black community as an entity. Hence, rather than mainstream race reform providing the material means for improving the housing, schools, cultural life, and economy of Black neighborhoods,[47] nationalists saw it as entailing "progress" only through Blacks moving into historically white neighborhoods, attending historically white schools, participating in white cultural activities, and working in white-owned and -controlled economic enterprises. "Even if such a program were possible, its result would be, not to develop the Black community as a functional and honorable segment of the total society, with its own cultural identity, life patterns, and institutions, but to abolish it—the final solution to the Negro problem."[48]

Accordingly, although there was nothing intrinsic to the liberal theory of integrationism that required public school integration to proceed by closing Black schools, firing Black teachers and administrators, and integrating Black children into formerly white schools,[49] the mainstream discourse of school integration perceived implementation in terms of "symmetry" and "quality," rather than in terms of the particular needs of the Black community to use schools as a base of empowerment and unity for the community as a whole. Given the integrationist analysis that racism stemmed from race consciousness, the effect of school reform on African Americans as a separate, integral community was categorically excluded from thinking about school reform.

From the nationalist viewpoint, integration has meant the loss of local institutions in the African American community geared to the needs and aspirations of African Americans, but integrationists did not even notice this consequence of a reform like public school integration. For them, African Americans do not compose a community at all, but rather are individuals who just "happen to be Black." Without the idea of racial difference, no space existed within integrationist ideology where one could conceive of African Americans as constituting a national community, as a group with common historical experience, cultural bonds, and aspirations for the future.

The correlate of the nationalist critique—that school integration meant not only the loss of an important institution in the Black community, but also the assimilation of Blacks into white cultural practices—likewise was invisible to integrationists. Just as integrationists translated the race consciousness of the nationalist focus on the need for Black institutional life as a form of reverse prejudice, integrationists largely also failed to comprehend the idea that racially integrated schools might manifest white culture. Instead, the images of expertise and professionalism that became the ideology of public education signified for integrationists the institutional face of the commitment to reason and impersonality at a philosophical level. In school integration, integrationists believed that Black children would be integrated into the aracial culture of quality education. The clinical computer printouts, reflecting the cognitive achievement level gleaned from standardized tests in statistical, percentile terms, symbolized the impersonality and hence cultural neutrality of the liberal reform of public education.

But where integrationists saw school integration in terms of transcending the bias at the root of segregation in favor of an "objectively" defined "quality education," nationalists saw that process as assimilating Black children to white middle-class norms. The nationalist perspective characterized the norms that constituted the neutral, impersonal, aracial, professional character of school integration as particular cultural assumptions of a specific economic class of whites. The vision of integration as a form of "painless genocide," then, stemmed from an analysis of integration as meaning not the liberation of the Black community from racial domination, but instead the transcendence of the Black community itself. In its place, "neutral" social practices would be imposed, ones that could only be identified as historically situated and culturally particular from the outside, by those for whom their supposed universality is experienced as a particular form of otherness.[50]

One can imagine a form of school integration that would have entailed consideration of the integrity of African American culture and recognition of the cultural assumptions of dominant public school practices. Nothing in the simple idea of racial integration necessitated that it be linked with universalist assumptions. But the critical nationalist analysis did correlate with the ways integrationism proceeded. The dismantling of dual school systems in reality meant closing Black schools and integrating Black children into white school systems. Moreover, for two reasons, the loss of Black community control over the education process did not even result in integration. First, whites fled urban schools in favor of predominantly white private or suburban schools, a move that left urban education with the universalist ideology of centralized professionalism, a segregated student population, and an insufficient tax base.

Perhaps more telling, in light of the nationalist critique of integration as a "subterfuge for white supremacy," even where integration has been "successful," it has largely meant resegregation within the walls of formally integrated schools. On the purported basis of ability, rather than race, the process of "tracking" utilizes various "objective" tests to segregate schoolchildren according to "cognitive ability." In school district after school district, the slower tracks are disproportionately composed of Black children and faster tracks are disproportionately composed of whites.[51]

The nationalist critique of integration highlights the ideological background against which this manner of conducting racial integration could seem plausible. Within the integrationist vision, once race consciousness (and other "biases") is removed, neutral, objective social practices remain. Thus, the logic of conducting school integration by closing Black schools and firing Black teachers and principals was premised on the ability to identify "quality" schools, teachers, and administrators in a neutral, objective way. In these neutral terms, Black schools were closed because they were inferior as a result of discrimination between white and Black institutions under segregation. Similarly, tracking supposedly measures an acultural, objective mental process called "cognitive ability." Signifying the transcendence of race as a meaningful social category, integrationists rationalize the disproportionate representation of Black children in decaying schools and slower educational tracks not as the manifestation of Black inferiority, but instead as the result of poverty, articulated bureaucratically as "low socioeconomic status (SES)."[52] Just as integrationists failed to recognize the cultural achievements of Black schools and saw them, as Cruse noted, simply as "products of racial segregation that should not even exist,"[53] they also failed to recognize the cultural specificity of white schools, which were instead seen only as "superior" education. The intense reaction on the part of liberals to Black nationalist movements for community control of schools and for the establishment of separate and autonomous African American Studies Departments[54] reflected the depth of the challenge nationalism posed to the dominant cultural ideology that linked rationality, enlightenment, and progress with racial integration.

For a brief period in the late 1960s and early 1970s, issues of public education policy crystallized the dramatic opposition between the nationalist ideology of cultural difference and organic community, and the integrationist ideology of universal reason and neutral institutions. In terms of community support and interest, nationalists produced their greatest organizational successes in the arenas of public schools and university politics. For low-income people of color, the nationalist approach to education unified popular movements for community control over schools in urban communities such as Harlem and Ocean Hill-Brownsville in New York City, and Adams-Morgan in Washington, D.C. In the middle class, nationalist activism took the form of demands for the establishment of African American Studies Departments in predominantly white colleges and universities across the country.[55] In each dimension, "the movement toward community control is a profound rejection of the core of liberal ideology" because liberal integrationism assumes that society is the "aggregation of independent individuals, rather than an organic compact of groups."[56]

Nationalists asserted that educational reform cannot be understood in terms of a "quality" education neutral as to race, but instead must be examined in terms of how schools serve the needs of an organic community held together by bonds of a particular racial culture and history. They thereby radically challenged the fundamental philosophical ideology that "knowledge" itself represents some acultural achievement and that schools could be evaluated according to some aracial standard based on how well they impart the neutral educational commodities of knowledge and reason. Rather, "the word 'better' can only be taken to mean better according to some secular standards, and it is precisely those standards that are now rejected."[57]

The equation of integration with assimilation, as drawn by Ture, Browne, Cruse, and many other nationalists, constituted the most threatening aspect of the nationalist critique. Here, the rejection of universalism took the form of an assertion that not only do African Americans constitute a distinct community—a "nation"—but white Americans correspondingly constitute a historically identifiable group within the structure of American race relations.[58]

Integrationists believed the transcendence of white supremacy would be achieved by eliminating the exclusion of Blacks from mainstream institutions, as if racism as a regime of domination and power consisted only of exclusion and did not inform the broader self-definition of white institutions. Nationalists sought to expose these limits of the integrationist vision and to focus critically on the manner in which white cultural assumptions extended to the everyday construction of institutional practices.[59]

Nationalism as a Critique of Liberalism

> It is necessary for us to develop a new frame of reference which transcends the limits of white concepts. It is necessary for us to develop and maintain a total intellectual offensive against the false universality of white concepts, whether they are expressed by William Styron or Daniel Patrick Moynihan. By and large, reality has been conceptualized in terms of the narrow point of view of the small minority of white men who live in Europe and North America. We must abandon the partial frame of reference of our oppressors and create new concepts which will release our reality, which is the reality of the overwhelming majority of men and women on this globe. We must say to the white world that there are things in the world that are not dreamt of in your history and your sociology and your philosophy.[60]
>
> Lerone Bennett, Jr., 1972

The alternative nationalist worldview embodied in the critique of public school integration manifested itself not only in an analysis of particular institutional practices, but also in a critique of each component of the integrationist worldview. At a more general and abstract level of nationalist analysis, the repudiation of the dominant ideology of public education corresponded to a thorough critique of the epistemological assumptions of liberalism as a whole. Black nationalists depicted the ideas of rationality, neutrality, and objectivity that integrationists associated with the transcendence of bias and prejudice as the particular cultural rhetoric of "the small minority of white men who live in Europe and North America." According to nationalists in the 1960s, these traditional categories of liberal and enlightenment thought do not constitute an aracial or culturally neutral standard that measures social progress in overcoming partiality, parochialism, and bias, but instead are simply parts of the dominant worldview of white elites.

The rejection of prevailing scholarly standards and methodologies represented one dimension of the challenge to the philosophic assumptions underlying liberal integrationism. Black nationalist scholars in the field of sociology, for instance, began to critique the social science norms of objectivity and value neutrality, and to draw a link between those general assumptions about the nature of intellectual and academic inquiry and the particular concepts that justified racial domination. Nationalist sociologists argued that American scholarly norms constituted a form of "academic colonialism" in which the discourse of universality and neutrality embodied an assumption of the superiority of white cultural practices and the corresponding inferiority of African American culture.[61] According to one line of attack, the mind/body dichotomy implicit in the distinction between intellectual and manual work, and the tradition of distinguishing scholarship as a specialized activity in the mental realm, represented an attempt at class rationalization—the elevation of mental activity symbolized the superior entitlement of the leisure class to the distribution of goods in society.[62]

Black nationalist sociologists further criticized the idea of impartiality and the notion of a sharp dichotomy between the detachment that marks good research skills and the emotionalism that constitutes a form of bias. The sociologists contended that the research norms that require a lack of empathy and existential connection with the subjects of sociological studies reflect a particular value orientation that ultimately helps to legitimize conditions of racial hierarchy. According to Black nationalist academics, the relationship between the "objective" researcher and his research subject mirrors the relationship between dominant and suppressed cultural groups. The researcher represents, vis-à-vis the social groups under study, the same rhetoric of rationality and objectivity that the powerful use to justify their domination generally.[63]

Many Black sociologists also sought to demonstrate a systematic bias in the ways mainstream sociological research was conducted, arguing that white culture represented the implicit standard in empirical research and Black cultural practices were represented as "deviations."[64] Similarly, nationalist sociologists criticized the analytic categories of prejudice and discrimination as based on a false image of reason and neutrality that embodied white cultural norms, and concluded that integration as understood in mainstream sociological analysis was premised on the annihilation of Black culture through assimilation into white American culture.[65]

The nationalists did not limit their attack on the idea of an objective, impersonal reason to a critique of academic work. Cleaver focused on the dominant image of rationality to launch a critique of white culture as manifesting a repression of sexuality, which provided the psychological ground for a deep fear of Blacks. Cleaver argued that the liberal contrast between reason and desire was part of a particular, historic language of power, within which dominant social groups differentiated themselves from those who are taken to be irrational, uncivilized, and ruled by myth. The white supremacist discourse that depicted whites as rational and civilized, and Blacks as irrational and lustful, was one manifestation of the reason/desire polarity. But, according to Cleaver, white supremacist ideology amounted to more than a failure to view the characteristics of reason and desire as symmetrically distributed among whites and Blacks. Instead, the very definition and content of rationality itself represented an ideology rooted in the sexual politics of race.[66]

Specifically, Cleaver argued that the manner of understanding reason in contrast to desire reflects the fear of Black sexuality that formed the infrastructure of white self-identity. The notion of reason as asexual was part of a legitimating rhetoric that itself justified white rule over Blacks by providing the conceptual categories within which whites represented the head and Blacks the body; in Cleaver's depiction of white racism, whites became the "bodiless Omnipotent Administrators and Ultrafeminines" and Blacks the "mindless Supermasculine Menials and Black Amazons."[67] That is, the rhetoric of superior evolution that characterizes explicit white racism was reflected in the reason/desire dichotomy through the differentiation of whites as rational and Blacks as ruled by passion. Such a filter in turn formed the basis for the projection of white male sexual anxiety through the image of unbridled Black sexuality. In this description, reason was understood not as the universal, objective transcendence of bias, but rather as the particular discourse by which whites justified their status in the social structure of racial domination as based on their asserted superior evolution from primordial sexuality. By denying "reason" to Blacks, whites eroticized Blacks as embodying the sexual license whites denied to themselves as "rational" administrators—explaining, Cleaver claimed, the fear and simultaneous attraction to Blacks that form the psychological infrastructure of white sexuality.[68]

In general, the radical critique launched by Black nationalist sociologists and cultural critics claimed that objective reason or knowledge could not exist because one's position in the social structure of race relations influenced what one would call "knowledge" or "rationality." The cultural differences between Blacks and whites could not be studied through a neutral frame of reference because any frame of reference assumed the perspective of either the oppressed or the oppressor, either African Americans or whites, either the sociologist or the subject. Cultural differences were not limited to particular social practices like religious activity or artistic production, but instead were infused more generally into how people perceived reality and experienced the world. There could be no neutral theory of knowledge. Knowledge was itself a function of the ability of the powerful to impose their own views, to differentiate between knowledge and myth, reason and emotion, and objectivity and subjectivity. In the historicizing perspective of Black nationalists, knowledge was necessarily a social construct. Understanding what society deemed worthy of calling "knowledge" depends on a prior inquiry into a social situation:[69] culture precedes epistemology.

This kind of generalized historicist challenge to reigning cultural assumptions also characterized Black nationalist perspectives on the debate about affirmative action. Rather than perceiving a conflict between "objective" merit and the goal of racial integration, the nationalist approach challenged the objectivity of the category of merit by viewing it in terms of the particular social practices by which whites historically distributed social goods. From the nationalist world-view, integrationist debates about affirmative action are a "subterfuge" for white supremacy. The debates focus on white cultural mores, present them as universal and objective, and then utilize them to characterize Blacks as not "qualified."

A contemporary example of this process can be found in legal education. As discussed in Chapter 1, in law schools throughout the country, admissions, hiring, and tenure debates proceed on the basis of standards of academic and scholarly merit that were constructed in a historical period when African Americans were excluded from mainstream law schools and when the very law to be studied sanctioned white supremacism. The notion that racism was limited to the exclusion of Blacks from law schools and was not part of the infrastructure for thinking about and constructing "qualifications" is emblematic of the limiting assumptions that nationalists perceived as underlying integrationism. The concepts of merit and qualifications have a function only in relation to existing social practices; Black nationalists insisted that the existing social practices should not be taken as the standard because those practices were created by a culture that considered it normal to exclude Blacks—that is, a culture itself in need of transformation.[70]

For example, imagine a legal challenge to the disproportionate racial impact of the LSAT. The use of the LSAT might be justified based on a functional correlation with performance in law school. But that functional defense views the status quo of legal education as the standard. Nationalists would argue that there is no intrinsic necessity to the current ways law schools conduct legal education and would emphasize the genealogy of existing law school practices in terms of their roots in white culture. To be sure, the status quo of legal education itself might be justified by a functional relation to existing legal practice (although I do not think many people claim that), but that merely pushes the controversy to another level—the nature of existing legal culture. And that is exactly what a challenge to the exclusionary aspects of the LSAT contests—the way the legal profession is currently constituted as a reflection of white culture. In short, the nationalist approach emphasized and criticized the self-justifying character of meritocratic assumptions about qualifications. Once we consider the possibility that existing social practices might reflect the domination of particular racial groups, those practices can no longer provide a neutral ground from which to defend existing definitions of either qualifications or merit as functionally correlated with necessary social roles.

Power, Subordination, and Colonialism

The assertion of nationhood on the part of African Americans also represented a declaration of alien-nation between races, an assertion that white culture is experienced as "other" to Blacks. Integrationists saw the transcendence of the structure of racism as replacing the same/other image of white supremacists with expansion of sameness to Blacks; nationalists conceived of the relations as other to other.

Integrationists located the roots of racism in consciousness, in the cognitive distortions of stereotype and prejudice. In contrast, the nationalist perception of whites and Blacks as occupying different national spaces entailed a view of racial domination as located in the particular power relations between Black and white communities, in the exteriors of social life, rather than the interiors of consciousness. Also, given the focus on social context, rather than consciousness, the "cure" for racial domination could not be centered on education and interracial contact to dispel stereotypes, but instead depended on the transformation of power relations between Black and white communities—or, in other words, on the achievement of "Black Power."

Similarly, because racism referred to the particular power relations between Black and white communities, there was no center of comparison from which to equate racial identity with other forms of identity, or to equate the domination of African Americans with discrimination against other groups. The significance of race in terms of social relations and the self-identity of people was seen by nationalists as having a particular weight and depth that could not be comprehended by abstracting from historical context and flattening out racial domination into one of many structurally equivalent forms of "discrimination." Nationalists asserted that a group identity that centers on race was not structurally the same as the "ethnic heritage" every American has because, in our social history, race has acquired a particular significance and centrality qualitatively different than the differences between, say, Italian Americans and Polish Americans.[71]

In contrast to the integrationist image of discrimination as the social practice of racism, the nationalist image was subordination—the hierarchy of the white community over the Black community. Rather than conceive of race reform in terms of affirmative action aimed at integrating formerly white institutions, nationalists sought to strengthen and develop institutions in the Black community that would serve African Americans. Thus, nationalists tended to see racial justice in terms of reparations[72] or foreign "aid" from developed countries to the Third World.[73] And that is why Malcolm X distinguished "segregation" from racial separation. According to his analysis, segregation amounted to a form of racial domination, in which the Black community was not only separate from the white community, but also ruled by it. As he saw it, if the power relations were changed, the meaning of the separation would be dramatically different.

In contrast to the integrationist image of segregation as a systematic form of racism, Black nationalists developed an analysis that relied primarily on an image of whites and Blacks constituting separate national communities. The systematic nature of American racism was described not as segregation, but as a form of colonialism.[74] According to Cruse's description, in the terms of the "domestic colonialism [analysis] ... instead of establishing a colonial empire in Africa, the United States brought the colonial system home and installed it in the Southern states.... Emancipation elevated the Negro only to the position of a semi-dependent man, not to that of an equal or independent being."[75] In the nationalist analysis, African Americans exist in a "neocolonial" relationship with whites—as a colonized people "dispersed" throughout North America:

> Black Power must be viewed as a projection of sovereignty, an embryonic sovereignty that Black people can focus on and through which they can make distinctions between themselves and others, between themselves and their enemies—in short, the white mother country of America and the Black colony dispersed throughout the continent on absentee-owned land, making Afro America a decentralized colony. Black Power says to Black people that it is possible to build a national organization on someone else's land.[76]

Comprehending the relations between Blacks and whites on a colonial model, 1960s nationalists asserted that even Black control of the Black community would be insufficient if it merely meant Blacks would administer the same structural power relations that previously existed between white and Black communities. The metaphor of colonialism thus symbolically placed 1960s nationalists outside the parameters of the pluralist wing of integrationism by suggesting that the racial diversification of existing American institutions and social patterns might simply be another form of the colonial relationship. A radical transformation of the status quo institutional practices would be necessary before identifiable Black and white communities could relate on a just basis.[77]

The colonialism metaphor unified the nationalist analysis by capturing, in one image, the totalizing sense of alienation between whites and Blacks that the rejection of common nationality represented, the depiction of structural and systematic power exercised by the white community, and the conviction that group solidarity was necessary to change existing power relations. Carmichael pointed to the colonialist relationship as an explanation of the apparent similarity between the material conditions of African Americans in diverse cities:

> The American city, in essence, is going to be populated by the peoples of the Third World, while the white middle classes will flee to the suburbs. Now the black people do not control, nor do we own, the resources—we do not control the land, the houses or the stores. These are all owned by whites who live outside the community. These are very real colonies, in the sense that they are capital and cheap labor exploited by those who live outside the cities.... It does not seem that the men who control the power and resources of the United States ever sat down and designed those black enclaves, and formally articulated the terms of their dependent and colonial status.... Indeed, if the ghettos had been formally and deliberately planned instead of growing spontaneously and inevitably from the racist functionings of the various institutions that combine to make the society, it would be somehow less frightening—one could understand their similarity as being artificially and consciously imposed, rather than the result of identical patterns of white racism which repeat themselves in cities as far apart as Boston and Watts.[78]

The colonialism metaphor also provided the rhetoric for a critical analysis of relations within the Black community between economic classes. Nationalists deploying a "neocolonialism" analysis accounted for opposition to the nationalist position in the Black community as the effects of "indirect rule," within which an elite was created among the colonized class, to administer and mediate on behalf of colonialist interests. According to many Black nationalists, the Black middle class played this role in America, and class differences with the Black poor and working class accounted for the middle-class support of integration. As Cruse saw it, the Black middle class was frightened of the masses, dependent on the white power structure, and ambivalent about their own identity; consequently, the installation of the Black bourgeoisie as administrators of the Black community did not necessarily serve the community's interests:

> The tragedy of the black bourgeoisie in America is not that it simply "sells out," since all bourgeois classes are prone to compromise their sovereignty during a crisis. It is rather that no class the world over sells out so cheaply as the American black bourgeoisie, whose nation, the richest in the world, wastes billions overseas buying the fickle friendship of unworthy allies.[79]

This orientation around colonialism connected various projects in the 1960s and early 1970s, including movements for community control over schools; Black political, economic, and police control over Black neighborhoods; race-conscious economic cooperation among African Americans; race-conscious reparations from the white community to African American communities; the establishment and control of African American Studies Departments and African American dormitories in universities; the preservation and transformation of Black colleges and universities; and cultural autonomy in arts, music, literature, and intellectual life.

CHAPTER 3
DIFFERENT MANIFESTATIONS OF INTEGRATIONISM AND NATIONALISM

To this point, I have described integrationism and nationalism as sharply distinct and diametrically opposed ideologies about race. My goal was to highlight the intellectual and cultural contexts within which integrationism is situated and to describe Black nationalism as a comprehensive analysis of racial power resting on a competing, interlocking set of ideas about what race means in American social life. Given the cultural dynamics through which integrationism became the mainstream ideology of race and nationalism was marginalized as extremist, it is necessary to contrast the two ideologies in these oppositional and bipolar ways to recover the integrity of the nationalist position as a possibly liberating discourse about race, and to counter the deeply held stereotype that Malcolm X, Kwame Ture, the Black Panthers, and other nationalists were simply reverse racists, and that Black nationalism and racism are synonymous.

But one of the difficulties in describing ideologies is that they can never really be captured in their lived and complex forms. Thus, these descriptions tend to sound like worked-out theories, rather than the more complicated and contradictory ways people in actual historic situations come to terms with social life. Although these polarized descriptions capture important differences between the two cultural stances, in actual social life few experienced or articulated their commitment to either nationalism or integrationism in the clean, philosophic manner in which I identified the worldviews.[1] Before beginning an analysis of the cultural dynamics underlying the rejection of nationalism in the 1970s,

I want to discuss other ways integrationism and nationalism have manifested and might manifest in the future.

Integrationism and Collectivist Consciousness

I have identified the structure of integrationist ideology as a cluster of ideas connecting belief in universalism, objectivity, and individualism, and I have suggested that integrationism consequently obscured consideration of the racial character of practices in institutions such as public schools. But this depiction itself tends to obscure the ways in which the demand for racial integration has often been radically oppositional, spiritual, and communal.

One important dimension of integrationism, as it manifested itself in American culture, was the manner in which the civil rights movement helped generate an authentic community of people who understood themselves as profoundly committed to the eradication of racial domination in American society. For them, the ideology of integrationism was not experienced as simply the working out of a liberal theory of enlightenment. Instead, integrationism provided a frame for articulating their more deeply rooted, existential revulsion to racial domination, and often to a range of other social and institutional practices of "the system" that also seemed under siege. The flattening out of integrationism as an ideological structure should not obscure the dramatic courage of its proponents, fueled by authentic spiritual connections between individuals and displayed by thousands of people involved with or inspired by the civil rights movement. Despite the cognitive dimension of integrationism that reflected assumptions of individualism and universalism, the goal of racial integration spawned a social movement based, ironically, on a sense of collectivist consciousness, communal support, and intersubjective recognition that transcended the ideological limits of integrationism as a "theory." The religious imagery of broad-based spiritual communion was intertwined with the more rationalist political and legal rhetoric of civic equality that symbolized the civil rights movement for many years; the combination captured real aspirations for human freedom and social decency.[2] As King stated: "As I stood with them and saw white and Negro, nuns and priests, ministers and rabbis, labor organizers, lawyers, doctors, housemaids and shop workers brimming with vitality and enjoying a rare comradeship, I knew I was seeing a microcosm of the mankind of the future in this moment of luminous and genuine brotherhood."[3]

Martin Luther King, Jr., and Black Power

The stark opposition between integrationism and nationalism I have drawn also lends itself to an overly simplified categorization of particular leaders and movements that were, in fact, much more complex. For example, by viewing race-relations issues as fundamentally organized around a clear opposition between nationalism and integrationism, one tends to associate King with the integrationist, rights-oriented wing of the Black liberation movement and to associate Malcolm X with the nationalist faction. But however accurate that depiction of Malcolm X might be, King's position was far more complicated and ambiguous.

There is no denying that King's rhetoric was organized around the universalist imagery of the "Beloved Community," drawn from both Christianity and American liberal constitutionalism, and that his articulated goal was the transcendence of race consciousness in favor of integration.[4] In addition, much of the King/SCLC discourse appeared "integrationist" insofar as it was framed as an appeal to morality and conscience as the framework for the achievement of racial justice, in contrast to the nationalist analysis that racial justice depended on achieving Black Power.

King has become more of an "integrationist" in death, however, than he was in life. With the elevation of King to the status of national hero, mainstream culture has focused exclusively on King's nonviolent, universalist rhetoric. But if integrationism means a commitment to transcend race consciousness, or if integrationism is tied to the rejection of Black Power as a goal of mass organization, then King cannot be neatly categorized as an integrationist. The domesticated, popularized image of King leaves out a critical aspect of King's work that might be interpreted as the more revolutionary dimension to his organizational strategy.

In terms of community organizing, King accomplished a critical dimension of the nationalist project while speaking the language of integration. In a profound way, King represented the symbolic message that African Americans could conceive of themselves as an organic community bound together by a unique history, a present whose power relations demanded solidarity and support, and a shared future that demanded collective action.[5] Thus, the civil rights movement under King's leadership assumed an important part of the nationalist worldview: the idea that African Americans could, as a community, self-consciously develop a strategy of social transformation through participation in politics on the basis of group power. This aspect of King's work is obscured when he is sharply distinguished from Black Power advocates. King's commitment to nonviolent means has come to signify the movement's goal as neutral reason and institutional impersonality, rather than community power.[6] But in contrast to the image of nonviolence, one of the most significant features of the civil rights movement under King's leadership was the manner in which civil rights activists actually transformed race relations in cities and towns across the South by exerting the power of African American community and acting in solidarity and through alliances with other groups, both within and outside the particular locale, to *force* social change.

This power challenge to the status quo manifested in an important way in Black protest and resistance itself. Major portions of the white community, especially in the South, had rationalized their own participation in racial domination in part through an ideological construction of African Americans as "happy," "smiling," and "contented."[7] Whites imagined that these images were confirmed, at the micro-level of daily interaction within the hierarchies of race, by the (coerced) deference, gratitude, and loyalty that formed the social language of public contact between whites and Blacks. One reflection of this dynamic was that many Southern whites saw Black resistance as the work of "outside agitators."[8]

King mobilized millions of Blacks to declare their alienation from this social structure; demonstrate that the peaceful, contented, and settled quality of race relations was a charade; show that the social structure of race had invaded virtually every relation between Blacks and whites; and give notice that the Black community *en masse* was prepared to assault the social structure through organized social power. The emphasis on nonviolence hides this power/confrontation dimension of King's organizing and tends to make invisible the threat to fundamental power relations manifest in the mass organizing of the Black community during the civil rights mobilizations.

This dimension of King's work might help explain why, for example, the late Thurgood Marshall initially opposed mass organizing to achieve school integration in favor of litigation.[9] The difference between the movement King led and the position represented by Marshall mirrors the contrast I have drawn between nationalism and integrationism more generally. In the legalist conception, racial justice was to be achieved, in a sense, through reason, by mastering the elite discourse of the white power structure to integrate that power structure. In King's direct action conception, racial justice was infused with the particular cadences of African American spiritualism. The roots of the civil rights movement in the Black churches symbolized the fundamental difference between integrationism as it became institutionalized in American discourse through the imagery of a secular reason and the vision of integration articulated by King.[10]

The image of King pleading with the conscience of white America on the grounds of morality leaves much out of the picture. King helped organize masses of Black people to step out of the daily roles of accommodation or defeat, and to utilize racial solidarity to boycott buses, banks, and stores; strike from jobs; disrupt the business-as-usual aspect of settled racial domination with small sit-ins and mass mobilizations; and demonstrate the power of African Americans to reclaim and transform streets, institutions, and communities. It is true that King's strategy clearly included a coalition with white liberals, moderates, and the federal government, but an important dimension of his organizing was implicit in the mass mobilization (often across class lines) of Blacks themselves. From the viewpoint of many whites, the formal fact of "nonviolence" was overwhelmed by the pervasive threat of the disintegration of the social structure of deference and subordination that Black mobilization embodied.[11]

Nationalism as an Influence within Integrationist Practice

An absolute association of integrationism with the discourse of universalism and individualism also obscures the ways that nationalist ideology might exert influence within integrationist ideology itself. The stereotypical public policy conflicts among integrationists—over affirmative action, whether to identify racism in terms of intent or impact, what roles "diversity" and "merit" should play in institutional decision-making, and whether to engage in race-conscious remediation—could represent a split between integrationist and nationalist interpretations of integrationism itself.

In this view, the "conservative" side of the controversies within integrationism—opposition to affirmative action, requiring intent to make out a claim of race discrimination, and belief that achieving racial diversity is not a legitimate public policy goal—form a particularly universalist and individualist version of integrationism. It makes particular sense to require intent to make out a claim of race discrimination when racism is seen as rooted in individual consciousness, in prejudice and bias. Here, "colorblindness" is the goal. Any deviation is suspect, and it is assumed that once we transcend intentional consciousness about race, we will be left with neutral, rational, and objective social practices and institutional forms.

On the other hand, the "liberal" discourse—consisting of support for affirmative action, an impact rather than intent standard to identify racism, and racial diversity as a legitimate goal for institutional life—can be interpreted in two ways. First, the liberal positions might simply represent a different means to the same normative end of integrationism. Second, they might constitute a more radical, nationalist-oriented challenge to the universalizing assumptions of integrationist ideology. In the first interpretation, the liberal wing of the integrationist argument appears as a tougher version of integrationism—for example, the demand for an impact standard can be understood to ensure more rigorously and cautiously that irrationality and bias have been eradicated. The racially identifiable results of a purportedly neutral selection procedure are simply taken as more reliable evidence of racial bias than the vague and subjective inquiry into intent. Affirmative action and the diversity commitment can be seen as empirically verifiable means to ensure that selection procedures are not biased because, through such special efforts, proportionate numbers of racial minorities are chosen.

Alternatively, the liberal wing of the integrationist conflict might be understood as a nationalist-oriented tendency within integrationism, or at least as an accommodation to the nationalist commitment that the focus of racial justice should be on the impact of social practices on the Black community as a whole. The impact perspective accordingly would signify not the possibility of "bias," but rather the qualitatively different view that "civil rights" means a transfer of opportunities and resources on a group basis—a view comprehending that race marks a culturally significant group. Rather than accepting the central commitment of integrationism (that is, a desire to transcend race consciousness), the progressive aspect of mainstream legal and political civil rights discourse might be interpreted as contesting the issue of race consciousness in the trenches of integrationist doctrine—as demanding that selection procedures, for example, be understood through their effect on the power of racially defined communities. Thus, liberal integrationist discourse can be understood as rejecting the individualist focus of the enlightenment assertion that race consciousness is irrational in favor of an interpretation of history through the prism of social groups.[12]

Extending this wing of liberal integrationism, one can imagine a sophisticated vision of racial justice that would systematically replace the individualist focus of traditional integrationism with a focus on cultural communities and would simultaneously view institutional practices as a reflection of particular manifestations of cultural power. Rather than comprehending identity in terms of the diluted practice of cultural pluralism, within which ethnic and racial difference become privatized to the home and marginalized to episodic public celebrations, this kind of ideology would interpret norms of diversity in terms of the creation of a "creole" or "cosmopolitan" institutional and public culture that would contain the elements of composite cultures, rather than flatten out difference into an assumed universal and neutral set of public practices.[13]

The Right-Wing Black Nationalist Tradition

Just as my description of integrationism as a universalizing ideology excluded its more complicated manifestations, my description of nationalism as fundamentally historicist in orientation takes the dominant, leftist form that nationalism took in the late 1960s to represent the general nationalist position. My opinion is that the nationalist ideology of that period in fact represented the "true" Black nationalist position, at least in terms of nationalism's opposition to liberal integrationism. But the discourse of Malcolm X, the Black Panthers, Kwame Ture, and others was arguably an unusually left-wing and revolutionary version of Black nationalism. The nationalist position has more often been occupied by authoritarian and right-wing ideologies, with the Nation of Islam a vivid contemporary example.[14] As I see it, the tradition of right-wing manifestations of Black nationalism motivated efforts by contemporary Black social theorists to distance themselves from the tradition.[15]

The relatively rapid transformation in formal community self-description (Colored, Negro, Black, Afro-American, African American) indicates one facet of a deeper controversy within nationalist sensibilities over what actually makes up "the concrete national culture" that Charles Munford evoked.[16] I believe the best way to differentiate critical, or left-wing, nationalism from right-wing versions is to focus on how this issue of group identity is answered and policed. In the terms I have used here, the more historicist the ideology, the more critical and left-wing the manifestation of nationalism—and the more essentializing, the more conservative and right-wing. In my lexicon, the key sign of right-wing nationalism is the demand for a particular, ahistoric version of authentic group identity. The more that nationalists insist on universal, essential characteristics of authentic African American group identity, the more similar their ideology appears to white racism.

One possibility for providing (fixed) content to the meaning of African American culture is to look to African cultures. Given that a structure of racial domination and oppression marks African American history, many nationalists, like integrationists, rejected the possibility of identifying with any particular culture Black people created in America on the grounds that such a culture reflects the pathologies of subordination and repression. Rather than view African Americans as constituting a particular and unique community whose culture has been deeply influenced by its formation in the context of American race relations, these nationalists define the community in terms of an earlier time of imagined purity, before the American experience.[17] In social life, this stance is reflected in an exclusive identification with African cultural symbols and a demand that community members Africanize according to some central, universal image of what an African heritage means.

One cultural manifestation of this dynamic occurred in the 1960s through the often repressive and authoritarian demand for conformity in African dress (e.g., dashikis) and "natural" hairstyles (i.e., Afros). But the "Back to Africa" consciousness was only one aspect of a continual tension within nationalist ideology between a historicized and an essentialized understanding of the self-identity of the Black community.[18]

Another manifestation was the insistence by many 1960s Black nationalists that patriarchy was a part of authentic Black culture, thus making problematic the opportunity of Black women to experience nationalism as liberating, rather than repressive. The essentialized identification of Black culture with patriarchy extended from the generally conservative ideology of the Nation of Islam to the otherwise countercultural mindset of radicals, such as many of the Black Panthers.[19] The same tension between an essentialist and a historicist conception of group identity also underlies conflicts between nationalists over whether to form coalitions with white groups[20] and whether to accept homophobia as part of the community's self-definition.[21]

In sum, Black nationalism ideology can and sometimes has been manifest in authoritarian, right-wing movements. It does not have to take the (mostly) historicizing form that I contend it took in the 1960s. In fact, as I describe in Chapter 4, the left-wing radicalization of the nationalist tradition was a dramatic achievement of the 1960s generation of Black nationalists.

Similarly, the association of Black nationalism with a historicized view of social relations obscures how nationalists often essentialized not only the Black community, but also the white community. The extreme manifestation of this tendency occurred in the rhetoric of mainstream Black Muslims, for example, which regarded the white community in monolithic and universal terms as the eternal "white devil."[22] But the tendency toward reductionism also was reflected in more subtle ways by a conception of the white community as a unitary, time-less entity, rather than a complex group of subcommunities and subcultures, organized around and within histories of conflict over issues of class, gender, ethnicity, age, religion, region, and sexuality. At least from the inside, there is not, except in the fantasies of white supremacists, any "white community" or white culture.[23]

Nationalism as a Frame for Integration

Just as integrationism could be interpreted with a nationalist tilt, so nationalism could be interpreted to contain a distinctly integrationist influence. Thus, Black Power could be understood not as the challenge to the fundamental premises for the distribution of power I described, but rather as a call for African Americans to integrate either into electoral politics by registering to vote and becoming an interest group in a pluralist polity,[24] or into the economy by becoming entre-preneurs and capitalists.[25] Under this kind of interpretation, nationalism could become such a limited and nonthreatening ideology that even Richard Nixon would call for "Black capitalism."[26] But even without a particular capitalist spin, it is difficult to distinguish this tendency within Black nationalism from the pluralist, group-based interpretation of integrationism that demands the respectful coexistence of diverse cultural groups within the existing structure of social relations.[27]

In addition, the nationalist position could overlap with integrationism to the extent that, in particular contexts, nationalists would conclude that integration was the best means to ensure community power. For example, a nationalist-oriented argument for school integration might advocate integration as the only way to guarantee that public education resources are actually distributed to the Black community equitably.[28] The idea that Black children must sit beside white children to prevent a mal-distribution of resources does not in and of itself contradict the nationalist commitment to a race-conscious focus on the impact of social arrangements on the Black community.

The point of all of this is that nationalism and integrationism are not them-selves analytically determinate "philosophies." As part of lived ideologies, they overlap and intersect. Nevertheless, my thesis is that, as indeterminate as the concepts might analytically be, this ideological opposition constitutes a critical frame through which to understand race relations in recent American history. Although a group-based integrationist perspective can accommodate nationalism—and a nationalist perspective can include integration to gain community power, as I discuss in Chapter 4—the struggle over the issue of race consciousness symbolizes the compromise underlying the institutionalization of the civil rights movement in the American cultural mainstream.

CHAPTER 4
THE CLASH BETWEEN INTEGRATIONISM AND BLACK NATIONALISM: 1966–1973

As I have suggested, there was no analytically necessary reason to identify social reform of racial integration with cultural assimilation, individualist norms, or the idea that race consciousness is evil. But racial integration and its oppositional relation to Black nationalism acquired this particular meaning in the crucible of the concrete struggle with Black nationalism in the period extending roughly from 1966 to 1973. The ideology of integrationism—with its analytic components of prejudice, discrimination, and segregation—emerged as the framework for American mainstream thinking about race. The plausibility of the range of cognizable arguments about racial reform being limited to the basic question of intent or impact, the rhetorical ground for the controversy over "affirmative action," and the commonsense understanding of calls for Black Power as reverse racism are all connected by the unifying cultural commitment to make race consciousness the very definition of racial oppression, and thereby relegate Black nationalism to an area outside the realm of serious possibility. Black nationalism—focusing on race relations in terms of racial power, social subordination, and domestic colonialism—has been exiled to the social margins, the outposts of artistic production, and the Nation of Islam.[1] To the extent that honoring and nurturing African American culture and community is recognized as a commitment of mainstream American life, it has been safely absorbed into the pluralist respect for everyone's "cultural heritage" or "different voice."[2]

The rejection of Black nationalism as reverse racism, with the corresponding idea that any race consciousness implies a form of domination and oppression, now forms part of the underlying structure of mainstream discourse about race in legal, political, and other "official" spheres.[3] When liberal positions within integrationist discourse (e.g., support for affirmative action or an impact standard for identifying discrimination) echo the remnants of race consciousness, they appear marginalized and inconsistent with the basic integrationist premise that race consciousness must be transcended.

The borders of contemporary political and legal discourse about race were formed in the cultural crisis that militant Black nationalism engendered when it was articulated on a mass scale in the late 1960s. Although there was nothing intrinsic in the concept of racial integration that demanded that it be understood according to the universalist ideology I described, and although there was no reason African American racial consciousness had to be equated with the racial consciousness of white supremacists, I believe that this way of thinking about race was produced in part to justify the rejection of Black nationalism.

On one level, the rejection of nationalism and the institutionalization of integrationism as the legitimate way to think about race relations can be accounted for as a philosophical choice; integrationists rejected nationalism out of a commitment to the liberal principle that race consciousness was a deviant and distorted way to look at the world because it was irrational. The shared opposition to white supremacy and Black nationalism accordingly reflected a commitment to objectivity, neutrality, and reason, whose background image was the universalism of our shared humanity.

But this kind of account takes the ideologies of integrationism and nationalism as predefined philosophical options from which people choose. My sense is that the mainstream ways to think about race in America were both produced in, and helped to produce, particular cultural conflicts and struggles. What I mean when I say this ideology was "produced" is that we cannot understand the integrationist worldview simply as a philosophy or a set of concepts that themselves demanded Black nationalism be translated in a particular way. We should understand the dominance of integrationism as at least in part an effect, as well as a cause, of the marginalization of nationalism—as a discourse created to justify the rejection of nationalism, as well as a discourse that simultaneously informed the way nationalism was perceived.[4]

Integrationism was supported by a wide spectrum of denouncers of the "Black Power" slogan. They formed a coalition between Black, predominantly middle-class moderates and white, predominantly middle- and upper-class liberals and progressives. Understanding themselves as specifically opposed to race consciousness, integrationists needed to reject Black nationalists because of the threat they posed to the cultural self-identity of both the Black, middle-class moderates and white, liberal supporters of civil rights. The commitment to a universalist vision of racial justice responded to the anxiety these two elite groups shared; to whatever extent their integration was "successful," Blacks worried they were assimilating to a white world, and whites, guilty about the benefits they had been enjoying on a racially exclusive basis, wanted to think their institutions were basically just except for the unfortunate history of racial exclusion.

The upshot of their implicit coalition was that they constructed and embraced a conservative race ideology that helped to contain the issue of racial liberation— together with other disruptive challenges to the assumptions of everyday institutional life, such as the feminist movement—by perceiving all of these challenges as part of a single discourse, unified around an idea of "discrimination." This integrationist ideology served simultaneously to recognize racial power as a formal matter and (yet) to set boundaries for its critique. Without attempting a complete account of how and why this coalition formed in this particular manner, I want to recall briefly the cultural politics of that period and to speculate about the dynamics that enabled today's mainstream ideology about race to achieve its dominant status.

The clash between nationalism and integrationism extended from the period starting in 1966, when the "Black Power" slogan first gained national prominence, and lasted until the marginalization of Black nationalists was complete in the mid-1970s. This was, to say the least, a particularly intense and significant historical juncture for both Black and white communities in America. The list of major events, in no particular order, is staggering: The Black Panther Party was organized on a national scale. Dr. Martin Luther King, Jr., spoke out against the Vietnam War and began criticizing capitalism. King and Robert Kennedy were assassinated. African Americans rioted regularly in urban ghettos across the country. The Vietnam War galvanized increasingly radical white and Black youth, who helped force a president out of office. Southern institutions had used up "all deliberate speed," and many were forced by federal courts to desegregate. George Wallace mounted two national campaigns for the presidency on a white supremacist platform. Gay men rioted when police raided the Stonewall Inn in Greenwich Village, marking the symbolic birth of the modern American gay liberation movement. The federal government was in the midst of civil rights enforcement. Richard Nixon was twice elected by the "silent majority." White, middle-class women were organizing on feminist issues on a mass scale. The

Woodstock nation was born. And the sexual revolution and the countercultural movement of white and Black youth were connected to antiwar and more general leftist projects in a large-scale rebellion of young against old.

Against this intense background, in which it seemed that so much in American society was up for grabs, Black nationalism achieved its most sophisticated articulation and its greatest mass appeal. Then, as various ruptures of American society were resolved in favor of the integrationist ideology, Black nationalism was pushed to the cultural margins.

To understand the particular way the conflict between nationalists and integrationists in the late 1960s and early 1970s constituted a pivotal, constitutive cultural moment for contemporary race discourse, it is important to comprehend what the conflict meant for the Black and white communities. In this section, I first trace the particular significance 1960s nationalism had in the Black community, arguing that in the 1960s, Black nationalism—for the first time in the 20th century—shed its historic association with a conservative, accommodationist, and disgraced separatist tradition. Moreover, this conflict within Black communities had sharp class and generational dimensions. For many middle-class and conservative Blacks, the universalist interpretation of integrationism was crucial to understanding their own position as not implying group betrayal. In the next section, I discuss what the Black nationalist position meant in the white community, and I contend that, for many white liberals and progressives, understanding racial justice through a universalist prism was crucial to avoiding deep-seated anxieties that they lacked the kind of rich culture and sense of community the nationalists asserted defined Black culture and that, in a distorted way, was also attributed to Blacks by white supremacist ideology.

The Transformed Meaning of Black Nationalism

One important aspect of the confrontation between nationalism and integrationism in the 1960s was that after decades of marginality within the African American community, Black nationalism achieved mass appeal and arguably overtook integrationism as the dominant ideology of racial liberation. Black nationalism in the 1960s represented both the reappearance of a long tradition that had begun at least as early as Martin Delany in the 1850s—a tradition that had been obscured by the unity created by integrationist-oriented leadership from the mid-1950s to mid-1960s—and also embodied a reinterpretation of

the nationalist ideology. This reinterpretation dramatically severed the associations between nationalism and accommodationism—a link dating back to the
confluence, under Booker T. Washington's leadership, of separatist organizing
and accommodationist relations with white domination.

The Continuity of the Civil Rights/Nationalism Opposition

According to Harold Cruse, "American Negro history is basically a history of
the conflict between integrationist and nationalist forces in politics, economics
and culture, no matter what leaders are involved and what slogans are used."[5]
This conflict has reappeared repeatedly; for example, when Delany articulated
the formation of Black colonies as a strategy for racial liberation in the mid-19th
century, his proposals were opposed by Frederick Douglass's discourse of militant
abolitionism, articulated in terms of American constitutional and civil rights.[6]
The nationalist strain subsided during Reconstruction, but was rejuvenated in
the post-Reconstruction world by the widely influential self-help and separatist
ideas of Booker T. Washington,[7] which W. E. B. Du Bois challenged at the turn
of the 20th century. In the tradition of Douglass, Du Bois argued for political
and legal equality as the proper vision of racial justice. From his influence, one
can directly trace the origins of the NAACP in the early 20th century.[8] And just
as the NAACP was consolidating its legal and political strategies in the 1930s
and 1940s, nationalist organizing reached a new mass base in Northern urban
centers through the leadership of Marcus Garvey.[9] Even in the late 1950s, when
King galvanized the African American community behind an integrationist
vision fused with images of religious and moral transcendence, the Nation of
Islam—articulating programs of economic cooperatives, cultural discipline,
self-help and solidarity, and African American separation from the United States
through a land grant—continued to contest the integrationist program, and attracted significant support in urban centers and among the most economically
deprived groups.[10]

Moreover, the tensions between integrationist and nationalist ideologies
were reflected within individuals and between political factions. Du Bois provided a vivid example of this inner conflict. Initially, he publicly represented
the integrationist/civil rights ideology in his critique of Booker T. Washington.
In fact, to this day, he is probably the person most responsible for the popular
image of Washington as a conservative accommodationist to Southern racial
apartheid.[11] Du Bois helped found and supported the NAACP, and he edited

its publication, *The Crisis,* for several decades, but he ultimately resigned his position, broke with the NAACP in the early 1940s in dramatic opposition to its policy of integrationism, and began to emphasize Pan-Africanism (the organization of economic cooperatives on a race-conscious basis) and "voluntary self-segregation" as the key ideas of Black liberation.[12] And this invocation of the highly publicized tension between integrationism and nationalism among community leaders does not even begin to describe the tensions and ambiguities that have traditionally characterized the popular, day-to-day culture of African American life. The demands and fruits of community solidarity are in constant tension with the ambiguity of simultaneous repulsion by and attraction to the possibility of assimilation into the white world.[13]

In short, the resurgence of Black nationalism in the 1960s reflected a long-standing conflict within the African American community that the brief unity around King's leadership temporarily obscured. But what made the struggle between Black nationalists and Black integrationists particularly significant in the 1960s was not its continuity, but its changed cultural meaning. Integrationism and nationalism traditionally have been the stark choices the African American community associated with racial politics, but that does not mean the two ideologies were always understood in the same way.

The 1960s Transformation of Black Nationalism

In addition to the conflict over nationalist and integrationist conceptions of race, the issue of "accommodationism" versus resistance embodies another central dimension of African American racial discourse.[14] The degree of resistance and opposition associated with either integrationism or nationalism was an independently important cultural issue—with its own history of conflict—in the perception of each stance.

Although the Black nationalist stance was unmistakably identified with a commitment to militancy—and eventually violent revolution—by the late 1960s and early 1970s, there was no necessary historic or analytic connection between Black nationalism and the desire to confront and resist the white power structure. To the contrary, virtually every other significant Black nationalist movement in American history bore marks of accommodationism. Early-19th-century colonization movements were framed in a historical context in which African American support for "Back-to-Africa" programs was linked closely to white supremacists who supported colonization as a means to deport Black people from North America.[15] In contrast to the colonists, the abolitionist/ civil rights/integrationist rhetoric of Douglass, for instance, appeared far more militant and oppositionist. Similarly, Du Bois based his critique of the self-help, racial-solidarity, and separatism rhetoric of Booker T. Washington on the manner in which Washington's approach amounted to a "submission" and "surrender" to the Jim Crow social structure, rather than a challenge to that structure.[16] Du Bois' differences with Garvey centered on the same issue, although Garvey was clearly more militant and confrontational than Washington.[17] By the time the integrationists' momentum increased in the 1940s and 1950s, Black national- ism, represented mainly by the socially and religiously conservative dogma of the Nation of Islam, had achieved the role of a kind of "traditionalism." Thus, in the early years of the civil rights movement, nationalist approaches, organized in the cultural margins of the Black community, seemed to many civil rights activists to imply an accommodation to the racial apartheid structure of white society through a retreat to the "isolation" of the Black community.[18] In generational terms, this meant that nationalist appeals to young civil rights workers were likely experienced as the conservative voice of an older generation saying "Don't make waves," and "Stick with your own people," in contrast to the sense within the civil rights movement of building a drive for resistance to and confrontation with the white power structure.

This symbolic association of nationalism with accommodationism and integrationism with resistance in the cultural perception of the basic choices facing Blacks helps account for how King could simultaneously represent the militant, confrontation-oriented aspirations of Black activists while speaking in the rhetoric of integrationism, moralism, and civil rights.[19] When King began in Montgomery, one could divide civil rights activists and groups according to whether they supported a legalist, litigation-oriented strategy of race reform or the approach of direct action and confrontation. As an early leader of mass direct action, King began his career representing the militant, nonaccommodation- ist wing of the civil rights movement, a faction whose strategies embodied the nationalist belief that racial solidarity and assertions of group power were the means to attain racial liberation.[20] That is, even while nationalist ideology was most marginalized in the Black community during the 1950s and early 1960s, one can detect aspects of nationalism within the integrationist civil rights move- ment itself. The historic opposition between nationalism and integrationism was reproduced in the conflict between the legalistic and direct-action factions of the civil rights movement.

Before the resurgence of nationalist ideology in the mid-1960s, this tension within the civil rights movement was understood to encompass only the strategic question of the degree of militancy. The decision to turn back the marchers at the Edmund Pettus Bridge in Selma became the cultural symbol of a split between Black activists over how far to extend confrontational organizing.[21] In retrospect, however, this argument over tactics can be seen to have contained the seeds of the later, more explicit opposition between nationalist and integrationist substantive ideologies. For a time in the early 1960s, in fact, the two tendencies merged in cultural perception. Militant, confrontational integrationists like Robert Williams, who advocated "armed self-defense" in his confrontationally titled *Negroes with Guns,* became associated with militant, confrontational nationalists like Malcolm X.[22] It was possible to perceive individuals and groups with such ultimately opposing and inconsistent ideologies as similar because the issue of militancy versus accommodation embodied central cultural significance in ways that transcended and eventually subsumed the split between nationalist and integrationist positions. It is therefore no coincidence that the most "direct action"–oriented groups within the civil rights umbrella—SNCC and CORE—would eventually renounce the civil rights analytics of prejudice, discrimination, and segregation in favor of the nationalist analytics of power, subordination, and colonialism.[23]

In short, Black nationalism in the late 1960s embodied two important African American traditions—on one hand, the long tradition of explicit nationalist ideology, and on the other hand, the long tradition of resistance by Blacks to racial domination. Given the different roles integrationism and nationalism played in relation to this separate conflict between resistance and accommodation, it would be a mistake to limit the historical antecedents of the nationalist presence in the mid- to late 1960s to groups, such as the Nation of Islam, that embraced Black nationalism as a formal ideology. In addition to roots in movements such as the Nation of Islam, Pan-Africanism, and Garveyism, an important historical antecedent for 1960s Black nationalism was the split in the 1950s and early 1960s between integrationists who advocated "direct action" and those who advocated legal and civil remedies for racial discrimination.[24]

The widespread invocation of the colonialism model to describe race relations[25] symbolized how 1960s Black nationalists linked nationalism and social struggle, and thus symbolically broke the traditional association of separatism with accommodationism. Previous nationalist movements, even militant Garveyism,[26] always could be associated with the humiliation of accommodationism to the extent that they seemed to accept American racial segregation. Rather than oppose the power dynamics between white and Black communities in the United States, the separatist proposals for a return to Africa (Delany and Garvey), creation of a separate land base in the United States (the Nation of Islam, the Republic of New Africa), or various proposals for the creation of a separate Black economic base (Du Bois, the Nation of Islam, Booker T. Washington) all carried a sense of retreat from mainstream American life into isolation and nonconfrontation. In contrast, the articulation of the relations between Blacks and whites as "neocolonialist" served as a bridge between the aspirations for community power that were always at least implicit in the nationalist ideology of racial solidarity and self-help, and the militancy and confrontationalism that had been the province of direct-action integrationists. Rather than representing a fantasy of separation or isolation from whites, the colonialism metaphor presented nationalists as engaged in the struggle for power in the United States; it posed the problem facing African Americans as the form of relations between white and Black communities, instead of asserting that the problem was that there were relations at all. And the colonialist analysis located the solution not in a retreat from the United States, but rather as a struggle to transform relations of subordination within America. Unlike the conservative aspects of earlier manifestations of Black nationalism, the colonialist analysis comprehended the imposition of an external power structure on the African American community and accordingly provided a symbolic mediation of the tendency for self-blame that a nationalist emphasis on self-help and personal discipline might otherwise imply.

In the 1960s, Black nationalists began to conceive of their project not as geographic separation from whites, but rather as the dismantling of the power relations between white and Black communities. Instead of the choices appearing as integration and assimilation on one hand or total geographic separation on the other, 1960s nationalists, led most notably by Malcolm X, developed a "third" way that combined militant engagement with the white power structure with the racial solidarity and anti-assimilationism traditionally associated with nationalism.[27]

In short, after embodying the opposite associations for most of the 20th century, nationalism became associated with resistance and militancy in the 1960s, and integrationism appeared the more accommodationist and conservative position. Early in the decade, Malcolm X symbolized this dimension of 1960s nationalism. By the mid-1960s, this reinterpretation of the Black nationalist tradition that Malcolm X began (and which helps explain his eventual break with the Nation of Islam)[28] was embodied by the "Black Power" movement, the explicit symbolic conjunction of the two traditions of nationalism and confrontation.[29]

In this new context, nationalist activism reproduced the class splits that historically characterized the opposition between integrationism and nationalism, and for the first time appeared poised to transcend those splits in favor of nationalism over integration.[30] In rough terms, before King's leadership, integrationism was the central ideology of the Black middle class, and the nationalist ideology primarily received support only from the Black poor and working class. Part of King's significance as a political leader was his ability to unite African Americans around integrationism across class lines for the first time in the 20th century.[31] Yet even during the period of King's greatest mass appeal, membership in Muslim temples continued to grow, and Malcolm X's militant nationalist appeals became popular in Northern urban centers. And as King started to lose Black support, it was the urban poor who most substantially challenged his leadership.

By the late 1950s, King had united virtually the entire Black community behind a program of confrontational direct action aimed at the achievement of integration, but the situation had changed by the late 1960s. Nationalists claimed the symbolic ground of militancy. They developed a sophisticated critique of dominant American culture and power relations that at least rhetorically connected African Americans to the Africans and Asians who were achieving independence from colonial rule, and they utilized a class-based neocolonialist analysis to identify Black integrationists with "moderate" and "assimilationist" middle-class accommodation to the white power structure. The respective reactions of integrationists and nationalists to urban riots in the mid- and late 1960s represent a dramatic example of these differences. In contrast to the attempt of those in the mainstream to interpret urban riots as unfortunate and irrational frustration with the slow pace of civil rights reform,[32] nationalists identified with and tended to support riots as decolonizing revolts against the white power and property structure.[33] These contrasting positions with respect to the hot issue of urban disruption were only one face of more thorough ruptures of the consensus King had achieved. Nationalists also contested the class unity King had achieved, so that by the mid-1960s, integrationism again bore the mark of the Black middle class and seemed to have little to offer the poor or working class. Furthermore, significant portions of the relatively small Black middle class, represented most strongly by Black students, repudiated integrationism. Integrationists were on the defensive within the Black community, and all the momentum seemed to be moving toward the nationalist position.[34]

The explicit ideological changes within organizations evidenced the sense of nationalist momentum. In the mid- to late 1960s, SNCC and CORE, which previously had been direct action–oriented civil rights groups advocating integration, adopted explicit nationalist positions.[35] In addition, the power of the nationalist drift was evident within the SCLC itself. King's decision finally to oppose the Vietnam War publicly in 1967 and the SCLC's shift in focus from civil to economic rights and from the South to the Northern ghettos shortly before King's assassination were arguably partly in response to the sense that King and the SCLC were quickly losing the support of both Black youth in general and the urban poor in particular.[36]

The conflict between these two groups soon became acute. Nationalists developed a rhetoric within which any association with whites was seen to be a sign of race treachery, captured by the epithet of "Oreo"; integrationists developed a rhetoric in which the nationalists represented a form of extremism akin to that of white supremacists and other hate groups. And, in fact, the polarization of the discourse between Black integrationists and nationalists was a manifestation of the ways each group threatened the other.

Nationalism upset the confidence the Black middle class had held since the turn of the 20th century in the achievement of civil rights and integration into dominant American institutions—a goal that to them had appeared a real possibility. Nationalist ideology threatened the self-identity of the middle class as the elite of Black society, who symbolized the achievement possible when Blacks are afforded opportunity. Nationalists also undermined the Black middle class's conception that their role in racial liberation was to help the "brothers and sisters" left behind to "escape" the ghetto and join mainstream institutions.

In the nationalist analysis, the very success of the Black middle class in American society betrayed the aspirations of the Black community because it reflected gains granted by a white power structure in exchange for Black administration of white interests. This rhetoric called to mind the shame of the long history of accommodationism by Black middle-class leaders and thus generated a kind of group anxiety. Integrationism, in the particular, universalist form it took in the 1960s, responded to this anxiety by denying that the world to which the Black middle class aspired was racially identifiable as a particularly white world, rather than a realm of universal, culturally neutral social practices.

Similarly, the very predominance and strength of the integrationist tradition engendered a correlate anxiety for nationalists, an anxiety that extreme and polar expressions of Black separatism helped resolve. According to Cruse, the particular violence and hateful rhetoric that came to characterize Black nationalist discourse by the end of the 1960s was rooted in a psychological attempt to overcome the ways Blacks had been conditioned historically to depend on whites in the realm of political action. To overcome the deeply ingrained inter-racialism that had characterized progressive coalitions for several decades, Cruse asserted that Black nationalists, particularly middle-class Blacks, had to muster hatred "to avoid the necessity of apologizing to whites for excluding them."[37] Thus, just as Black integrationists gravitated toward a particularly universalist interpretation of racial justice to help resolve anxiety that nationalists raised about their self-identity, so Black nationalists gravitated toward particularly extreme exclusionary interpretations to overcome their anxiety about their own relation to whites. And, in this cultural posture, each group tended to confirm the suspicions of the other. The more universalist the integrationist ideology, the more nationalists saw an apologia for assimilation into the white world and a corresponding betrayal of the Black community. The more hateful the nationalist rhetoric became, the more integrationists saw the same bitterness and parochialism as they saw in white supremacists.

Black Nationalism and Whites

The ultimate marginalization of Black nationalists from mainstream discourse reflects several historical factors. One important feature was the overt and covert state repression that groups like the Black Panthers faced.[38] Another was the way in which the increasingly extremist and revolutionary rhetoric and social actions on the part of the Black and white left began to appear more and more fantastic as time went on.[39] Furthermore, limitations in ideology often led to a rigid, otherworldly revolutionary dogma gleaned from a conglomeration of Karl Marx, V. I. Lenin, Mao Zedong, Frantz Fanon, and others—a dogma that took on an extremist, righteous tone that began to associate anyone who had a job with the white power structure. This approach alienated masses of African Americans and others who were not prepared to engage in an armed guerrilla campaign in America.[40] In addition, just as the economic health of Black communities generally deteriorated during the recessionary periods of the late 1960s and mid-1970s, the Black middle class expanded with the advent of integrationism as a national policy, and they largely abandoned traditionally Black neighborhoods.[41] By the mid-1970s, successes in struggles for political influence in or control of many cities, combined with an emerging national commitment to "cultural diversity," began to echo features of the nationalist program. American mainstream institutions seemed to accommodate a diffused and limited version of Black race consciousness. Such developments tended to obscure the nationalist position as a sharp alternative to integration.

Whatever else "caused" the decline of nationalism, however, there can be no question that its near-total rejection[42] by whites played a critical factor in its exclusion from mainstream American discourse. As indicated above, the overt analytic framework for this reaction was the identification of race consciousness with the evil of racism and the consequent perception of Black nationalists as racists. In this section, I now want to speculate about what led whites to adopt this view of race and to mistranslate Black nationalism as the Black equivalent of white supremacy.

Various factors partially explain why white liberals and progressives in particular rejected nationalism as a way to analyze race relations. First, at least early in the 1960s, there is no doubt that nationalists (including Malcolm X) tended toward explicit racism and hatred in their depictions of whites.[43] Second, unlike the long tradition of progressive Black nationalism in African American communities, the only major white groups that explicitly perceived race as a significant feature of group identity were white supremacists—a group historically composed of a loose cultural coalition of Southern well-to-do whites and major segments of the white working class across the country. In their congruence of race and nationalism, race consciousness was tied to an interest in racial domination—specifically, the perpetuation of white domination—and, in more recent years, fears of Black domination should African Americans achieve significant social power in American society. One factor that led to the failure of white liberals to comprehend Black nationalism as a liberating, rather than repressive, movement was that race consciousness had been historically associated with precisely the segments of the white community from whom enlightened whites wished to distinguish themselves.[44]

Moreover, because Black nationalism before the 1960s was largely separatist and isolationist, almost by definition whites had little or no contact with the tradition of race consciousness among African Americans. In terms of their perception of the Black nationalist position, most white liberals and progressives were influenced by the conventional understanding of the racial separatism advocated by Booker T. Washington as Black accommodationism to segregation. Like most Black activists, white civil rights supporters in the early 1960s took the confrontation-oriented direct-action wing of civil rights protest as the very definition of committed struggle. They perceived that the choices were between moderation and activism—or (put another way) between legalism on one hand and street action coupled with community organizing on the other—and that these choices defined the parameters of political and ideological issues posed by race.

Before the 1960s, whites who were serious about race reform worked with, supported, and often directed the legalist strategies of the NAACP and the Urban League, and the direct-action integrationism of groups like the SCLC, SNCC, and CORE.[45] This decades-long civil rights tradition carried on by white liberals and progressives, with longer roots to 19th-century abolitionists, defined racial enlightenment in relation to the staunch and often violent opposition of white supremacists. By the mid-1960s, when Black nationalism reached its height of popularity within the Black community, white liberals and progressives still understood the issue as a choice between militancy in support of immediate integration and the conservative stance of foot-dragging. While Black integrationists with any connections to the Black community simply could not avoid confronting the Black nationalist analysis of race in the 1960s, it is striking that, except for some relatively isolated leftist factions, whites as a group never considered the possibility that race consciousness might have a liberating, rather than repressive, meaning.

Against this historical background of nonengagement with, and ignorance of, the Black nationalist tradition, Black nationalism confronted white integrationists in the 1960s through the militant rhetoric fist of Malcolm X and Black Power proponents. Although the particular form nationalist rhetoric took in the 1960s was largely responsive to the struggle between integrationists and nationalists within the Black community, an obviously significant factor in the white response was the rejection and repudiation that whites experienced from Black nationalists.

One important episode that marked the white response to 1960s nationalists was the expulsion and exclusion of whites from civil rights organizations like SNCC and CORE when the organizations took a nationalist turn in the mid-1960s.[46] According to Cruse, a discourse of race hatred on the part of many new nationalists:

> resulted from the particular ideology of interracialism that had become inculcated into the Negro's mind: Even before the average Negro attempts to

undertake any action himself, he assumes, almost involuntarily, that he must not, cannot, dare not exclude whites, because he cannot succeed without them. He has been so conditioned that he cannot separate personal and individual associations with individual whites ... from that interior business that is the specific concern of his group's existence.... But with LeRoi Jones and his young Afro-American nationalists, anti-interracialism was equated not only with anti-whiteness, but with hatred of whiteness. In other words, Negroes had become so deeply mired in an institutionalized form of political interracialism that they could not break with it unless sufficient hatred were mustered to avoid the necessity of apologizing to whites for excluding them. That this was a paranoia-producing rationalization was not understood. If Negroes were actually thinking and functioning on a mature political level, then the exclusion of whites—organizationally and politically—should be based not on hatred but on strategy. It would be much like the tradition that no one outside one's immediate family is ever admitted into a discussion of intimate family problems. It is, therefore, an unfortunate development in Negro life that political interracialism has become so doctrinaire that certain nationalistic Negroes have been forced to resort to race hate in order to block out the negative effect of interracialism on ethnic consciousness.[47]

This dynamic helps to account for what appears to be, in retrospect, the particular and often seemingly gratuitous extremism of middle-class Black nationalists during the 1960s. It is possible that the extreme militancy many others experienced as "posturing" played a defensive role in helping to repress the actual cultural ambiguity that has historically marked the Black middle class self-identity.[48] While many Black nationalist groups and individuals adopted the "hate whitey" rhetoric that had historically characterized the Nation of Islam ideology, others, like Cruse, saw the developments as part of a pathology rooted in the historic commitment to interracialism on the part of the Black middle class. According to Cleaver, who on behalf of the Black Panthers actively advocated and organized coalitions with radical whites, the expulsion of whites from SNCC resulted from a "paranoid fear" of white domination rooted in the fact that SNCC nationalists had to wrest control of SNCC from whites, a situation the Black Panthers never faced.[49]

This rage-filled rhetoric of hate against whites adopted by many nationalist groups and leaders seemed to confirm to whites the idea that Black nationalism and white supremacy were identical manifestations of irrational and indiscriminate hate. As the nationalists began to achieve power within the former direct-action wing of the civil rights movement, liberal and progressive whites who had participated in the movement either withdrew from racial politics altogether or made alliances with "moderate" and mostly middle-class Blacks around the commitment to integrationism, understood as the transcendence of race consciousness.[50]

But the image that whites were simply repelled by Black nationalists does not fully account for the ways in which white liberals and progressives reacted to nationalism as an ideology of race reform. Their embrace of integrationism in the particular universalist form it took in the 1960s was also, arguably, more subtly related to anxieties about their own cultural self-identity than can be accounted for solely by the pain of exclusion and rejection by Blacks. For this group of whites, the nationalist assertion of the particularities of Black culture brought to the surface unresolved anxieties that "nonracist" whites had about their own feelings regarding both Blacks and themselves.

With respect to Blacks, the nationalist assertion of difference and the location of that difference in terms of the particularities of culture simultaneously connected to two key issues for whites: First, whites committed to nonracism had expended energy and concentrated on overcoming the teachings of a society permeated with racist ideology that Black difference—specifically inferiority—justified racial hierarchy. Second, to the extent that a residue of racist dogma remained in white liberal consciousness, it existed as a vague sense of *envy* that Blacks were different from whites specifically because Blacks possessed a rich and spiritual culture filled with music, dance, religion, and passionate sexuality—qualities that whites experienced most strongly as lacking in the dominant white American culture.

In other words, for white liberals and progressives, the nationalist assertion of a particular African American culture immediately brought to the surface white anxiety that, in fact, the nationalists were right—Blacks had the kind of cohesive and rich culture whites felt they themselves lacked. It simultaneously created feelings of guilt about believing such a thing because that kind of attribution of characteristics to Blacks seemed just like the racist ideology these whites had worked so hard to overcome. More specifically, the culture whites secretly feared Blacks possessed looked like the symbolic structure as envisioned by white supremacist ideology: a particular primitive culture having a folk life, spirituality, and sexuality that stood in opposition to rationalism, objectivity, and civilization. Black nationalism, particularly in the machismo and Africanist forms it took in the late 1960s, specifically exposed the deepest inner anxieties whites as a cultural group possessed—anxieties that white liberals and progressives had worked hard to repress.

Integrationism, understood as the transcendence of race consciousness, provided a vehicle for resolving the anxiety nationalists raised by denying that Blacks or whites as such had any identifiable culture at all. People "happen to be Black" or "happen to be white." In the integrationist mindset that white liberals and progressives adopted, it made no sense to think about institutional practices in racial and cultural terms because there were no cultures tied to racial identity. And so it came to be, paradoxically, that for whites, integrationism actually constituted an indirect defense of status quo social and institutional practices to the extent that integrationist ideology was constructed to foreclose consideration of these cultural manifestations of racial power.

Seen in this way, the psychological identity issues engendered by Black nationalists were in some ways similar for both Black and white integrationists. The otherwise paradoxical coalition between Black moderates and conservatives on one hand and white liberals on the other hand had its roots in the way that universalism helped resolve the identity anxieties of each group. Black integrationists could identify with a commitment to an objective, aracial set of social norms, rather than perceive themselves as assimilating into the white world. And white integrationists could understand themselves as advocating the equal distribution of opportunity, rather than asserting the superiority of white social norms or acknowledging their more deep-seated fears about Black passion, culture, and sexuality.

In short, enlightened whites helped construct and deploy a liberal understanding of racial justice that incorporated universalist and objectivist assumptions. This understanding rejected race consciousness as a categorical matter, in part as a way to avoid issues of white cultural identity that Black nationalism brought to the fore. The near-universal rejection of a nationalist understanding of race was not required for whites to oppose white supremacists, and it was not based on simply a "philosophical" commitment to integrationism, because the repudiation of racial domination could have taken many other forms. Instead, the particular view of race embraced during the 1960s reflected a cultural response on the part of white liberals and progressives, not only to white supremacists, but also to Black nationalists.

The embrace of integrationism did not represent the only way that the broad avoidance of white racial identity took place. Although the mainstream white response was to denounce Black nationalists as reverse racists, significant elements of the white liberal and progressive community attempted to embrace nationalists as allies. A roughly identifiable group of Northeastern liberal elites, depicted in Tom Wolfe's account of this cultural phenomenon in *Radical Chic & Mau-Mauing the Flak Catchers*,[51] sympathized with nationalist groups and personalities, but their comprehension of the issues did not extend to the actual substantive programs or theoretical commitments of the nationalists. Instead, they perceived Black nationalists from a civil liberties standpoint within which nationalists appeared as militant and aggressive civil rights groups who were wrongfully repressed by the State.

On the other hand, radical white groups such as the Students for a Democratic Society (SDS) did embrace the nationalist critique of existing American cultural forms and the critique of the conservative underside of liberal integrationism. In fact, during the 1960s, there was a great degree of reciprocal influence between the developing social analysis that came to be known as the "New Left" and the developing Black nationalist approaches. But relations between white radicals and Black nationalists in the 1960s and early 1970s tended to have a distorted and pathological dynamic; White radicals often approached nationalists as representing an oppressed group that possessed, by virtue of their oppression, the unique insight and entitlement to determine how the social struggle should proceed and to decide virtually any other issue that arose. Lacking success with the traditional left constituency—the working class—white radicals began to substitute a "Third World-ism" for an economic analysis. Black nationalists, in turn, approached white radicals as representatives of historic white power.

The relationship was repetitive in nature; Black radicals made more and more demands for control of white groups as evidence of white commitment, and white radicals continually deferred to Blacks as acts of white atonement. The more general cultural manifestation of this stance of white radicals was the constant tendency to make Blacks the paradigms of political and cultural insight. In interracial contexts in radical circles, this tendency led to the development of a dynamic of Black self-assertion and racial critique, and white submission and deference—colloquially known as white "self-flagellation"—that came to define race relations among radicals.

These predominant relations to Black nationalism[52] linked manifestations of a central dynamic that characterized the liberal and progressive white community— the inability to come to terms with white self-identity. The virulence with which white liberals denounced Black nationalism as reverse racism, patronizing tolerance of Northeastern liberal elites, and self-effacing submission that characterized many white radicals who engaged nationalists reflected a similar cultural position among "nonracist" whites during the 1960s. In fact, the widespread embrace of integrationism and the idea that racial enlightenment consisted of transcending race consciousness were only the reigning ideological faces of a more diffuse and widespread cultural avoidance that seemed to include measures of guilt, desires for atonement, and needs for absolution.[53]

This discomfort with whiteness has led to a kind of self-negation. One manifestation is the attempt to construct racially neutral settings—for example, public education—where the problem of interracialism is imagined to be resolved by effacing any culture at all. Another manifestation is the attempt to embrace Black culture by making it one's own—that is, by talking and acting according to how whites think Blacks act. At the individual level, this flight from racial identification appears as the exaggerated need for acceptance from Blacks on the ground that one is not like the rest of the whites—that one is not really white. And the broadscale ideological dimension is a commitment to integrationism in the particular form that has characterized mainstream race discourse for the last two decades—integrationism understood as the transcendence of race consciousness.

Black nationalism caused great anxiety and turmoil for whites in part because of the violence that nationalists symbolized, but also because nationalism represented whites as constituting a community with particular cultural norms. As whites articulated their rejection of Black nationalists, they complained of "reverse racism" because they experienced the nationalist depiction of a white culture as the same kind of essentializing and stereotyping that white racists utilized in describing Black culture. And, to be sure, much of nationalist rhetoric was reductionist with respect to the complexity of group relations within the white community. But through the identification of racial identity and group consciousness as central to the structure of American social relations, the Black nationalists of the 1960s also identified the particular aspect of avoidance and denial that white support of Black liberation assumed—the commitment by whites to deny the centrality of race as a historically constructed, and powerful, factor in the social structure of American life. Understanding racism as a form of "discrimination" from an assumed neutral norm was the cognitive face of a widespread cultural flight from white self-identity. The resurgence of ethnic group consciousness on the part of whites during the 1970s, although in part a liberating attempt to reclaim cultural authenticity in the face of the mainstream culture of neutrality, was also in part a reflection of this same dynamic; being Polish, Italian, or Irish meant, to a degree, not being simply white.

The upshot of this cultural situation is that, despite the fact that race has worked as such a powerful element of the economy and culture of social relationships, no group of whites has formed who could identify themselves with the white community without also associating whiteness with either paralyzing guilt or interest in racial domination. Explicit white racial identification was left to lower-class, "ignorant" whites; the implicit racial identification was left to the universalizing aspirations of the culturally dominant white upper-middle class.

The broad-scale effect of this particular resolution of the "race" issue within mainstream discourse was that the very whites who might otherwise have been allies of Black nationalists during the 1960s were motivated, in terms of their own cultural identity, to avoid racial identification altogether. Without the development of white race consciousness, no significant group of whites understood themselves as struggling to transform the white community itself in terms of race relations or as supporting African Americans as a people or a nation. In terms of national policy, tremendous energy was committed to the centralized policy of integration, but little attention was paid to the integrity and health of Black neighborhoods and institutions. Integration of dominant institutions, rather than reparations from one community to another, became the paradigm for racial enlightenment, at least until the emergence of "multiculturalism" in the 1980s, as the next chapter considers.

CHAPTER 5
THE RACIAL IDEOLOGY
OF EQUAL PROTECTION LAW

> *Brown* symbolized the Supreme Court's proper role as the articulator
> and defender of America's fundamental constitutional values.... Fifty
> years after *Brown*, much has changed. But what has not changed is the
> iconic status of *Brown* itself. It remains a central symbol of American
> constitutional law and constitutional equality. Nowadays we no longer
> fight about whether it was correct...."[1]
>
> Jack Balkin, 2001

The integrationist ideology I have been describing—as well as its eventual disag-
gregation into its component parts—is exemplified in mainstream American legal
discourse about race. In this chapter, I consider the ways the Supreme Court has
interpreted the Equal Protection Clause of the Fourteenth Amendment over the
past 50 years or so with regard to racial inequality. This discourse is presented
as "legal" or "principled," rather than political or ideological, as judicial rather
than legislative. In fact, however, any sense of the "rule of law" quality of the
American legal discourse about race depends on taking as self-evident, rather than
political, the ideology of integrationism that I outlined in earlier chapters.

I begin with the Court's 1954 decision in *Brown v. Board of Education*[2] and
the initial controversy among legal elites that it spawned. In *Brown*, the Court
overturned the "separate but equal" doctrine that, for more than half a century,
defined equal protection law with respect to race and legitimated the regime of
American racial apartheid as constitutional.

The *Brown* decision was at first highly problematic for the American legal mainstream; however, as the quote from Professor Balkin above reflects, dominant legal culture eventually embraced the decision. By translating *Brown* in integrationist terms, liberal legal elites succeeded in transforming it from a problematic to an emblematic example of judicial review. The universalist assumptions of integrationism resonated with the particular need for a recently impugned American rule of law to appear neutral, rational, and objective. *Brown* became the centerpiece of a broad revamping of constitutional theory around the basic idea that the judiciary's "activist" protection of racial (and other) minorities—and of political participation rights in general—could be consistent with, and even supportive of, democratic rule. *Brown*, in some ways a path-breaking example of the progressive possibilities of judicial review, was ultimately de-radicalized as it was transformed into an "icon" of mainstream constitutional law.

The ideological framework within which American judges and lawyers have conducted doctrinal debate about equal protection since *Brown* has developed over time. Early on, there was little tension within the different prongs of the integrationist worldview. It was just assumed that colorblindness in consciousness and equal treatment in practice would lead to racial integration in institutional life. Once school officials and employers stopped discriminating, integration would "naturally" follow. When that assumption proved false,[3] one could differentiate conservative from liberal judges and lawyers by whether they chose colorblindness or racial integration as the more important integrationist norm.

In sum, in the struggle over the *Brown* ruling's meaning and legitimacy that followed the decision, distinctive conservative and liberal legal positions emerged with respect to the key doctrinal issues of constitutional interpretation—whether intent to discriminate on the basis of race should be required to make out an equal protection violation,[4] whether racial affirmative action is permissible,[5] and how broad to make remedies for institution- and society-wide constitutional wrongs. What is striking about the decades of doctrinal contestation over the constitutional treatment of race, however, is that the debate among (virtually all-white) legal elites occurred entirely within integrationist assumptions. The ideas that race is an arbitrary characteristic, racial justice consists of equal treatment according to race-neutral norms, and racial integration should be the institutional goal of race remediation made concern for the interests of African Americans *as a community* seem exceptional and its justifications defensive.[6] The "legal" quality of the legal discourse about race depended on a suppressed political and ideological choice of integrationist, rather than nationalist, accounts of race.

Brown as Part of the Postwar Rejection of Formalism

> We consider the underlying fallacy of the plaintiff's argument to consist in the assumption that the enforced separation of the two races stamps the colored race with a badge of inferiority. If this be so, it is not by reason of anything found in the act, but solely because the colored race chooses to put that construction upon it. The argument necessarily assumes that if, as has been more than once the case, and is not unlikely to be so again, the colored race should become the dominant power in the state legislature, and should enact a law in precisely similar terms, it would thereby relegate the white race to an inferior position. We imagine that the white race, at least, would not acquiesce in this assumption.
>
> *Plessy v. Ferguson*, 1897[7]

> To separate [Black students] from others of similar age and qualifications solely because of their race generates a feeling of inferiority as to their status in the community that may affect their hearts and minds in a way unlikely ever to be undone.... Whatever may have been the extent of psychological knowledge at the time of *Plessy v. Ferguson*, this finding is amply supported by modern authority. Any language in *Plessy v. Ferguson* contrary to this finding is rejected.... [S]eparate educational facilities are inherently unequal.
>
> *Brown v. Board of Education*, 1954[8]

In *Plessy,* the Court upheld a Louisiana law mandating racially segregated passenger rail cars against a challenge asserting that such a law violated the Equal Protection Clause of the Fourteenth Amendment. As long as the facilities were "separate but equal," no constitutional violation could exist, according to the opinion. The *Plessy* doctrine governed equal protection cases for the first half of the 20th century.

In *Brown,* the Court struck down a Topeka, Kansas, law mandating racially segregated school assignments. While formally limited to the field of public education, *Brown* was quickly understood to overturn the "separate but equal" doctrine that *Plessy* had announced when *Plessy* had helped rationalize, as consistent with the "equal protection of the laws," racial segregation on rail cars and in social life more generally. In fact, although *Brown* involved a specific challenge only to racial segregation in public education, in the ensuing years, the Court routinely found other governmental segregation unconstitutional on a *per curium* basis (without issuing opinions in the cases).

Brown was decided in the context of, and became central in, an emerging postwar reconstruction of American legal discourse. The contrast between the reasoning in *Brown* and *Plessy* highlights how at least one dimension of *Brown* (a unanimous decision of the Court) was of a piece with a main current of postwar American legal thought: a "realist" rejection of the "formalism" of the *Plessy* era.[9]

The legal realists had attacked the "formalism" of the *Plessy* era in cases in which the Court struck down economic regulation on the ground that it interfered with the "liberty of contract" rights supposedly enjoyed equally and symmetrically by all parties, workers and owners alike.[10] The realists contended that owners and workers were equal in legal form only. Predatory and exploitative labor practices reflected disparate real-world power regardless of the legal form it took. The realists claimed that they criticized the Court's decisions in the liberty of contract cases in order to defend the purportedly democratic choices of (progressive) legislatures. But in the *Brown* setting, the realist approach would set the Court *against* a presumably democratic legislature—the school board and city council of Topeka, which had mandated school segregation by statute. The elite criticism of *Brown* on *institutional* grounds showed how such a functional, realist stance was particularly difficult to maintain with respect to judicial review of the constitutionality of legislative action.

In terms of formal argument, the *Plessy* Court's interpretation of equal protection was not illogical. If members of respective races were treated separately and equally, it was hard to conceive exactly how they were being denied the "equal protection of the laws" under legislation mandating racial segregation. If Blacks and whites were symmetrically barred from each other's facilities, and if the facilities themselves were equal on all quantifiable measures, then the Jim Crow regime of Southern segregation appeared literally to accord Black and white citizens "equal protection of the laws." The idea that this legal regime imposed a badge of inferiority on Blacks *might* have been just in their heads, as the *Plessy* opinion suggested, and it *could* have been that Blacks did "choose to put that construction upon it." This same kind of reasoning could apply to anti-miscegenation, school assignment, and many other segregation laws.

But this logic was merely *formal* because, like the equal contract rights of owners and workers that the Court posited at the turn of the 20th century, there is little doubt that Black and white rail passengers, Black and white students, or

Blacks and whites in general were not *in fact* accorded equal services and facilities, at least in most places. And even if facilities were occasionally physically equal, racial segregation meant racial inequality in the social system of American apartheid in all kinds of intangible ways. The point of racial segregation was to regulate Blacks, who several decades before had been held openly and legally as slaves, and specifically to keep Blacks away from whites, not the other way around.[11] To maintain that the law mandating rail car segregation in Louisiana in 1897 reflected *equal* protection of the laws is akin to Holocaust denial. Nevertheless, under *Plessy,* the formal interpretation of "equal protection of the laws" as a practical matter put the burden on victims of the American racial caste system to prove tangible inequality in a place-by-place, isolated, and piecemeal fashion—a practically impossible, even if theoretically conceivable, task.

As part of its long-term legal strategy, in the years before its frontal assault on the constitutionality of school segregation in *Brown,* the NAACP had successfully challenged law and graduate schools of state universities for failing to provide Black students the equality required under the "separate but equal" doctrine.[12] That litigation had pushed the "separate but equal" analysis beyond consideration of the relative physical facilities or even a comparison of spending to consider elements of educational opportunity that were more difficult to quantify.

In *Sweatt v. Painter,* the Court had held that the dual law schools run by Texas were not equal because of differences between "intangible factors" at the two schools, such as the ability to meet and engage with the state's future political leaders, an opportunity only available in Texas's leading law school and an opportunity accordingly denied by the restriction of Blacks to the all-Black school.[13]

Similarly, in *McLaurin v. Oklahoma State Regents,* the Court had found that even when Blacks were admitted to study at the same graduate school as whites, equal opportunity was denied by internal segregation within the school, which there consisted of racial restrictions on places a Black student could sit, study, and eat. Among the "intangible factors" the Court found necessary to consider in evaluating whether a Black student was afforded equal protection was the ability to share ideas with fellow classmates in graduate school, an opportunity virtually foreclosed by definition when the school imposed internal segregation requirements.[14]

This litigation strategy of pushing the "separate but equal" doctrine in a functional, realist direction by introducing into the analysis the social meaning of attendance at law school or the real benefits of peer learning in a graduate

school culminated in *Brown's* proclamation of the *inherent* inequality of segregated schools. Regardless of how many books the library of the Black law
school that Texas ran possessed, how many teachers it employed, or how many
classrooms it had, it could never be "equal" to the law school in Austin if the
University of Texas is where the state's future powerful elite went to school.
The cases leading up to *Brown* (in retrospect) showed that a more "realist," less
formal interpretive stance had already been adopted in equal protection cases,
so that, even under the rubric of the "separate but equal" doctrine, the Court
could have held unconstitutional virtually all racial segregation then practiced
in the United States. One virtue of the *Brown* formulation that segregated
schools were *inherently* unequal was that the unconstitutionality of segregated
facilities need not be proved on a case-by-case basis, in that the Court defined
the constitutional violation as segregation itself, rather than the inequality the
segregation was supposed to reflect or effect.

It is noteworthy that the *Brown* opinion did not present any analytic counter
to the formal, logical claim in *Plessy* that any "badge of inferiority" associated with
segregation *might* be in the heads of Blacks themselves, and it did not present
any support for its assertion that "separate educational facilities are *inherently*
unequal." The response to the formal equality argument in *Plessy* was, instead,
implicit in the opinion's *functional* (how it worked) focus on the harmful *impact
and effects* of segregation on Black children as school segregation was actually
conducted:

> Segregation of white and colored children in public schools has a detrimental
> effect upon the colored children. The impact is greater when it has the sanc-
> tion of the law; for the policy of separating the races is usually interpreted as
> denoting the inferiority of the Negro group. A sense of inferiority affects the
> motivation of a child to learn. Segregation with the sanction of law, therefore,
> has a tendency to [retard] the educational and mental development of Negro
> children and to deprive them of some of the benefits they would receive in a
> racial[ly] integrated school system.[15]

The *Plessy* ruling was attributed to the undeveloped "state of psychological
knowledge at the time."[16]

Brown rested on this rejection of formalism in favor of a *functional* assessment
of laws mandating racial school segregation. In these terms, the *Brown* argument depended on the social-science evidence it cited purporting to establish

that segregation was psychologically harmful to Black children[17]—evidence like
the so-called "doll studies," in which Black children's preferences for white dolls
were supposed to demonstrate the pernicious effects of school segregation.[18] The
Brown argument also depended on the recognition of the historically contingent
racial hierarchies within which school segregation laws were situated.[19]

To the extent that the consideration of the psychological damage or social
meaning of segregation involved "intangible factors," this dimension of *Brown*
overlapped with, rather than broke from, the more sensitive and functional ap-
plications of the "separate but equal" doctrine reflected in the law and graduate
school cases, which were in turn themselves continuous with the post–New Deal
reconceptualization of American law on more functional bases. The problem,
however, was that the more functionalist, realist style associated with post–New
Deal descriptions of the realities of the judicial role had become particularly
problematic in the practice of judicial review.

The Controversy over *Brown* among (White) Liberal Legal Elites

> Is it alternatively defensible to make the measure of validity of legislation
> the way it is interpreted by those who are affected by it? In the context
> of a charge that segregation with equal facilities is a denial of equality, is
> there not a point in *Plessy* in the statement that if "enforced separation
> stamps the colored race with a badge of inferiority" it is solely because
> its members choose "to put that construction upon it"?
>
> Herbert Wechsler, 1959[20]

Brown was, to say the least, highly controversial. Billboards were mounted across
the South calling for Chief Justice Earl Warren's impeachment.[21] Southern gov-
ernors mapped out strategies of "massive resistance" to implementation of the
ruling. Segregationists asserted that federal court power to nullify local school
laws violated states' rights to legislate segregation, and vowed to resist.[22]

In addition to the familiar opposition by segregationists, and despite the lack
of dissent on the Court, *Brown* was also controversial within mainstream legal
discourse, even among elite white liberal lawyers. For example, Learned Hand,
one of America's most famous jurists (and the most evocatively named) was an
esteemed federal judge on the U.S. Court of Appeals for the Second Circuit and
a leading symbol of the early-20th-century progressive transformation of American legal discourse from formalism to realism. Yet he argued in his 1958 Oliver

Wendell Holmes Lectures at Harvard Law School that *Brown* was illegitimate because it dishonored democratic choice. Insofar as constitutional language like "equal protection" was vague and open-ended, it could not be interpreted without discretionary choices by judges. But such choices, not constrained by "law," were illegitimate. Deference to the legislature was warranted. Hand's lectures were published as *The Bill of Rights* and became a national bestseller.[23]

The next year, Columbia University Law Professor Herbert Wechsler, himself an eminent mainstream postwar scholar and lawyer, criticized the *Brown* decision in his 1959 Oliver Wendell Holmes Lectures. The lectures were published as an essay, "Toward Neutral Principles of Constitutional Law," and have become one of the most widely cited law review articles in history.[24]

Wechsler focused his criticism on the Court's concern with psychological harm to Black schoolchildren from school segregation. According to Wechsler, the problem was that the decision was not supported by what he called "neutral principles," rather than these historically and factually contingent psychological reactions of children. The finding that segregated schools were "inherently unequal" was not a principled ground for the constitutional ruling because the finding of inequality was actually fact-specific to the sociological testimony in the particular case. Expert witnesses in other school cases testified in contrary ways, and (in any event) Wechsler contended that the social-science evidence was relative to the specific research upon which the conclusion of inequality and harm rested and to the specific questions posed to social-science experts.[25] But that would mean that the very same practice—governmentally imposed racial segregation—might be constitutional in some places or at some times, but not others, which was a geographic and historic contingency that Wechsler assumed was inconsistent with the idea of constitutional rule.

Wechsler speculated that the decision was not really based on the sociological evidence of harm to Black children from segregation, but instead rested on the view that racial segregation must necessarily entail denial of equality to the minority, "the group that is not dominant politically and, therefore, does not make the choice involved."[26] But this ground also could not be principled because it made constitutionality turn on the subjective motive of the legislature or on the subjective interpretation of the legislation by those subject to it, who "choose" to see segregation as inequality or who "resent" segregation. A principled analysis would make the constitutional determination turn on the objective character of the legislation itself. If there were objectively equal facilities, Wechsler argued, the question of whether racial segregation entailed inequality necessarily depended on one's point of view, implicating a value choice that the judiciary did not have the institutional competence to make.

According to Wechsler, *Brown* actually involved a "conflict of human claims" in the application of the "freedom to associate."[27] Legislated segregation denied freedom to associate on an interracial basis to those who wished it, but integration forced association on those for whom interracial association might be "unpleasant or repugnant."[28] What was involved was a conflict between different social interests, one that no neutral principle could resolve.

Wechsler was a political liberal and law reformer, best known for his work on modernizing the Model Penal Code and on rationalizing the federal court system.[29] Hand was a progressive judge, best known for setting forth a functional cost-benefit test with which to define the common law negligence standard in tort.[30] To understand how it came to be that these two mainstream legal modernists joined with never-say-die segregationists in questioning the Court's legitimacy in *Brown*, it is necessary to comprehend how, in the early 1950s, the charge of "judicial activism" was still being launched by liberals against legal conservatives.

Brown and the Evil of "Judicial Activism"

Brown was decided in the context of postwar American legal discourse and the emergence of the "counter-majoritarian difficulty" as the central issue for the legitimacy of constitutional law. Wechsler and Hand were part of a generation of lawyers who had learned constitutional law in the midst of conflict between a conservative turn-of-the-century Court and politically progressive legislatures. The conflict was epitomized by cases in which the Court interpreted the due process clauses of the Fifth and Fourteenth Amendments to protect an individual's "liberty of contract" against legislative regulation, striking down maximum hour,[31] minimum wage legislation,[32] and other Progressive and New Deal reforms.[33] Like other liberal lawyers of their generation, Hand and Wechsler embraced the dominant scholarly criticism that the Court acted illegitimately because it interpreted the Constitution to obstruct democratic control over economic policy. Thus, they made the issue of "judicial activism" central to their understanding of what was wrong with the old constitutional order.

Through this *institutional* lens, white elites such as Wechsler and Hand presented their criticism of the *Brown* decision as a principled stand; as much as they might sympathize with the result in the case (as a matter of social policy), their opposition to the conservative Court of the 1890–1937 period on the grounds that it had imposed its own value judgments on its interpretation of the Constitution to forbid legislative regulation of the economy demanded that they also oppose judicial activism by a liberal Court. And, again, what made the *Brown* decision activist, in their minds, was that it rested on necessarily discretionary judgments about intangible and historically contingent social dynamics such as the *impact* of school segregation on Black children.

In sum, *Brown*'s anti-formalist reliance on sociological evidence of school segregation's harm to Black children's self-esteem was of a piece with the general tenor of American law in the postwar period. The "Brandeis brief" symbolized this aspect of the fall of formalism, as Louis Brandeis famously marshaled sociological research regarding the working conditions of women in support of legislation regulating their working hours. The answer to whether economic and social regulation violated the Constitution could not be found in determinate deductions from starting-point principles (e.g., the idea that every party had a right to contract as they saw fit); Brandeis presented empirical data to demonstrate social effects that warranted legislative response.

What made *Brown* different was that, unlike Brandeis' argument in *Muller v. Oregon*,[34] the sociological evidence in *Brown* was not advanced to support the rationality of labor laws, but rather to show the *unconstitutionality* of (segregation) legislation. And, for the generation of lawyers who had resisted and helped impugn what they saw as the anti-democratic activism of a right-wing judiciary— one that had been striking down and obstructing economic regulation under the idea that "due process" included "liberty of contract" rights that legislatures could not abridge—this institutional difference made all the difference. Because judges were unelected, there was no legitimate basis for making the value judgments inevitable in setting social policy. Only democratically elected legislatures could legitimately decide issues about which there is reasonable disagreement.

The 1950s lawyers presented fidelity to "judicial restraint" as flowing from a deep commitment to democracy and to the protection of democratic self-determination from judicial power. Justice Felix Frankfurter's concurring opinion in *Dennis v. United States*[35] was one of the notable early examples of this focus on the relative institutional competence of courts and legislatures as a way to resolve substantive issues of constitutional law. In *Dennis* (coincidentally affirming a decision by Judge Hand[36]), a member of the Communist Party of the United States of America challenged the constitutionality of his conviction under the

Smith Act, which made it a crime to knowingly conspire to teach and advocate the overthrow or destruction of the U.S. government. Because outlawing such (mere) advocacy would be consistent with First Amendment free speech rights only if the party posed a serious threat to ordered government (under some version of the then-extant "clear and present danger" test), and because *that* issue depended on the evaluation of historical events and their significance that could not be conducted in a principled way, Judge Hand (on the Court of Appeals for the Second Circuit) and Justice Frankfurter (concurring on the Supreme Court) both upheld the Smith Act on the idea that appropriate judicial restraint required them to defer to Congress on the key historical and evaluative issue of whether a dangerous worldwide Communist conspiracy against democratic government existed.

I have presented this background to provide the intellectual context for the opposition to *Brown* of Hand, Wechsler, and other 1950s legal elites. The Frankfurter concurrence in *Dennis* illustrates that their concern was not specific to *Brown*; instead, it reflected the emerging proceduralism in American legal thought, a new mainstream that, after the realist movement, sought to base the rule of law on *institutional competence* and *procedural regularity*, rather than on substantive grounds.[37] In this view, when it reviewed the constitutionality of legislation, the judiciary's legitimacy depended on staying within its appropriate sphere of authority, itself gleaned from the judiciary's institutional characteristics. Because it was unelected, it had no authority to decide issues that were not capable of a principled resolution because, by definition, in its constitutional review of legislation, an elected legislative body has already decided policy and value questions. So whatever the *substantive* merits of the *Brown* Court's interpretation of "equal protection," its reliance on a functional evaluation of the social significance of school segregation rendered it illegitimate because that kind of evaluation— that procedure for resolving the conflict—was beyond its *institutional competence* as understood by Hand, Wechsler, and many other legal elites who had earlier sided with the "realists" in criticizing the formalism of the *Plessy* era.

But why didn't the actual distribution of wealth, jobs, political power, intellectual prestige, educational opportunity, housing, and social status between whites and Blacks in 1950s America prove the inequality that Wechsler could not find from the fact of segregated schools in *Brown*? More generally, why wasn't the fact that school segregation in *Brown* was only a part of a pervasive social structure of state-supported, institutionalized racism enough to justify the Court's conclusion that segregated public schools were part of the social subordination of Blacks? Were Hand and Wechsler also against the functional, realist application of the "separate but equal" doctrine, as applied in *Sweatt* and *McLaurin*, so that, in their view, the Court should also not consider real, but "intangible" factors of inequality? Why wasn't it immediately obvious that the Wechsler and Hand positions, flowing from the formal identification of relative institutional competencies, were just as formalist as the *Plessy* approach?

As Wechsler posed the issue of equality, it was either explicable in terms of an objective, principled comparison of concrete facilities, such as school buildings, or it depended on the personal and subjective, even psychologically based, reactions of Blacks who "choose to put that construction upon" racial segregation. The imagery of choice and psychological resentment contrasted with the imagery of the comparison of facilities in the same way values were different from facts. The "equal facility" comparison could be factual and objective, not a matter of individual opinion, psychology, or will.[38] Because any determination of whether segregation was part of a system of social inequality would inevitably require the consideration of subjective factors, it would necessarily involve a substantive evaluation of society.

Because these kinds of judgments were outside the judicial competence when engaged in judicial review of the constitutionality of legislation, the only principled way to resolve the case was to treat it like a "political question," and therefore neutrally to decide, on institutional competence grounds, that the legislature was the appropriate institution to resolve the issue. In the view of these 1950s legal elites, in so upholding the constitutionality of school segregation, the Court would not be ruling on the value question—whether such segregation involved a denial of equality—but instead would be holding that the issue was not amenable to judicial procedures of dispute resolution. In this discourse, it followed automatically that if there was no neutral way for the judiciary to resolve the issue of racial segregation, it was to be left to the legislature.

The Incoherence of the "Judicial Activism" Charge

I do not want to press too far the idea that 1950s legal elites were trapped in some historically determined mindset. As I have argued elsewhere, nothing demanded that legal elites in the early 20th century pursue the particular institutional path of critique of the old constitutional order they followed, and even within their own framework, nothing determined that they apply their analysis to find *Brown* illegitimate.[39] In fact, at least in retrospect, Frankfurter's approach in *Dennis* and the opposition of Hand and Wechsler to *Brown* epitomize the analytic incoherence of their "judicial restraint" stance. The predicate for judicial restraint was supposed to be the democratic character of the legislature, in contrast with the unelected nature of the judiciary, but the democratic character of the legislature was simply presumed. There was, in fact, no necessary analytic link from the proposition that it was a value question, whether school segregation was a form of social inequality, to the conclusion that deference to legislative judgment was in order. Finding that the issue in *Brown* involved a value judgment constituted merely half the analysis—before deference to the legislature was in order, the judiciary would have to decide that the legislature actually employed the procedures that made it competent to decide the issue. Deference was only appropriate if the legislature was truly democratic. In the imagery of "the counter-majoritarian difficulty,"[40] the basis for the Court's limited competence in the role of judicial review was inferred from a comparison of the relative competence of the judiciary and the legislature. The constitutional court was confined to a principled, value-free analysis because it lacked the democratic legitimacy the legislature enjoyed; therefore, when it confronted legislative choices, it could not legitimately impose its own values.

A critical analysis of the democratic legitimacy of the legislature would have exposed the inevitable indeterminacy and circularity of this institutional logic. If the determination of the institutional legitimacy of the legislature ultimately depended on a substantive and value-laden analysis of the actual power relations existing in society, the limitation of the judiciary to a neutral principles analysis meant that the judiciary would never be able to determine whether the legislature was in fact democratic or whether society was instead rife with social and political domination. The institutional competence analysis ultimately rested on this analytic loop; the judiciary had to defer to legislative value judgments because the judiciary was unelected and therefore incompetent vis-à-vis the legislature to make value choices. However, the democratic character of the legislature, the ground for deference, could never be determined by the courts because the determination of whether the legislature was truly democratic depended on the resolution of issues of value that were beyond the judicial competence. The limitations on the judiciary that were inferred from the democratic nature of the legislature prevented the judiciary from determining the democratic legitimacy of the legislature to justify those limits in the first place. The determination of the institutional legitimacy of the legislature, from which the circumscribed power of judicial review was inferred through the "counter-majoritarian difficulty," was beyond the competence of the judiciary given the "counter-majoritarian difficulty."

This analytic circularity belies the notion that Wechsler's or Hand's opposition to *Brown* was determined by the conceptual structure of postwar intellectual discourse. Their institutional rhetoric could only be appealing if one already possessed a particular outlook and attitude toward the legitimacy of the social arrangements of American society, such that one could believe that the norms that characterized the democratic rhetoric of their institutional discourse also characterized day-to-day life in the actual institutions that Hand, Wechsler, and the others considered. Rather than being the "source" for substantive value choices made in American institutional life, the intense commitment by 1950s scholars such as Wechsler to institutional procedures was the effect of a particular, benign view of American society within which the possibility of social domination had been defined away.

It is striking that the 1950s constitutional law theorists who made the "counter-majoritarian difficulty" the centerpiece of their entire theoretical approach never bothered to consider the legitimacy of legislative action. Although Wechsler's argument for "neutral principles" reflected his commitment to an institutional competence analysis, and although his analysis concluded that the lack of a principled resolution required deference to the legislature, he failed to complete the analysis by applying the institutional competence calculus to the legislature itself. Hand, Wechsler, and the others provided no means to distinguish between truly democratic legislatures and imposters. Their advocacy of "judicial restraint" rested instead on the most formalist of ways for identifying legislative choice; decisions flowing from institutions formally designated as the "U.S. Congress" or "New York Legislature" were taken, without critical analysis, to be democratic decisions.

Further, even when the issue under consideration was the possible denial of free speech rights, as in *Dennis,* or the caste-like exclusion of Blacks from mainstream American life, as in *Brown,* it apparently never occurred to this group of legal elites that if free speech had been denied and a caste social structure enforced, then one could not simply conclude that legislation reflected democratic, rather than despotic, rule. This analytic aporia would be addressed by the emergence of a new structure of justification for judicial review that emerged in the 1960s and 1970s, one that found a theoretical basis for the judiciary's competence to ensure the democratic legitimacy of the legislature.

Reinterpreting *Brown* as Protecting "Discrete and Insular Minorities"

> It is unnecessary to consider now whether legislation which restricts those political processes which can ordinarily be expected to bring about repeal of undesirable legislation, is to be subjected to more exacting judicial scrutiny under the general prohibitions of the Fourteenth Amendment than are most other types of legislation.... Nor need we inquire whether similar considerations enter into the review of statutes directed at particular religious, or national, or racial minorities; [when] prejudice against discrete and insular minorities may be a special condition, which tends seriously to curtail the operation of those political processes ordinarily to be relied upon to protect minorities, and which may call for a correspondingly more searching judicial inquiry.
>
> *United States v. Carolene Products,* 1938[41]

Hand and Wechsler represented only a first wave of mainstream and elite legal thought about *Brown*. Soon afterward, there emerged a new, liberal discourse supportive of *Brown* and many of the other decisions of the Warren Court that had been criticized as "activist." This framing placed *Brown* within the outlines of judicial review described in the famous footnote 4 of the Court's decision in *United States v. Carolene Products.* In this re-reading of the *Brown* decision, *Brown* was consistent with a more sophisticated, institutional competence analysis than what was reflected in the question-begging pronouncements about judicial activism of Hand and Wechsler.

The *Carolene Products* conception was ingenious in that it found the bases for "activist" judicial review in the very starting premise of "judicial restraint"— judges should respect the value judgments of democratically constituted legislatures. If the analytic shortcoming of the "judicial restraint" advocated by Hand and Wechsler was that it was based on an unexamined assumption that legislatures were democratic and therefore worthy of deference, exceptions to judicial restraint could be identified from the requirements of democratic rule itself— justifying judicial "activism" (articulated as "heightened review") about issues regarding free speech, voting rights, protection of minorities, and the like. The procedural interpretation of the Constitution reflected in the famous footnote 4 of *Carolene Products* required the courts to defer to legislatures generally, but not, in this more refined version of postwar proceduralism, when the issues presented concerned the democratic character of the legislature itself.

Under this resolution of the "judicial activism" controversy, the *Brown* ruling (but not necessarily the opinion itself) became the leading exemplar of the new conventional thinking about constitutional law. In this conception, *Brown* was legitimate because the judiciary had a special obligation to protect the interests of "discrete and insular minorities" like Blacks who were the subject of "prejudice" (and therefore the usual democratic process of deliberative democratic debate could not be assumed), whose discreteness made it easy to identify them for negative treatment, and whose insularity made it difficult for them to protect themselves in the give and take of interest group, pluralist politics. One could infer from the *majoritarian* structure of democratic institutions that they might systematically fail to reflect the interests of such minorities. One could infer from the fact that a group was subject to prejudice that the normal processes of constitutional decision-making had been distorted. Therefore, one could conclude that while the judiciary should generally defer to the legislature because of its democratic character, such deference is not warranted for certain kinds of issues that democratic procedures are not well suited to consider.

Liberal and progressive legal elites, politically on the side of integration in the acute social struggle led by the civil rights movement, needed a way to understand *Brown* as a legitimate, even heroic, application of law. The *Carolene Products* conception provided them with that. It gave them a general, background confidence in the legitimacy of judicial action to protect Blacks and other "minorities," and if one did not look too critically, it also seemed to provide a principled basis for the *Brown* ruling that liberals had demanded. So successful was this read of *Brown* that, as quoted above, by 2001, a mainstream liberal constitutional scholar could claim that *Brown* "remains a central symbol of American constitutional law and constitutional equality. Nowadays we no longer fight about whether it was correct."[42]

In fact, though, the *Carolene Products* conception was at too high a level of generality to dictate the resolution of the critical doctrinal questions: How should the court identify when the interests of Blacks are at stake? How should they be protected? Should judicial activism on behalf of Blacks be triggered only by legislative action, or should there also be review of legislative inaction? Should all governmental action affecting Blacks be subject to heightened review, or only when the government intends to affect them? Should governmental action to benefit Blacks be subject to the same heightened review as when the government acts to burden Blacks? And so on.

I argue in the next section that the opposition between formalism and functionalism that the institutional focus seemed to resolve simply reappeared within the *Carolene Products* reconceptualization of American constitutional law in the guise of competing views of how to identify the democratic breakdowns that, under *Carolene Products,* justified some measure of judicial activism.

The Conflict over *De Jure* and *De Facto* School Segregation

> "Freedom of choice" is not a sacred talisman; it is only a means to a constitutionally required end—the abolition of the system of segregation and its effects. If the means prove effective, it is acceptable, but if it fails to undo segregation, other means must be used to achieve this end. The school officials have the continuing duty to take whatever action may be necessary to create a "unitary, non-racial system."
>
> Justice William J. Brennan, *Green v. County*
> *School Board of New Kent County,* 1968[43]

> Racial balancing is not transformed from "patently unconstitutional" to a compelling state interest simply by relabeling it "racial diversity" ... avoidance of racial isolation, [or] racial integration.... The way to stop discrimination on the basis of race is to stop discriminating on the basis of race.
>
> Chief Justice John Roberts,
> *Parents Involved in Community Schools v. Seattle*
> *School District No. 1 (PICS),* 2007[44]

The Court's rulings in *Green* and *PICS* are respectively representative of the liberal and conservative wings of integrationist ideology as they developed after *Brown*—positions that I call here the *de jure* and *de facto* (or, alternatively, the *intent* and *impact*) approaches to identifying constitutional equal protection violations.

The conflict between these identifiably liberal and conservative approaches initially arose in cases concerning the appropriate remedies for school segregation. There, the constitutional issues generally revolved around whether the *Brown* ruling and the Equal Protection Clause solely prohibited school officials from assigning students to schools based on race (the *de jure* view reflected in *PICS*) or whether it imposed an affirmative duty to integrate schools, a duty that might require school officials to make race-conscious decisions (the *de facto* view reflected in *Green*). The *Carolene Products* idea that the judiciary should apply "heightened scrutiny" to protect the interests of Blacks as a discrete and insular minority was too abstract to help decide whether to identify their interests on a *de jure* or *de facto* basis when carrying out the assigned judicial task.

The Court's ruling in *Brown* was met by strategies of "massive resistance" in several Southern states, and the ensuing legal battle over the appropriate remedies for school segregation occupied one front in what would become "the civil rights movement."[45] The need to choose between different *de jure* and *de facto* approaches soon became apparent because one strategy many school systems pursued to avoid school integration—arguably the motive for the plan in *Green*—was to enact "freedom-of-choice" plans under which parents chose what school their child would attend. Typically, as in *Green,* such plans failed to succeed in meaningfully integrating the schools. Integrationists were then forced to choose between colorblindness on one hand and integration of schools on the other once it became clear that race neutrality on the part of the government would not itself lead to school integration; conservatives chose colorblindness, and liberals chose integration.

The school system challenged in *Green* had legislatively mandated racial segregation of its two schools until it adopted its freedom-of-choice plan. In the 3-year period during which the freedom-of-choice plan had been in effect, no white child had chosen to attend the school formerly segregated for Black pupils, and about 85% of the Black children remained in that school.

Under a thorough *de jure* approach, racial segregation continuing under the freedom-of-choice school assignment policies would not have been constitutionally cognizable to the extent that such segregation was not traceable to affirmative governmental actions. By adopting and implementing an official policy of governmental neutrality with respect to race in school assignments, the state was no longer acting to foster school segregation—and desegregation plaintiffs in the case were apparently not able to show that, despite its official policy, the government was taking other racially discriminatory actions with respect to school assignments or that continuing segregation was causally traceable to prior governmental acts.

Nevertheless, again acting unanimously, the Court in *Green* struck down the freedom-of-choice plan and ruled that school systems that had operated *de jure* segregated schools came under an "affirmative duty" to achieve integrated schools, not simply a duty to cease state-sponsored segregation.[46] Once school officials were under an affirmative duty to integrate schools, it did not matter whether current segregation was imposed by law (*de jure*) or by purportedly private choices and factors, such as residential racial segregation not dictated by law (*de facto*). In other words, under *Green,* one could (almost) conclude that the constitutional *right* was an affirmative right to attend integrated schools, not simply a right to have the government be colorblind in school assignment.

The debate over the choice between *de jure* and *de facto* standards for identifying equal protection remedies in the school desegregation context had its fullest articulation at the Supreme Court level in the 1973 *Keyes v. Denver School District* decision,[47] a case in which Justice Lewis Powell proposed that the Court no longer require proof of *de jure* segregative intent or purpose, but rather that it should order desegregation "where segregated public schools exist within a school district to a substantial degree."[48] According to Justice Powell, the recognition in *Green* of an affirmative duty for school systems to remedy *de facto* segregation once they had been proven to have engaged in *de jure* segregation could not be limited to the remedial context without imposing indefensibly different duties in the North, which often did not have legally required school segregation, and in the South, where legislation had typically mandated it. Justice Powell concluded that, after *Green,* the *de jure/de facto* distinction "no longer can be justified on a principled basis." The fact that school segregation in the South was mandated by explicit law, while in the North it was not, was defined as merely a *formal* distinction in the face of empirical facts about the racial identity of public schools.

Given his center-right jurisprudential stance, Justice Powell's 1973 opinion in *Keyes* is significant in demonstrating how close the Court had come to a *de facto* definition of equal protection requirements in the school context. However, in contrast to the 1968 *Green* mandate that school officials must adopt race-conscious assignment policies to ensure the actual racial integration of public education, by 2007 the *PICS* Court would *forbid* school officials from considering race in school assignment plans where existing racially disproportionate schools had not been traced to past unconstitutional racial discrimination. *PICS,* in which the Court prohibited race-conscious school assignment plans to achieve integration, completes an arc in the re-interpretation of *Brown* from a realist, functionalist case concerned about the real world impact of race policies on Black students to a "principled" symbol of the evils of race consciousness in general. *PICS* marks the contemporary triumph of the colorblindness principle over racial integration in American law.

The Triumph of the *De Jure* Approach

[W]e have difficulty understanding how a law establishing a racially neutral qualification for employment is nevertheless racially discriminatory, and denies "any person . . . equal protection of the laws," simply because a greater proportion of Negroes fail to qualify than members of other racial or ethnic groups. Had respondents, along with all others who had failed Test 21, whether white or black, brought an action claiming that the test denied each of them equal protection of the laws as compared with those who had passed with high enough scores to qualify them as police recruits, it is most unlikely that their challenge would have been sustained. . . . Respondents, as Negroes, could no more successfully claim that the test denied them equal protection than could white applicants who also failed. The conclusion would not be different in the face of proof that more Negroes than whites had been disqualified by Test 21. That other Negroes also failed to score well would, alone, not demonstrate that respondents individually were being denied equal protection of the laws by the application of an otherwise valid qualifying test being administered to prospective police recruits.

Washington v. Davis, 1975[49]

The *PICS* ruling is noteworthy because it prohibits "benign" race consciousness in public school assignments to achieve "diversity," a justification that the Court had approved in upholding limited race-conscious admissions to college and graduate schools. Because, like *Brown* and *Green, PICS* also involved the public school context, the Court's ruling forecloses speculation that the public school context would also be recognized as another of the limited sites where government officials could take account of race. However, the Court's rejection of the *de facto* view implicit in *PICS* had actually occurred explicitly decades before, in the 1975 case of *Washington v. Davis.*

In 1971, before *Davis,* the Court in *Griggs v. Duke Power Co.*[50] had imposed a disproportionate impact standard for identifying employment discrimination under Title VII, a statute that forbids employment discrimination on the basis of race. If a particular employment criterion had a disproportionate racial impact, it was presumptively illegal for an employer to utilize it unless he could show it was a *"bona fide* occupational qualification"—that is, that it was really necessary for the job. "If an employment practice which operates to exclude Negroes cannot be shown to be related to job performance, the practice is prohibited."[51]

But *Griggs* applied to the *statutory* context. The issue in *Davis* was whether the same impact test would apply in the *constitutional* context. In terms of the test at issue in *Davis*, the application of the *Griggs* standard would have meant that, because of its racially disproportionate impact, the City could not use test results to deny jobs to Black applicants unless it could show that the skills tested for were really required for the job, which was in sharp dispute in the litigation. While the City asserted that the communication skills evaluated by the tests were useful for police officers, it apparently could not demonstrate they were a *bona fide* occupational qualification under then-applicable standards.[52]

In light of its rulings in *Green* and *Griggs*, and considering Justice Powell's opinion in *Keyes*, discussed above—all suggesting support for a *de facto* approach—there was speculation among civil rights lawyers and equal protection advocates that, by the mid-1970s, a majority of the Court might be ready to extend *Green* beyond the remedial context of school segregation to define disproportionate impact as an equal protection violation in the first instance. In *Davis*, the Court made clear that it would not.

The plaintiff in *Davis* challenged a standardized, written qualifying test that the Washington, D.C., police department used in hiring police officers, alleging that its racially disproportionate results and lack of proven relationship to the performance of the jobs for which it applied made its use an equal protection violation. At the time, Title VII, which *Griggs* had interpreted to impose a disproportionate impact test for identifying a *prima facie* case of employment discrimination, did not then apply to municipal employees. In holding that, in contrast to Title VII's statutory standard, disproportionate impact was not a sufficient basis for a *constitutional* claim of discrimination under the Equal Protection Clause, the Court held that *de jure* proof was required, meaning proof of a purpose or intent to discriminate on the basis of race.[53] The *Davis* Court contended that a *de facto* standard "would be far reaching and would raise serious questions about, and perhaps invalidate, a whole range of tax, welfare, public service, regulatory, and licensing statutes that may be more burdensome to the poor and average Black than to the more affluent white."[54]

The *Davis* opinion concluded with this "slippery slope" argument. However, the Court never made explicit what would be wrong with invalidating "a whole range" of laws disproportionately burdening Blacks.[55] It was taken for granted that that consequence was out of the question.

The Intent and Impact Alternatives

The competition between the intent and impact standards might be seen to involve simply a (particularly important) burden of proof issue; the impact standard puts the constitutional burden of justification on proponents of racially disproportionate practices to show that the practices are really necessary (e.g., "job-related" in the employment context). The intent standard puts the burden on those who would challenge the results of purportedly fair practices to show that they have been infected by racism.

However, the choice was not merely procedural. The choice of one standard over the other implies a view about the nature of the status quo of race relations. The impact standard assumes that a practice with a racially disproportionate impact that cannot be shown to be necessary for other purposes should be unconstitutional. The intent standard assumes a benign background in which disproportionate racial impact by itself has no constitutional significance because there is no particular reason to believe that a racially disproportionate impact is a result of the exercise of racial power.[56]

Even from within the terms of liberal race consciousness, I think there are many reasons to prefer the more critical burden of proof allocation of the impact standard. Proponents argued that it helped to flush out "unconscious racism," including the failure to consider the effects on a group of which one is not a member. In addition, it could only seem controversial in the abstract to presume that a practice with a disproportionate racial impact and no compelling rationale is the result of racial power. In light of the history of American slavery, the Jim Crow era of American apartheid, and the continuing failure to integrate African Americans into mainstream American institutions, it may just make more sense to set the presumption in favor of the putative victims.

To return to the slippery slope that the *Davis* Court invoked to conclude its opinion, what was apparently supposed to be self-evident about the Court's conclusion was, as far as I can determine, that it would be beyond the competency of the judiciary for it to apply "heightened scrutiny" to the "whole range" of governmental action (and there does not seem to be any reason to exclude government inaction, for that matter) that leaves African Americans less well off.

Such review would involve the judiciary in "activism" without limit.[57] Only the intent standard could limit judicial discretion. In this reading, the Court was deriving the limits of its review of the *Carolene Products*–type legitimacy of the legislature according to the predefined limits of judicial competency, reproducing the analytic circularity of the Hand and Wechsler approaches (i.e., because the limits of judicial competency were themselves derived from the assumed existence of a legitimate, democratic legislature).

De Jure, De Facto, and Affirmative Action

> The most pernicious feature of racial prejudice and discrimination is their underlying premise that members of some racial groups are less worthy than members of others. The antidiscrimination principle holds that this assumption is fallacious because race has no moral salience. For administrative purposes, some remedies for racial discrimination are triggered by disproportionate racial impact or treat persons according to membership in racial groups; but group membership is always a proxy for the individual's right not to be discriminated against. Similarly, remedies for race-specific harms recognize the sociological consequences of group identification and affiliation only to assure justice for individual members.... [M]ost societies in which power is formally allocated among racial and national groups are strikingly oppressive, unequal, and unstable.
>
> Paul Brest, 1976[58]

While *Davis* formally involved solely the issue of how equal protection violations would be identified, the same conflict between proponents of *de jure* and *de facto* standards structured each of the other well-known equal protection controversies. In the debate over the constitutional legitimacy of affirmative action, for example, the choice of a *de facto* impact test for defining a constitutional violation in the first place would have essentially mooted the entire debate. From the baseline definition of unconstitutional discrimination as limited to intentional or purposeful discrimination, affirmative action appears as the government intervening in the results of an otherwise aracial realm. However, the issue of affirmative action conceptually never comes up in the alternative, impact-based definition of discrimination. Instead, had that standard been adopted, there would be a constitutional *duty* to conduct the "affirmative action" that is now taken as exceptional, to correct unnecessary racially disproportionate outcomes.

Had unconstitutional discrimination been defined on the impact basis rejected in *Davis*, so-called affirmative action would appear in legal discourse merely as the constitutionally required remedy for unconstitutional discrimination, rather than as a controversial *exception* to the norms of nondiscrimination and individual merit.

Liberal equal protection arguments were defensive and apologetic because the race consciousness necessary to apply the *de facto* standard violated the foundational belief in the rationality of colorblindness, and because the strongest arguments for a *de facto* standard—the distributive justice claims of minority communities to proportional participation in American life—could not be articulated within the confines of integrationist ideology. In the context of *Davis*, for example, the best argument against continued use of a test that disproportionately screened out Black applicants for police positions might have been the Black *community*'s interest in having its members serve on the armed force that would be patrolling their neighborhoods, particularly in light of the history of tension between white police officers and residents of the Black neighborhoods that white officers patrol. The District of Columbia itself was only a few years away from the widespread riots of the late 1960s. However, to articulate the Black community's interest in community control over the police who came into their communities, one would have to think in terms of the continued vitality of the Black community, a concern literally outside the language of integrationism. The deep embrace of integrationist ideology precluded consideration of such nationalist concerns.

The quote from eminent legal scholar and former dean of Stanford Law School, Paul Brest, at the introduction to this section exemplifies mainstream legal liberal integrationist thinking in law. While liberals acknowledge the white power structure's dominance in society, they take the structure in which whites have been privileged as the fixed background against which race-conscious remedies are to be seen as exceptional. In this view, race-conscious state action can be appropriate, but only as a remedy for conscious racial bias. Despite the well-documented, systematic attacks on Black culture, achievement, and pride throughout American history, Brest asserts that "race-dependent decisions are [now] forbidden," thus defining and cementing as unexceptional all the other existing rules for distributing wealth, prestige, and power. Any frontal attack on this domination is dismissed as not being consonant with the liberal assumption of a "neutral" society based on "merit."[59] Further, the idea that a *de facto* standard could lead the Court to remedy "a whole range of tax, welfare, public service, regulatory and licensing statutes that may be more burdensome to the poor and to the average black than to the more affluent white"[60] is reason enough to banish the doctrine to the realm of exception, to be "used selectively and perhaps be modified to create rebuttable rather than conclusive presumptions of discriminatory intent."[61] The assumption, then, is that most policies with racially disproportionate impact are based on "merit," and merit is a meaningful, valid, aracial arbiter; racist "intent" is the real target, even of a disproportionate impact test, within the blinders of integrationist ideology.

In sum, the great doctrinal debates between liberals and conservatives in American legal discourse over the past five decades have taken place virtually entirely within the terms of integrationist ideology as I have described it. While one can imagine a nationalist, group-oriented justification for the racial proportionality assumptions of a *de facto* equal protection standard and, similarly, for racial affirmative action policies, the only justifications that entered mainstream legal discourse were either remedial, prophylactic, or aimed at the purported social benefits of "diversity." Liberals and conservatives differed on how far the causal effects of racial discrimination against Blacks ran, and liberals argued for an impact standard of racial affirmative action to remedy effects they saw broadly in society. However, both sides assumed that the evil to be remedied was race consciousness itself, rendering exceptional the arguments for the race consciousness required for remediation or diversity. Even as American culture generally accepted the limited race consciousness implicit in a multiculturalism that treated racial identity as the marker for a culturally distinct community, as the next chapter discusses, legal discourse moved in the other direction, toward the embrace of colorblindness as the central definition of racial justice. Equal protection discourse over the past 50 years has depended on an underlying ideological choice of integrationism as the exclusive way to understand racial justice.

CHAPTER 6
MULTICULTURALISM, IMPERIALISM, AND WHITE ANXIETY

> *Brown* in itself did not need to rely upon any psychological or social-science research in order to announce the simple, yet fundamental truth that the Government cannot discriminate among its citizens on the basis of race.... As the Court's unanimous opinion indicated: "In the field of public education the doctrine of 'separate but equal' has no place. Separate educational facilities are inherently unequal." ... At the heart of this interpretation of the Equal Protection Clause lies the principle that the Government must treat citizens as individuals, and not as members of racial, ethnic or religious groups. It is for this reason that we must subject all racial classifications to the strictest of scrutiny.
>
> Clarence Thomas, 1995[1]

This chapter considers the transformation from the colorblindness ideology that Justice Thomas, like Dean Brest, claimed was embodied in *Brown v. Board of Education*[2] to the more recent emergence of "cultural pluralism" and "multi-culturalism" as the dominant categories through which progressive American whites think about racial justice.

For many left-leaning lawyers and activists throughout the 1960s and 1970s, the Supreme Court's *Brown* text and the eventual federal court enforcement of school desegregation policies were emblematic of progressive law reform, if not idealized as the epitome of liberatory social change through litigation. However, as I have discussed in earlier chapters, the kind of racial integration envisaged in the construction of *Brown* as a cultural icon actually embodied conservative assumptions about culture, identity, and difference. The contemporary (though belated) embrace of "colorblindness" by the right, exemplified by Thomas's writings about racial justice, is linked to a "principled" reading of what *Brown* stood for and of what the opinion meant as a broader symbol of civil rights reform in American society—a reading that includes some of the very ideals that moderate and left-leaning whites used to champion but, in the ensuing decades, came to experience as backward and regressive.

The rejection of "colorblindness" in favor of "multiculturalism" as the frame through which progressive whites understand racial justice is, to my mind, a positive development in recent American racial dynamics. One strand of this chapter traces the discursive terrain traversed by progressive whites in the decades since *Brown* and, conversely, maps the route by which *Brown* was symbolically appropriated in the 1990s by a new racial conservatism, articulated by Thomas and others. The aim is to reread *Brown* through the lens of contemporary assumptions about culture, race, and ethnicity to explain its recent ideological realignment.

In this chapter, I also highlight a particular link between the multicultural sensibility and the recent lack of progressive white activism around issues of race. A paradoxical tendency toward cultural isolationism has often been associated with the embrace of multicultural ideology by whites. As I see it, intense anxiety about the risks of exercising "cultural imperialism" over "other" groups has led many whites to view cultural nonintervention as the guiding norm for their social practices. This response is understandable in light of the belated realization that the racial consciousness symbolized by *Brown* represented a false form of universalism blind to the mores of white American culture, as they were embedded in the everyday life of workplaces and schools. Self-doubt is preferable to the worst forms of cultural presumptuousness characterizing the racial dynamics of the recent past. However, anxiety about the limits of our own cultural position also tends to leave progressive whites silent and passive in the face of politically conservative and often authoritarian representations of the interests of minority communities, like those presented by Louis Farrakhan and other leaders of the Nation of Islam.

The first part of this chapter describes, in very general and basic terms, the ways progressive whites today tend to view racial and ethnic difference and the central place that the injunction to avoid "cultural imperialism" occupies within that contemporary racial ideology. Next, I relate the multicultural sensibility to the Thomas/Anita Hill controversy in the 1990s, focusing on how the image of African American cultural particularity—"playing the race card"—was deployed to immunize Thomas's harassment of Hill and to immobilize white criticism. The noninterventionist posture is then contrasted with the broad-scale regulation of Southern life that *Brown* represented and that progressives of the period proudly supported. The chapter proceeds by tracing the genealogy of contemporary progressive white race ideology from *Brown* to the Black nationalist' critique of *Brown*'s integrationist assumptions, and, through their contrasting interpretations of *Brown* and the general course of the school desegregation effort, to the various features of the 1960s Black nationalist ideology that have been appropriated by both conservatives and progressives today.

Next, I argue that the general idea of deferring to the self-determination of "other" cultural groups is incoherent; this imagery of deference and nonintervention echoes, at the level of groups, the assumptions that liberal free-market ideology makes about individuals—assumptions progressives have already properly rejected as incoherent. I also suggest there is a link between this *"laissez-faire"* way of thinking about relations between cultural groups and the conservative presentation of group identity that marks recent right-wing appropriation of 1960s Black nationalist rhetoric. The chapter concludes by suggesting an alternative way to think about race—a "postmodern" attitude about cultural difference and nationalist integrity that seeks to retain a liberatory aspect of *Brown*—the social will to intervene, even forcefully and coercively, to transform oppressive social structures.

In this chapter, I treat *Brown* as a cultural symbol for a set of recognizable, though constantly reinterpreted and contested, ideologies about race in America. There are many other ways to approach *Brown*—as standing for particular philosophical principles[3] or social policies that might be debated, as posing a specific doctrinal approach to the legal issue of the appropriate interpretation of the Constitution, or as the actual causal agent for public school desegregation. Part of the significance of *Brown*, of course, is that its literal text was produced in the American legal arena, so that its meaning is bound up with more general notions about legal authority and specific, localized controversies about legitimacy and the role of neutral principles in judicial decision-making. Here, however, I take *Brown* to signify a broader "text" as well—one that includes not only the specific moment of the Court's opinion, but also the ways that *Brown* consequently has been interpreted, constructed, rejected, and appropriated in American racial ideologies. While the debate about the legal or institutional legitimacy of the Court's ruling in *Brown* and its progeny is important, my focus here is on reading *Brown* as both a still-contested and highly charged cultural icon, and more specifically as a historical demarcation point from which to analyze the ideological dynamics of transformation over the last several decades. From this perspective, *Brown* is both a reflection of and a constituent factor in ongoing struggles over how to comprehend and describe race and its place in the social world. The particular legal institutionalization of the racial ideology reflected in *Brown* is only one part of that story.[4]

Finally, given my specific interest in viewing *Brown* through the lens of contemporary multiculturalism, I take as starting-point assumptions that there is such a thing as cultural difference between groups in American society and that African Americans and whites in general inhabit significantly—though, of course, not totally—different cultural spaces.

The Racial Predicament of Progressive Whites

Later in this chapter, I trace the steps that progressive whites followed in the decades after *Brown* that led to the adoption of multiculturalism as the organizing norm of racial justice. Rather than start chronologically with *Brown*, however, I want first to depict, in very general terms, the problem of "cultural imperialism," as it is situated in contemporary progressive white consciousness to provide a point of contrast for the *Brown* history.

As I use the term, "multiculturalism" refers to a recognizable ideology that is associated with left-of-center politics and social style and manifest in a loosely connected set of attitudes and practices sharing, in one way or another, the notion that American society should be understood as a collection of diverse cultural groups, rather than a single, unified national body on one hand or as simply an aggregate of atomized individuals on the other. It is distinguished from the traditional liberal civil rights vision evoked by Thomas in the passage that opens this chapter in that it takes the status of group membership as a positive, meaning-generating value, rather than an irrational or arbitrary attribute. Unlike the governmental colorblindness Thomas advocates, a multiculturalist sensibility implies that the government must recognize and respect, if not nurture, the diversity and integrity of racial and ethnic communities.

Stated in this amorphous way, I am suggesting that a wide range of social phenomena—the appearance of Afro-centric schools, political support for bilingual education, university campaigns for "diverse" faculty hiring, legal consideration of the "culture defense," campus hate-speech codes, the official institutionalization of "Black History Month," sidewalk tolerance of "Free Mike Tyson" sweatshirts, and so on—are linked by a recognizable, shared ideology about the nature of race, ethnicity, and difference. The point is not that this is all new—clearly, bits and pieces have been contained in past efforts at "cultural appreciation" and the like—but rather that, by the mid-1990s, a notion of respecting cultural integrity had replaced antidiscrimination as the primary frame through which progressives understood racial justice. Multiculturalism in this sense is not meant as a philosophical position or social theory, but rather a vaguer, less worked-out, background sensibility.

It is within this new sensibility—that racial justice means respecting the integrity of diverse cultural groups in the social fabric—that the idea of "cultural imperialism" assumes a central place. Again, it is not as if this notion is new by any means—it is, after all, a metaphor referring to the classic colonial relationships between "nations"—but instead that it has been centered in a recognizable and particularly contemporary racial ideology.

The idea of "cultural imperialism" is that one cultural group will impose its norms on another. The "cultural" side reflects the notion that colonialism is not always imposed by visible material force or according to the boundaries of formally constituted nation-states. The "imperialism" side embodies the understanding that disparate power is at issue.

The well-known controversy over whether Westerners should oppose female genital mutilation—despite claims that it is an integral ethnic ritual when seen from within particular African tribal worldviews[5]—puts the cultural imperialism issue in clear focus, given the international context and clear history of European colonial domination in Africa. However, the international rights debate is only one, relatively distanced (for virtually all Americans) site where the colonialism framework operates; anxiety about cultural imperialism is also more local and common. There is a sense in which it looms in the background of everyday relations between whites and Blacks, Anglos and Latinos, straights and gays, and so on, as less a worked-out ethical dilemma and more an undercurrent of social interaction in America.

Anxiety about exercising cultural imperialism is the manifestation of two different kinds of impulses that progressive whites want to respect. First, as progressives, we strive to make the world a better place, relieve suffering, and effect a more egalitarian distribution of wealth, power, and recognition. These commitments suggest active intervention in the social world. Second, we simultaneously believe in community self-determination and the correlate principle that white/Euro cultural norms should not dominate the cultures of other people, particularly historically disempowered groups. The prevailing norm is to defer to the mores and wishes of other cultural groups.

Given these two impulses, progressive whites have faced a repetitive dilemma. The substantive impulse to reform the world in a progressive fashion is met by a procedural impulse—with its own progressive pedigree in the language of anti-imperialism—to respect and celebrate, or at the very least tolerate, difference. The result of this tension has often been paralysis—the inability to resolve, in a series of particular contexts, whether it is acceptable to criticize and intervene in an attempt to influence another group, or whether this intervention constitutes cultural imperialism; whether progressive whites should actively intervene in race politics, or whether they should simply defer to the decisions of people of color; and so on.

A general consequence of progressive preoccupation with this set of issues has been that, while conservatives in America have articulated a substantive and existentially evocative vision of how the world should be, liberals and progressives have instead struggled over whether it is acceptable to take a position at all. Conservatives have staked out a stance in the "culture wars" and clearly marked their territory—as repressive and false as their picture might be to a left-leaning constituency. Liberals and progressives, however, have spoken less in terms of substantive visions and more in terms of procedural-type values such as inclusion and respect for other cultures. This phenomenon is particularly evident among white, straight males, who do not identify as members of structurally victimized communities (indeed, not as members of any socially constructed group at all), and it is also apparent with respect to how whites relate more generally to people of color.

I believe that the injunction to respect the autonomy and self-determination rights of other cultural groups reflects real progress on the part of progressive whites. It was not long ago, after all, that liberal whites unselfconsciously dominated and directed major civil rights organizations or, as I discussed in Chapter 1, integrated public schools primarily by closing Black schools and replacing Black teachers. After years of painful critique on this score, it is widely understood that well-intentioned "help" can itself constitute a form of domination.

On the other hand, it is also possible that the centering of cultural imperialism has provided a discursive framework that seems to confirm it is progressive not to act in many instances when intervention would make the world better. The idea of avoiding "cultural imperialism" cannot resolve the difficult but inevitable issue of what whites should do with the racial power they actually possess; not exercising this power affirmatively does not make it disappear.

To clarify at the outset, I am not claiming either that the kind of white anxiety I am describing is the most important problem of contemporary race dynamics (I think that designation should go to the maldistribution of wealth and income) or that whites should stop paying any attention to these concerns. I address "cultural imperialism" simply as one trope among the many complex and cross-cutting strands of our racial landscape; my particular interest is in exploring how this belief structure has helped disempower progressive forces in cultural and political conflict with conservatives.

This general description of "multiculturalism" and "cultural imperialism" is meant to evoke a recognizable piece of our cultural landscape. More than a set of "ideas" or "premises" in a theoretic model, the point is that, as a social ideology, this sensibility is a lived part of and helps constitute everyday psycho-cultural experience. Accordingly, its range of influence sets the boundaries not only for what is considered acceptable in the realm of public policy and official institutional culture, but also for the terms of micro-encounters in everyday social life. Think of the phenomenon of whites adopting Black vernacular in integrated social settings, for example, as at least partly epiphenomenal behavior constituted and regulated by the social construction of (the meaning of) race.[6]

In the next part of this chapter, I explore how the "ideas" I've just described helped frame social perception and regulate political energy in the context of the Thomas/Hill confrontation during Thomas's 1991 confirmation hearings.

Clarence Thomas, Anita Hill, and a "Down-Home Style of Courting"

> With his mainstream cultural guard down, Judge Thomas on several misjudged occasions may have done something completely out of the cultural frame of his white, upper-middle-class work world, but immediately recognizable to Professor Hill and most women of Southern working-class backgrounds, white or black, especially the latter.... I am convinced that Professor Hill perfectly understood the psycho-cultural context in which Judge Thomas allegedly regaled her with his Rabelaisian humor (possibly as a way of affirming their common origins), which

is precisely why she never filed a complaint against him.... [S]he has lifted a verbal style that carries only minor sanction in one subcultural context and thrown it into the overheated cultural arena of mainstream, neo-Puritan America, where it incurs professional extinction.... [M]ost of Professor Hill's supporters seem to be middle-class white women. My own daughter, Barbara, a post-feminist young woman brought up by two feminists who came of age in the 60's, believes along with her friends that Judge Thomas did say those raunchy things, should have been told at once what a 'dog' he was and reported to the authorities by Professor Hill if his advances continued to annoy her. But they cannot see the relevance of Judge Thomas's down-home style of courting to his qualifications for the Supreme Court.

Orlando Patterson, 1991[7]

To get a more concrete sense of the contemporary ideological situation I want to evoke, consider the 1991 confirmation hearings for Thomas. In what became the central focus of that widely followed cultural spectacle, Hill, a Black law professor who had worked under Thomas when he was an official at the Department of Education and at the Equal Employment Opportunity Commission, came forward during his confirmation to accuse him of sexual harassment in that workplace. She charged that he had made numerous unwelcome sexual overtures to her and that "he spoke about acts that he had seen in pornographic films involving such matters as women having sex with animals and films showing group sex or rape scenes.... On several occasions, Thomas told me graphically of his own sexual prowess." In one instance, "Thomas was drinking a Coke in his office, he got up from the table at which we were working, went over to his desk to get the Coke, looked at the can and asked, 'Who has pubic hair on my Coke?'"[8]

The televised Thomas/Hill hearings transfixed the country. They helped to center the issue of sexual harassment during a period of general (white) feminist upsurge, both reflecting and confirming the dominance of radical, rather than liberal, feminist projects. I believe they also completed the arc, begun with the 1970s expulsion of whites from Black radical "civil rights" groups, marking the symbolic end of liberal whites' involvement with the Black community.

One of the explicit charges made against Hill was that she represented white feminism, directly in the sense that white feminists were putting her up to testify and advising her while the controversy went on, and indirectly because a white feminist ideology had made "sexual harassment" a problem as a legal and cultural trope in the first place.

Orlando Patterson, an esteemed Black male Harvard sociology professor, articulated this analysis of Hill explicitly in the *New York Times* op-ed piece from which I have quoted. His argument is an exemplar of what is commonly called "the culture defense," the idea that taboos are culturally specific, and thus what would be a transgression in one culture may not be in another. Underlying its deployment is the premise that a dominant cultural group should not impose its norms on a minority.[9]

Patterson's text is actually a vivid example of the twists and turns required by an argument based on an accusation of cultural imperialism and invoking the authority of the "subcultural group." Patterson's overt argument is that Hill, in a sense, perpetuated a culture fraud on mainstream America by pretending she did not recognize Thomas's behavior simply as "down-home courting," rather than sexual harassment. Patterson's authority to expose her fraud is, apparently, his own status as an African American, signifying a culture he claims they share.

However, as soon as that authority is expressed, it is immediately evident that it is insufficient. If this were an issue of possible *gender* domination, it makes no more sense for a male like Patterson to adjudicate it than it would for "[white] mainstream, neo-puritan America" to adjudicate the mores of Hill and Thomas, two African Americans.

Given this reflexive tendency of Patterson's brand of the culture defense to turn on itself, it is not surprising that he then awkwardly deploys the authority of "my own daughter … along with her friends." However, even that deployment is suspect, from the viewpoint of sensitivity to the risk of imperialism; he gives as his "post-feminist" daughter's main credential that she was brought up by "two feminists," reverting obliquely around to his own authority as a "good male" while manifestly claiming to be invoking the authority of females. His daughter's feminist authority is derivative of her upbringing by properly feminist parents, one of whom is Patterson himself. So, ultimately, Patterson's authority to define the feminist position is himself—not necessarily a problem, unless one is claiming to be speaking against the attempt of a more powerful group to impose its mores on a weaker subcultural group.

It is not that one should ignore Patterson because his "argument" has these internal tensions and contradictory meanings that undermine the authority or the coherence of the positions he asserts. These limitations in a sense did not matter because the effectiveness of his intervention depended on the particular anxiety about cultural imperialism whites *already* experienced. Patterson's editorial was one example of the many ways this dynamic played out during the

Thomas/Hill confrontation. The gist was that Hill represented white feminism, and thus supporting her meant violating the norm of cultural and racial self-determination. It is a sign of its strength that it is not only progressive whites who honor the principle, but moderates as well: Senator Sam Nunn, a centrist from Georgia, openly justified his vote by pointing to the overnight poll results showing overwhelming support for Thomas among Blacks in Georgia.[10] There was, in all of this debate, no need to justify or argue about the underlying premise of cultural deference because cultural deference was a key implied component of the reigning multicultural sensibility.

The Thomas/Hill confrontation also implicated a second dimension of the "culture defense"—its deployment in service of a conservative, traditionalist, and allegedly authoritative representation of a "culture." The force of Patterson's argument against intervention depends on two assumptions: first, the idea that whites must respect the cultural integrity of the African American community, and second, that Patterson himself was authentically representing the Black community's "courting" mores. Given the cultural geography that multiculturalism celebrates, most whites are in no position to challenge the accuracy of "indigenous" descriptions of native cultural space. However, if Hill's depictions were accurate, as Patterson assumes, it does not *necessarily* reveal a courtship ritual practiced across distant cultural boundaries. Instead, her account describes a common, recognizable—albeit particularly awkward and bizarre (the "pubic hair on the Coke can")—genre of male sexual acting-out with subordinates with which most people in both Black and white culture are familiar. (This is not to say it is a universal or inevitable phenomenon.)

From this perspective, it is possible to explicate Patterson's use of the term "courting." It does not seem likely that he is asserting that "courting" is the term indigenous to (or even used by) "down-home" Blacks themselves, except with the frame of irony that whites also recognize. The "courtship" reference is recognizable across cultural space as the ways privileged *white* Southerners conceived of dating; its limited use by the Southern working class, both Black and white, is derivative and self-mocking, accentuating the ways their own dating lacks the formalized manners they project onto the rich. However, by calling Thomas's awkward behavior with Anita Hill "courting," Patterson is committing his own culture fraud, using "courting" to try to give the behavior an anthropological status it does not possess. Assuming the truth of Hill's testimony, Thomas just appears to be a member of some culture who actually *failed* to learn to deploy the culture's "courtship" rituals. That is the pathetic, vulnerable aspect of Thomas's behavior that was so humiliating for him to have exposed—his incompetence at "courtship" in *any* permissible cultural frame.

The progressive white community, however, was (and is) politically and culturally vulnerable to the accusations of improper intervention as exemplified by Patterson's editorial. It would be silly to claim that Patterson as an individual contributed in a significant way to Thomas's confirmation. On the other hand, the attitude expressed by Patterson was, I believe, part of a wider point of racial confrontation that undercut the will and confidence of white opponents of Thomas and contributed to his ultimate confirmation.[11] Patterson's accusation that Hill was a tool of white feminism directly addressed white liberal anxieties about engaging in cultural ethnocentrism; it equated feminist reformism with white imperialism, thus linking feminist criticism to the "lynching" metaphor of Thomas's own testimony.[12]

The high-profile nature of the Thomas/Hill confrontation made the deployment of cultural difference against white progressives particularly obvious. However, progressive whites face this same hurdle of cultural legitimacy at various points of cultural contact, ranging from broad doctrinal questions in legal discourse about various forms of the "culture defense" or debates about American foreign policy, to specific questions of how whites ought to react to Minister Louis Farrakhan, to Black celebration of the O. J. Simpson verdict, to the valorization of the Jena Six (Black teenagers who were accused of beating a white classmate and were overcharged by prosecutors), to the abusive sexuality and consumption-centered values promoted by many hip-hop artists, to the Afro-centric fundamentalism of the Reverend Jeremiah Wright, to the fact that symbols of the Black bourgeoisie such as Barack Obama and Oprah Winfrey would patronize his church, and so on. As crystallized in the Thomas/Hill confrontation, the question was what white progressives thought Senator Nunn should have done when presented with the apparent self-determination of the Black community manifesting approval of Thomas. Within what understanding of racial and cultural justice was Nunn to oppose Thomas, without reverting to the discredited tradition of vicious Old South paternalism represented by Nunn's Georgia predecessor, Herman Talmadge?

In the remainder of this chapter, I will ultimately defend an "interventionist" orientation against the reigning notion that whites must defer to the dominant voice of "other" communities or be guilty of cultural imperialism. The motivation for this argument is a general belief that, under the rubric of "respecting the self-determination rights of cultural communities," whites have often neglected some of the best aspects of the progressive tradition—the willingness to intervene to create a more just social world, as well as a general observation that the Black community is in deep trouble.[13]

Brown and the Colonization of the South: Replacing "Down-Home" Schooling with New South Technocracy

> Local control is a major cause of the dull parochialism and attenuated totalitarianism that characterizes public education in orientation.
>
> Myron Lieberman, 1960[14]

In this section, I utilize the multicultural sensibility I have sketched above as the framework to describe the enforcement of *Brown's* desegregation ruling as a colonialist intervention of Northern (more specifically, white Northeastern) power and cultural ideology in the South. My aim is to provide a point of contrast from which to reconsider today's reflexive deference to "other" cultures.

Contemporary caution about the dangers of cultural intervention is markedly different from the confidence and sense of righteousness that characterized the specific federal enforcement of *Brown's* desegregation ruling in the South, and that marked the more general assurance, openly expressed by Lieberman and others, that the parochialism of Southern culture could be transcended by centrally administering Southern schools. Seen through the filters of later concerns about "cultural imperialism," the relationship between the Northeast and South during the 1960s looks, in retrospect, classically and unabashedly colonialist. *Brown* appears as one face of a broad Northeastern intervention into what might be seen as the indigenous culture of the South as it existed before the mid-1950s, an intervention that included elements of physical and material coercion; the delegitimation of the justificatory ideology of natural order and divine authority; the substitution of the discourse of technocracy, professionalism, bureaucratic expertise, and competent management; and the associated replacement of the former ruling aristocrats with a New South leadership more pleasing to Northeastern sensibilities.[15]

The material dimension of Northern intervention was dramatic. Armed troops enforced the *Brown* ruling, albeit after official legal delay and massive resistance including "Impeach Earl Warren" billboards sprinkling Southern highways. The famous Little Rock television coverage—the nationally broadcast images of coolly professional, armed federal officers protecting a frightened Black girl arriving for the first day of school with a book bag and a lunchbox, facing a venomous mob of screaming white adults—remains powerful and compelling even today. The visual images combine the dramatic quality of the intervention through coercive, militaristic power with a moving portrayal of the existential basis for the exercise of that power.

Less dramatic versions of the Little Rock scene were re-enacted in school after school across the South in the mid- to late 1960s. Even after the first wave of white parental resistance subsided, students often started the first school year in desegregated schools under the shadow of bayonets held by federal or national guard soldiers perched on the roof "in case of trouble." The presence of troops to enforce federal court desegregation orders was a particularly visible and clear reminder that power was being exercised from the outside, by an authority structure external to and superior to the locals who had administered the Southern version of American apartheid.

However, the "takeover" of the South did not consist simply in the enforcement of legal rulings under *Brown,* although that was its most dramatic point of visible coercive intervention. *Brown* was part of a broader critique of and intervention into the status quo culture of Southern life; in general terms, the trajectory of Northern regulation was to replace the all-white, Old South patriarchal ruling class with a somewhat integrated, rationalist, and technocratic New South leadership, literally in terms of political office and more generally in terms of everyday cultural and ideological legitimacy in diverse institutions.[16]

Accordingly, it made sense that federal courts banned school prayer—a common and significant ritual in Southern schools—at about the same time they implemented *Brown.* In the ideology of federal intervention, both reforms consisted of replacing the parochialism and narrow-mindedness of Southern schools with the rationality of Northern professionalism and expertise. At the level of cultural symbolism, racism and religiosity were linked as irrational and ignorant belief structures, to be contrasted with the face of Northeastern legitimacy, enlightenment of science, and rationality of the rule of law.

By the time the various facets of Northern intervention had played themselves out, the transformation of everyday Southern culture was striking, particularly with respect to schools. By the mid-1970s, public education in the South proceeded for the most part on a legally desegregated basis.[17] Virtually all school prayer had ceased, and (more generally) the kind of centralized professionalism advocated by Lieberman replaced virtually any semblance of local Southern influence over schools. Significantly, the rest of the traditional school practices—paddling, singing, an informal maternal network of educators, curricular education in moral virtues and social values—were, without any legal compulsion from the North, replaced with the latest in standardized instruction, evaluation, curriculum, and administration.

Ultimately, the schools in Southern cities and suburbs, and to some extent even in rural areas, became in most respects—with the notable exception of the students' and faculty members' accents—indistinguishable from those in the Northeast. The colonization of Southern schools was accomplished over little more than a decade between the appearance of armed troops and the ultimate administration of the modernization project by a heralded New South suburbanite class recruited to manage the new order. In terms of the exercise of cultural power, it was as if alien educational institutions designed in the Northeast had simply been placed in the midst of Southern communities by an occupying force with superior might and ultimately the ability to impose a new ideology of legitimacy and authority.

Support for the federal government's coercion of local Southern school boards on matters of race and religion, and the correlate critique of traditional Southern white culture as parochial and backward, constituted an important part of what identified one as a progressive during the 1960s and 1970s. As the image of the thickly accented "redneck" was explicitly utilized by the popular media as the comical signifier of uncivilized stupidity, the possibility that one should respect the "cultural differences" of white Southerners simply did not appear on the progressive ideological screen.

The point here is not to bemoan the destruction of the dominant Southern white culture of the pre-*Brown* period, or to condemn the implementation of *Brown* and the associated reform of the South on the grounds that it all constituted a form of colonialism with respect to the region's "traditions." As I discuss, what might be called the *Brown* intervention is properly understood as in many ways heroic and virtuous; it was a good thing to topple the old regime. Aspects of the intervention also were colonialist and imperialist as well. My aim in framing the description in these terms is to highlight how much white progressives' assurance about the legitimacy of coercive intervention has changed from support for the explicit regulation of the Southern social structure to today's reigning anxiety about the risks of engaging in cultural imperialism.

It is possible, of course, that *Brown* was not experienced as a colonialist intervention because the group being coerced consisted of other whites (or other

"Americans"), and thus white Northerners did not experience themselves as exercising power over an "other" cultural group. Alternatively, perhaps Southern culture was seen as so bound up with racism that it was deemed worthy of destruction—or, to say it differently, "the issues were so much clearer then." However, I do not believe that either of these possibilities adequately accounts for the contrast between progressive whites' enthusiasm for the regulation of the South in the 1960s and 1970s and the contemporary, generalized anxiety about cultural intervention.

The next section of this chapter examines the substantive racial ideologies progressive whites held at the time of *Brown* and their subsequent repudiation to suggest that the universalist and rationalist racial norms of integrationism and colorblindness that *Brown* for a time represented were ideologically linked with the social willingness to intervene across cultural boundaries. While this section treated the *Brown*-oriented transformation of the South as a possible form of cultural imperialism when viewed from the viewpoint of status-quo, white Southern traditionalism, I next consider *Brown* as emblematic of the imposition of culturally imperialist power vis-à-vis Blacks themselves, a charge that has, I believe, propelled progressive whites to reconsider and repudiate the ways racial justice was understood at the time of *Brown*.

The Construction of Multiculturalism and the Reinterpretation of *Brown*

> [I]f we can get an all-Black school that we can control, staff it ourselves with the type of teachers that have our good at heart, with the type of books that have in them many of the missing ingredients that have produced this inferiority complex in our people, then we don't feel that an all-Black school is necessarily a segregated school. It's only segregated when it's controlled by someone from the outside.... So, what the integrationists, in my opinion, are saying when they say that whites and Blacks must go to school together, is that the whites are so much superior that just their presence in a Black classroom balances it out. I just can't go along with that.
>
> Malcolm X, 1963[18]

> It never ceases to amaze me that the courts are so willing to assume that anything that is predominantly black must be inferior.... First, the

court has read our cases to support the theory that black students suffer an unspecified psychological harm from segregation that retards their mental and educational development. This approach not only relies upon questionable social science research rather than constitutional principle, but it also rests on an assumption of black inferiority ... the idea that any school that is black is inferior, and that blacks cannot succeed without the benefit of the company of whites.... Given that desegregation has not produced the predicted leaps forward in black educational achievement, there is no reason to think that black students cannot learn as well when surrounded by members of their own race as when they are in an integrated environment. Indeed, it may very well be that what has been true for historically black colleges is true for black middle and high schools.... [B]lack schools can function as the center and symbol of black communities, and provide examples of independent black leadership, success, and achievement.

Justice Clarence Thomas, 1995[19]

To understand the stakes of the cultural imperialism charge for progressives today, it helps to consider the genesis from "colorblindness" to "difference" as the dominant way of understanding race. When Malcolm X opposed school integration, the civil rights movement, led by the Reverend Martin Luther King, Jr., was near its apex. Malcolm X spoke against school integration in the same year as the March on Washington, where King's "I Have a Dream" speech movingly summarized the moral basis for colorblindness.[20] Further, the country had just symbolically committed itself to the coercive enforcement of school desegregation in the South in Little Rock and other places. Although Malcolm X's rhetoric actually represented a revitalization (and radicalization) of a tradition of Black nationalist ideology with long roots in the mid-19th century, he was experienced, at least by virtually all liberal and progressive whites, as a militant and somewhat crazy reverse racist, as the Black equivalent of the never-say-die segregationists in the South. Both white racists and Malcolm X violated the reigning moral norm that color makes no difference between people and that only irrational and prejudiced people thought it did. In the dominant perception of liberals and progressives, the key racial conflict was between enlightened integrationists and ignorant segregationists. Malcolm X was simply off the map.[21]

The transformation of reigning racial assumptions over the last three decades is dramatically manifest in the way that Thomas's rhetoric in 1995 echoes Malcolm X's critique of integrationism. Thomas represents a neoconservative ideology fundamentally at odds with the left-leaning and revolutionary worldview of Malcolm X, Stokely Carmichael, the Black Panthers, and other Black Nationalists of the 1960s and early 1970s. No one interprets his rhetoric as suggesting the same thorough critique of American society that 1960s radicals lodged, but both Thomas and Malcolm X, from opposite ideological commitments, target the (predominantly) white liberal administration of race reform as it was practiced in the desegregation era.

The ingeniousness (if ultimate incoherence) of Thomas's reconstruction of conservative race ideology is that he has melded an individualist-oriented legal rhetoric of governmental neutrality and colorblindness onto the group-based racial self-determination assumptions of contemporary multiculturalism. In doing so, he is able to appropriate strands of Black nationalist discourse—particularly the self-help thematic—in service of right-wing legal ideology. His view is traditionally conservative in its depiction of the government as a "night watchman" over society, basically staying out of the "private" marketplace except to enforce the ground rules of social competition and struggle. The difference between this view and its traditional 19th-century antecedent is that the private marketplace is now conceived as made up of discrete cultural groups, such as African Americans, rather than discrete individuals. In this vision, colorblindness serves to permit Blacks to establish their own schools and determine their own community needs, rather than providing the justification, as it did in the 1960s and 1970s, for coercive federal intervention to integrate schools.

It is difficult for progressive whites to oppose rhetoric like Thomas's because, in many ways, it actually matches the implicit assumptions of their own embrace of multiculturalism. To understand how they have arrived at this rhetorical juncture, it is instructive to consider the twists and turns that white progressive race ideology has taken in the last three decades. What follows is a summary and somewhat impressionistic account of the recent history of progressive white race consciousness. *Brown* and the widely shared moral imperative to end school segregation is an obvious and useful demarcation point against which to contrast the multicultural sensibility and from which to trace its development through the succession of racial ideologies held by moderate and left-leaning American whites in the recent past.

As Thomas states, *Brown* is now conventionally understood to have embraced two basic justifications for its ruling that state-enforced school desegregation was unconstitutional. The first, celebrated by Thomas and other conservatives in contemporary discourse (if not at the time of the *Brown* decision itself) was based on the formal principle that government may not take race into account in making decisions about social policy because race is an irrelevant and arbitrary attribute of individuals, and thus virtually any governmental decision based on race reflects a distortion of legitimate decision-making procedures and a violation of an individual's right to be treated on his own merit. The emphasis in this read is on the statement in the opinion that school segregation was "inherently" unequal.

As discussed in the preceding chapter, the other justification—more controversial within traditional understandings of the appropriate grounds for constitutional interpretation—was that segregation produced psychological ill effects in Black children. This conclusion was supported in the *Brown* opinion by cites to social-science research and the famous "doll studies" purporting to show that Black children in segregated educational settings viewed white characteristics as superior.[22] Thomas asserts that, given the *principle* against race consciousness, "*Brown* did not need to rely on any social science evidence."

As a reflection of what would become the dominant moderate and progressive white view of race, however, these jurisprudential distinctions were at first technical and legalistic. For progressive whites and (one supposes) most members of the Court, the two strands of *Brown* were complementary and consistent. Segregation in principle was wrong, and social science confirmed its pernicious effects. It was not until the principle of colorblindness seemed to be insufficient to produce desegregation that the two bases diverged into two different and recognizable ways to understand racial justice, with conservatives embracing colorblindness, governmental neutrality, and formal equality, and progressives advocating affirmative governmental action to achieve substantive racial equality—an equality of results understood as integrated social institutions.

As described in Chapter 5, this divergence emerged as a clear ideological opposition in the legal arena with respect to the enforcement of *Brown* itself. It soon became clear that simply forbidding the state from enforcing racial school segregation would not achieve integrated schools; colorblindness in official policy—say, by adopting "freedom-of-choice" plans permitting students to go to whatever school they chose or adopting neighborhood attendance policies—by itself did not produce an end to segregation in fact.[23] At that point, liberal and progressive legal discourse began the first stages of rejecting colorblindness and, ultimately, its associated assimilationist assumptions. Linking the issues of school desegregation and race discrimination generally to the formalism/

realism opposition already extant within legal ideology, progressives within the legal arena began associating the colorblindness approach with formalism more generally. Colorblindness became linked to the formal equality espoused by the Court in the discredited "liberty of contract" era, within which laborers and capitalists were said to have equal rights to contract with respect to wages and other working conditions.[24]

According to this kind of "racial realism," color consciousness was required to identify whether racial discrimination was being practiced or whether remedies were being implemented in good faith. In the school context, progressives argued for a *de facto* test that would make constitutional requirements turn on the actual achievement of integration, rather than merely a cessation of intentional segregative practices on the part of the government. In the employment context, they advocated a disparate effects test that made the identification of discrimination turn on the racial results of alleged job qualification criteria. In the emerging affirmative action context generally, they contended that a period of benign color consciousness was required practically to offset the effects of years of malign racism and to compensate for the "deprivation" Blacks suffered under the segregation regime.[25]

Within the terms of this advocacy of "substantive," rather than "formal," equality, the social-science research relied on by the *Brown* Court came to symbolize a real-world jurisprudential alternative, opposed to the abstract and formal quality of the conservative commitment to "principled" decision-making. The social-science stand of *Brown* became a new, positive symbol of realism in law, of making law correspond to the actual social conditions to which it applied, rather than to the abstract idealization of formal equality in the face of empirical inequality.[26] In this alternative reading, *Brown* could be interpreted to stand for the proposition that constitutional law must consider racial history, power relations between groups, social meaning of particular governmental acts, and so forth. Looking to social science signified opposing formalist and universalist abstraction.

This splitting of *Brown* between a formalist and realist (or functional) interpretation constituted only the first stage of a progressive reinterpretation of *Brown*. The second part consisted of the less explicit, more subtle rejection of the social-science side as well, as it became apparent that the "realism" depicted by social-science research itself rested on what we would today call "Eurocentric" assumptions.

From "Cultural Deprivation" to Cultural Difference: Accounting for Black Underperformance

> The problem, stated as simply as possible, is that the environment [in] which lower-class Negro children ... [have] grown up does not provide the intellectual and sensory stimulation they need in order to benefit from the conventional kindergarten and first-grade curricula.... [M]iddle class children do, in fact, come already equipped with these skills; they acquire them quite unconsciously from their environment, more or less by osmosis. But the lower class child, as a rule, has not acquired these skills because of the intellectual and sensory poverty of his environment.... For example, the Negro youngsters ... have much less auditory discrimination [because] the noise level in a household tends to be so high that the child is forced to learn how not to listen and [fails] to develop an ability to distinguish relevant and irrelevant sounds.... [The] lower class child has not had the experience of having adults correct his pronunciation ... or ask about school.... The nonverbal household [in which] adults speak in short sentences ... and give orders in monosyllables ... means that youngsters' memory, as well as their attention span, receive less training.... Given this poverty of experience, it is almost inevitable that the Negro child will fail when he enters school.[27]
>
> Charles Silberman, 1964

The irony of the opposition that progressive legal commentators drew between the formalism of the colorblindness principle and the "real world" depicted by social-science research was that the social-science paradigms of the *Brown* period were themselves, in historical retrospect, quite universalist and ethnocentric. "Cultural deprivation" was the reigning paradigm in sociology in the late 1950s and early 1960s for comprehending the underachievement of Black students in integrated educational settings. As the phrase suggests, Black underachievement was explicitly understood on cultural grounds as the inferior quality of a Black culture rooted in poverty.

Although he would later renounce the thesis as racist,[28] Silberman, writing as a concerned liberal sociologist, was a leading exponent of the cultural deprivation thesis. In his account, Black schoolchildren failed in integrated educational environments because they tended to come from more crowded living conditions, providing the material frame for a whole slew of learning problems.

The "cultural deprivation" ideology was more than simply the thesis of academic sociologists. It became, for a short time, the dominant framework for a liberal American understanding of race.[29] The idea that Black children were culturally deprived and therefore needed enrichment to fare well in the educational process underlay the institution of programs during the War on Poverty, such as Head Start,[30] and the basic, early justifications for affirmative action in many contexts.[31]

The furor that erupted over the 1994 publication of *The Bell Curve*[32] and its thesis of Black genetic inferiority is but one notable example of how far mainstream culture had come from the kind of discourse Silberman employed. The kinds of claims made by Silberman in the 1960s seem downright racist and totally "ethnocentric" today in that he explicitly used the mores of the white middle-class, two-parent family as the baseline norm from which deprivation was determined, and he arguably made patronizing assumptions about different verbal and familial styles across racial boundaries.

Like the lack of consciousness about the possible imperialism implicit in the denigration of Southern culture generally, Silberman and other white liberals of the period similarly had little apparent consciousness about the possible imperialism implicit in their depictions of the "plight" of Blacks, and they displayed no sense of the positive, sustaining elements of the Black community. Progressive whites thus experienced militant nationalists like Malcolm X as ideologically indistinguishable from deferential "Uncle Toms" in the Black community who opposed segregation because they had bought into the ideology of white supremacy or were too scared to oppose it. In other words, whites saw in Black life only the harmful consequences of racial hierarchy and simply never considered the possibility that African Americans had constructed a cultural community worth preserving. When nationalists argued for the preservation of Black institutions, whites heard only resistance to liberatory change.

The embrace of the idea of "cultural deprivation" also illuminates the particular manner in which the school integration policy was actually implemented. Nothing in *Brown* (the formal legal decision) or within the analytics of integration as a social policy dictated that it would proceed primarily by closing formerly Black schools, terminating Black teachers and administrators, and virtually wiping out, for a generation, almost the entire class of educators in the Black community—a class with a long and important influence in constituting Black middle-class culture.[33] Well-intentioned white liberals could think that such a social policy was not problematic from an ideological framework within which the ethnocentric cast of the "cultural deprivation" thesis was invisible and from which, conversely, white schools appeared as superior on neutral, acultural terms.

In other words, the assumption was that schools themselves did not embody cultural norms, and thus pursuing an integrationist policy that largely integrated Black children into formerly white schools did not raise issues of cultural assimilation—or, as Robert Browne, a Black nationalist intellectual of the late 1960s put it, "painless genocide."[34]

By the mid-1960s, Silberman and other liberals publicly renounced the "cultural deprivation" thesis as racist in its implications. Instead, mainstream sociologists such as Silberman and Kenneth Clark began embracing what became known in sociological jargon as "labeling theory"—the general idea that Black children's underachievement resulted from the discriminatory way schools responded by expecting them to fail.[35] In this reading, the very labeling of Black children as "deprived" made their educators expect less of them, imperceptibly communicating to the children themselves that they did not have an equal chance at educational success.

This transformation from "cultural deprivation" to "labeling theory" and "lowered expectations" focused attention away from alleged inadequacies in lower-class African American culture and toward the inadequacies of mainstream public schools. It was symbolically, in my reading, the first step in the ultimate rejection of the assimilationist assumptions of integrationism as it was understood by white proponents of *Brown*. Also, this implicit rejection of the social-science basis of *Brown* was concurrently the last step in the implicit progressive rejection of *Brown* as resting on ultimately conservative assumptions about the range of cultural norms of institutional life.

While it would be impossible to account definitively for this change in perspective, it was correlated with, and I believe largely responsive to, the simultaneous explosion of anti-integrationist, nationalist militancy in the Black community. While white progressives were, in the legal arena, struggling to extend integrationist norms by requiring actual integration as the test of remedying past segregation and disparate impact to identify present discrimination, and had in general embraced the cultural deprivation account for understanding Blacks' relative inability to assimilate successfully into white schools, the nationalist posture of Malcolm X and newly emerging Black radicals such as Carmichael and the Black Panthers put the rejection of colorblindness on a more fundamental, substantive plane.

As more fully described in Chapter 2, Black nationalists in the 1960s and early 1970s explicitly asserted that the integrationist policy mainstream America had by then adopted was colonialist and racist. In their analysis, the institutions into which Blacks would be integrated were specifically white in character and culture. Racial integration accordingly meant a further loss of Black control over the institutions of their community, insofar as integrationism implied that Blacks would be integrated into white schools, economic institutions, and neighborhoods.

With respect to the rejection of the idea of culture deprivation, Black nationalist and liberal academic sociological discourse had similar structural elements. Most importantly, they both located the cause of the problem in the institutions into which Black integration would be conducted, rather than in the culture of Black people—although they pointed in very different directions.

For the liberal sociologists of the mid-1960s, heirs to the colorblindness ideology of racial justice and integrationist social policy, the problem Black children were having in integrated classes could be accounted for by bias in how integrated public schools approached them. The problem, from the liberal integrationist point of view, was one of deviation from a supposed neutral norm of how teachers should relate to students in a classroom, "regardless of race." In this discourse, when teachers do not expect as much from Black children, Black children get the message that they are not expected to do as well. According to labeling theory's contribution, people tend to adapt to the category in which they are classified, and thus Black children did not do as well as whites in integrated schools.[36]

The alternative view articulated by Malcolm X and other radical Black nationalists of the 1960s and early 1970s differed at the basic starting point of analysis. While traditional liberal pro-*Brown* integrationists saw the goal to achieve neutral public institutions, purged of specificity and neutral to a diverse population, "regardless of race, religion, creed, etc.," nationalists asserted that institutions like schools were inevitably culturally specific and identifiable as white institutions. Borrowing from the independence discourses of emerging African nation-states, Black nationalists saw school race issues not as concerned with the identification of bias from a position of neutrality or objectivity, but rather as an instance of colonialism through which a national community was being robbed of important cultural, economic, and educational institutions. The model of racial power in the Black nationalist analysis located racial hegemony outside individuals who may have "biases," to institutions and social structures, conceived in terms of separate white and Black cultures. The colonialism framework was vastly different than the model of integrationism because it assumed there *are* differences based on race and that the proper goal was not to integrate what was wrongly segregated, but rather a kind of respectful coexistence, like friendly nations on the world stage. Malcolm X dramatized this ideological message when, with some degree of seriousness, he sought relief for African Americans as a colonized nation from the United Nations.

It is amazing, in light of how vilified nationalists were in the late 1960s and early 1970s in mainstream discourse, that they ultimately won the cultural/ philosophical dimension of this particular ideological struggle. Over the last few decades, American culture in general, and white progressives in particular, have moved ever closer to the basic assumption of the nationalist depiction of the inevitable cultural character of institutions like public schools. While there is no clearly obvious demarcation point akin to the "cultural deprivation" idea or the adoption of "labeling theory" within academic discourse to chart this transition, the trajectory for white progressives has been a subtle and incremental rejection of the colorblindness model of racial justice in favor of at least a version of the nationalist analysis.

As described above, the first analytic step in this process was clearly contained within the frame of the substantive vision of colorblindness itself; color consciousness was necessary properly to identify discrimination on the basis of race and to ensure compensation for past exclusion. It was the way to ensure in a real-world way that integration was actually taking place. The gradual extension of this idea, that institutions discriminated whenever their processes affected people differentially based on race, would over time lead to the premise from which Black nationalist analysis began—that institutions themselves embodied inevitable cultural assumptions. Accordingly, rather than conceive of the continual application of antidiscrimination norms to "purify" schools and other places of their "biases," progressives came to believe instead that schools must be "multicultural" and "inclusive" of various cultural traditions and assumptions.

Of course, this dynamic did not consist simply of a progression of ideas leading logically to "multiculturalism." These transformations all occurred in the social/ cultural context of the heated appearance of nationalist ideology on the American scene in the late 1960s, explicit and implicit expulsion of whites from dominant positions in what remained of the "civil rights movement," disintegration of racial liberation politics in the late 1970s and early 1980s, rebirth of nationalist ideology in the African American community continuing through the 1990s, appearance of a radicalized feminist movement simultaneously criticizing antidiscrimination ideology in the gender context as "formal equality" because gender marked real cultural "difference," and emergence of other ethnic nationalisms, particularly with respect to Latino culture. In addition, this ideological transformation has not been complete and total, by any means. As I see it, white progressive race ideology today still contains bits and pieces of the antidiscrimination vision, even as "multiculturalism" has become the public slogan for understanding racial justice. Progressive whites bemoan the failure of the current Supreme Court to vigorously enforce school desegregation decrees and its adoption of the *de jure* model of unconstitutional discrimination—all analytically based on the *Brown* model of integrationism—while they simultaneously celebrate Afro-centric schools and honor ethnic assertions of difference and cultural integrity. The dominance of norms of inclusion, diversity, celebration of difference, Black History month, and the like in contemporary American discourse about race reflects at least a diluted version of the Black nationalist project in refusing integration on the model of the sameness of all students before a neutral institutional face. However, it is also true that the multicultural sensibility sits alongside the image of racism consisting of bias and prejudice—as if its adherents still believed there was some neutral, acultural, aracial way to constitute institutional life, to set admissions criteria for universities and qualifications for jobs.

The contemporary emergence of multiculturalism is ultimately traceable to various historical factors, and it is only partial. Nevertheless, it also seems clear that one of its main, established tenets has been the idea of acknowledging and respecting difference, rather than assuming, like the *Brown* consciousness seemed to, that there was a neutral, acultural institutional reality, in public schools or any other places, that would transcend race. From this vantage point, the social-science paradigms of "cultural deprivation" embraced in *Brown,* as well as the confident assertions of colorblindness and integration into "quality" schools, seem embarrassingly naive to contemporary progressives. Both of these justifications for the *Brown* ruling have, at least implicitly, been recast as ultimately resting on conservative cultural premises; from a multicultural sensibility, both strands of *Brown* posed as universal assumptions about social reality that over time have come to be seen as culturally specific.

This history of ideological development, I think, accounts most profoundly for progressive white sensitivity to charges of "cultural imperialism." It was, in a sense, culturally traumatic to have confidently embraced as liberatory a way of understanding racial justice as an ideology of integrationism that would soon be turned on its head and alleged to be yet another form of white domination.

In addition, it also seems clear that another dimension of contemporary white anxiety is rooted in the lack of any perceived substantive basis upon which intercultural activism could be based. That is, taking seriously the ideas

of multiculturalism means acknowledging there may be no transcultural normative basis by which to judge the social practices of another culture. The sense of
righteousness and confidence with which progressives supported the coercive
enforcement of *Brown* was, in this interpretation, linked to the very universalist
premises of the colorblindness principle and the "realism" of cultural deprivation
that seem so problematic from a contemporary multicultural perspective. The
topic of the next section is whether "deference" to the cultural self-determination
rights of culturally identifiable groups is a coherent response to this history.

Laissez-Faire Multiculturalism

The image of cultural self-determination implicit in the reigning anxiety over
"cultural imperialism" presents a false picture of distinct cultures existing outside
the discourses in which they might be recognized. However, there is no doubt
that, if there is coherence to the idea of an "African American" community, it
must certainly be at least partly an *effect* of racial ideologies. The issue is whether
the dichotomy I have just described—between a belief in an objectivist, neutral,
moral imperative like colorblind integrationism linked with the will to intervene
on one hand, and a belief in relativistic, multicultural assumptions about differences in mores and an accompanying deference to other identified cultural groups
on the other—exhausts the realistic possibilities for a coherent understanding of
race on the part of whites.[37] Is it plausible to believe simultaneously in the "rela-
tivist" norms of multiculturalism and nevertheless be willing to intervene across
cultural boundaries to influence and even coerce other cultural groups? Is the
Brown intervention into Southern culture defensible only from now-discredited
universalist premises about the possibilities for cultural neutrality on the part of
schools and other institutions?

I approach this issue in a negative fashion: rather than provide an affirmative defense of cultural intervention in specific contexts, I want first to consider
the possibility that the opposition between deference and intervention is a false
way of framing issues of interracial and intercultural dynamics. Mutual respect
and cultural self-determination are too indeterminate to themselves provide a
justificatory compass. The respectful, deferential aspect of multicultural sensibility depends on there being some transcultural basis upon which to identify the
cultural boundaries of the other group, and to distinguish between authentic
and fraudulent representations of that group's mores. To carry out the deference

injunction, in short, some way of identifying what is being deferred to is necessary. The more formalist, essentialist, ahistoric, and traditionalist the definition of the other culture's mores, the more compelling the case for deference will seem to be, in that intervention would be posed against a clearly delineated, fixed practice. At the same time, the more formalist, essentialist, ahistoric, and traditional the definition of the other culture's mores, the more it will appear that the practice in question is a contested one within the other group, and that the practice's survival depends on the continued domination of a segment of the community, rather than the reflection of the culture as a whole.

The background analytic that informs this approach to cultural issues is an analogy to similar images of deference and self-determination in liberal market ideology. That is, the progressive commitment to the importance of cultural self-determination embodied in the contemporary multicultural sensibility closely tracks, in both substantive motivation and analytic structure, the political and economic theory of the "invisible hand" in *laissez-faire* market ideology.

In free-market ideology, the norm of government neutrality vis-à-vis the private market was based on the notion that, if the government stayed out of the private sphere, individual actors would freely choose the terms and conditions of their relationships. Through the workings of the market's "invisible hand," society would end up enjoying the fullest possible level of social satisfaction.

The problem, compellingly demonstrated through the American legal realist scholarship of the 1920s and 1930s, was that it was analytically impossible to conceive of the state playing merely a background role in protecting private property, enforcing contractual agreements based on free will, and refusing to enforce agreements that were the result of fraud, duress, or incompetency. As the realists showed, the "framework" rules of the private market were not merely background, but necessarily regulative as well. The legal rules for identifying what would or would not be protected as "property" served to establish the bargaining position of individuals in the market, and yet there was no way analytically to leave such questions to the market itself because any market must proceed on the basis of such rules already being in place. Similarly, the identification of the free will of a market actor depended on legal rules that distinguished the permissible from the impermissible deployment of coercive pressure, and yet rules for determining duress, fraud, and incompetency could be drawn in a variety of ways without violating the underlying notion that the voluntary decisions of market actors would be decisive. Again, however, the specific ways that legal rules distinguished free from coerced transactions "regulated" the market to the extent that they favored some transactions at the expense of others.[38]

In short, the legal realists concluded that the central ideal of a private market free from the regulatory effects of state power was incoherent. The social power of the state, manifest in the choice of a certain delineation of interests that would be protected as private property, or a certain definition of permissible and impermissible market pressure, constituted what *laissez-faire* economics falsely understood as the private market. The idea of deferring to private-market actors was analytically indefensible because the private market itself was constituted by social power. The conclusion that the state constituted the very market it purported merely to facilitate and defer to was hidden from view, the realists argued, only by *formalism*—the assumption that the particular legal rules for identifying property and free will somehow matched up with their actual existence in the world.

The same kind of analytic applies to the identification of and deference to the self-determination of cultural groups. This aspect of the multicultural sensibility depends on the ability to identify an independent culture, just as free-market ideology had to identify a private market actor, and to distinguish what is really an integral part of that culture from what is an illegitimate imposition of external and distorting power, just as a *laissez-faire* approach must distinguish free from coerced market transactions. Short of a formalist or essentialist definition of particular cultures, however, there is similarly no way neutrally and aculturally to identify what practices are worthy of deference because they represent the intrinsic integrity of independent cultural groups. Just as the state inevitably regulated when it appeared simply to facilitate an independent private market, so a similar form of regulation is implicit in the idea of cultural deference.

Take, for example, the issue of African female genital mutilation as it has been constructed in mainstream Western human rights discourse. The common way the imperialism concern is articulated is with respect to the mores of, say, tribal Sudanese culture. However, identifying the relevant self-determination interest as implicating indigenous culture is a contingent and culturally loaded judgment.

In the international context, we conventionally identify culturally relevant entities in terms of geography, identifying culture with the boundaries of land and territory in which an identifiable group lives. However, there is no analytic reason to identify the culturally relevant group in terms of land or the inclusion in a particular nation-state. In fact, in many ways, in this age of worldwide digital communication, it seems quite formalist and old-fashioned to think that the most relevant cultural association must be based on physical proximity or national borders. Just as there were, within market ideology, alternative ways to identify and protect private property, so there are alternative ways to slice the cultural pie.

While we tend to think of culture in terms of a people who have a particular geographic solidarity within which they share cultural mores, there actually are virtually infinite ways to define a culture for the purpose of ensuring respect and deference to the culture of others. For example, it is possible to conceive of a "female" culture that exists in the world and flows, perhaps, from experiences that females across traditionally defined cultures share. That is a fairly abstract and general definition, but it is sufficient to see that, from this alternative way of identifying culture, the issue of deference and intervention looks qualitatively different. From this perspective, to the extent that Sudanese males are encouraging or requiring genital mutilation practices, *they* are regulating, dominating, and intervening in the culture of females. Honoring the principle that no group should impose its power on another cultural group, any female is part of that international culture of females, and therefore (from this cultural angle) has a basis under self-determination principles to "intervene" in Sudanese life.

Alternatively, we could identify culture not by geography, but by age. This approach would build from the realization that, across land-based cultures, there are youth subcultures, there are cultures of the elderly, and age also is an important determinant of the way we look at the world. To the extent that Sudanese rituals are practiced on adolescents, one must decide whether to respect the land-based culture of Sudanese tribes or the age-based culture of rebellious youth. Nothing in the idea of "respecting cultural difference" can determine which cultural frame to utilize.

The point is not that these alternative ways to divide cultural boundaries are equally meaningful or that the choice between them is arbitrary. It is rather that *analytically* nothing in the general idea of respecting difference can determine how difference will be identified. As the realists demonstrated with respect to the claims that the Constitution protected "liberty of contract," there is a broad range of ways to identify the voluntary free will of the contracting party, ranging from the formalism of a seal on a document to a substantive inquiry into the fairness of an exchange itself. Also, the choice of one point over another on the continuum implicated the social power of the state into the "private" market. Similarly, there is a broad range of ways to identify the boundaries of a culture and its authentic mores; the difference between ways that seem silly and ways that make sense flows from within *our* own assumptions about what culture consists of—that is, of the identity of others.

To carry this analogy to another stage, just as it was necessary to distinguish between coerced and free exchanges within market-oriented legal theory, so the idea of cultural deference requires a distinction between cultural practices that are authentic expressions of the cultural community from those that are merely reflections of a culturally contingent victory of a particular group of dominators. For example, consider again the Northern intervention into Southern culture associated with the enforcement of *Brown*. To highlight the arguably colonialist character of the intervention, I described it earlier as if it were clear that there was a "Southern" culture that had authentic cultural mores of racial segregation and subjugation, along with religiosity and other characteristics not directly connected to race. However, it was possible to describe the whole process in different terms. Utilizing the frame of an "American" culture, the Old South rulers could be seen to have thwarted the self-determination rights of a general American culture. Alternatively, their rule could be characterized as a takeover and domination of an authentic Southern culture of kindness and gentility by a particular, small class of white aristocrats who had themselves perverted its true expression—say, because of their economic drive for free and cheap labor. Just as the possibility of nonenforcement on the ground of duress helps constitute the bargaining power of "private" market actors, the possibility of nondeference, when an alleged "cultural practice" is actually a sham cover for domination over the cultural group itself, helps constitute power *within* the group. Recognizing self-determination "rights" of Catholics, for example, requires taking sides on that group's internal struggle between the formally constituted church hierarchy and those they designate as dissidents and insurgents who claim to speak for the true interpretation of their community's faith. Again, the point is not that these descriptions are equivalent in any sense, other than that they pose the analytic indeterminacy of the idea of deference on the grounds of cultural self-determination.

Finally, the realist idea that the private sphere is constituted by state power also seems applicable in the cultural context. The point is easiest to see with respect to African American culture. The image of deference to African American norms, as it was deployed, say, in the Thomas/Hill confrontation, implies that the African American culture was developed outside and independent of white American culture, as if Black cultural norms had a freestanding, intrinsic life of their own. However, despite some nationalist attempts to invoke a distant African past as the basis for cultural self-identification, the fact is that African American culture has been constructed in large measure in a dialectical engagement with whites in America. Some of the terms of this engagement have been horrific; others have been ambiguous and complicated. However, it is impossible simply to define an African American culture that does not acknowledge engagement, albeit often unwilling, with whites.[39]

In fact, one of the sad ironies of the current racial scene is that, while progressive whites seem anxious to honor the principle of community self-determination and thus publicly to defer to the otherwise objectionable anti-Semitic, homophobic, and sexist ideology of the Nation of Islam under Farrakhan, it is not clear that the current domination of this authoritarian form of Black Nationalist ideology is simply reflective of African American self-determination. From another perspective on the recent history of race relations, the strength of Farrakhan is in some measure because of whites themselves, in the sense that whites helped empower Farrakhan by rejecting and repressing more progressive and sophisticated expressions of Black nationalism in the 1960s and 1970s, leaving the Nation of Islam as the only major nationalist group with the means for institutional survival.

Similarly, even if Patterson is right about Thomas, the very "down-home" tolerance of a pathetic Black male attempt to "court" a Black woman cannot be divorced from the history of white power over the Black community. Since at least the 1960s, a current of Black female discourse has explicitly claimed that the white emasculation of Black men put Black women in different relations to Black men than white women had to white men, with the general idea that feminist concerns often have had to give way to overriding concerns of the Black community.

Implicit in the comparison of the idea of deference to the self-determination rights of cultural groups and the idea of deference to the wishes of market actors is an analogy between the state in *laissez-faire* economic theory and whites in American racial dynamics. The basis of this comparison is the idea of *power*. Whites in contemporary racial dynamics are in an analogous role to the state in liberal market theory to the extent that, as a group, whites currently possess significantly and qualitatively greater social, political, and economic power than any other identifiable cultural group. That is why, of course, the cultural imperialism anxiety runs in a specific direction; I am unaware of progressive people of color, similarly committed to multiculturalism, anxious about the risks that they will culturally dominate whites.

This final link in the analogy—the correlation between the state and whites—is the most troublesome for progressive whites. It brings together the issue of the connection between a substantive basis for intervention with the terms of white identification within a multicultural sensibility. To the extent that the comparison between the position of whites in a race-stratified society and the position of the state in market ideology makes sense, it exposes the problematic character, from within the ideological development of progressives since *Brown,* of whites exercising their racial power.

Since *Brown,* the demonstration that a particular institutional practice was rooted in white or Eurocentric cultural assumptions has been understood to delegitimate that social practice on the grounds that it embodied hidden biases against racial minorities. When *Brown* was understood to rest on acultural norms of colorblindness and a rationalistic case for integration, the basis for its coercive enforcement was not seen to emanate from culturally specific white norms. When, within the assumptions of multiculturalism, the only basis for action seems to be culturally specific frameworks for perceiving the world, whites are hesitant to act on the basis of white cultural traditions whose identification as white has always been in service of their delegitimation.

Another way of saying this is that, in the multicultural sensibility, there is a missing ingredient—the cultural integrity and self-determination interests of the dominant group of whites in American society. Identification with white-ness has traditionally meant an interest in racial domination. No alternative traditions have developed from which whites could understand themselves as acting as whites in a liberatory, nonimperialist, and nonracist fashion. Yet, if this picture of the racial landscape is persuasive, whites must be seen—regardless of their various subcultural and other group identifications—to be constituted in the dynamics of American race relations as a specific, identifiable group, one that has an enormous amount of power on various axes of measurement. It is the anxiety over facing this fact of their own status as a socially constructed cultural group that has characterized the recent isolation of progressive whites with respect to race politics. They do not want to act *as whites,* and yet no other basis for action seems available from within their own ideological assumptions and historical position.

One way to understand the current ideological situation of progressive whites is to see that they are, in a sense, between ideological paradigms. They have em-braced multiculturalism as the norm of racial justice, but perhaps because of the historically imperialist use of race by whites in America, they have not located

themselves within the multicultural social fabric. Instead, their cultural "affili-
ations" have in a sense been privatized to subcultural groups—as Jews, Irish,
gays and lesbians, workers—within the larger white community, groups that
seem to be in no direct engagement with the overall racial economy. Progressives have sympathy with postmodern admonishments that cultural groups not
be essentialized, that cultural meaning be recognized as contested, in flux, and
subject to diverse interpretation. However, they simultaneously seem to defer
to a formalized presentation of the self-determination of other cultural groups,
perhaps in response to their own anxiety that intervention will be a form of
imperialism and paternalism, and therefore deference is in order.

As I see it, the problem is that deference is simply not analytically available.
Having racial power, however unwilling whites may be to admit it, means necessarily acting one way or the other, to delegitimate social practices as forms
of domination or to privilege them as forms of cultural integrity, to accept
the existing community's dominant voice representing its cultural mores or
to support insurgents fighting for change. The option of simple deference to
some independently constituted cultural community is, by and large, an empty
set—just as empty as the idea of deferring to the "private" market because of
its efficiency properties or deferring to a legislature because of its democratic
character in legal thought.

Comprehending whites and Blacks in terms of culturally distinct communities
is a major ideological victory for what I would describe as the most progressive
faction of the struggle for Black liberation. From a leftist perspective interested
in challenging the reigning distribution of wealth, power, and prestige, and its
ideological justifications in terms of merit, the Black nationalist analysis is superior
to the conventional integrationist interpretation of race issues. Specifically, the
exposure of the Eurocentric assumptions of mainstream institutional life is an
important stage of racial development in which the culture of the dominant white
community, long invisible as simply the background assumptions for social and
institutional life, is brought into relief, undercutting the universalist pretensions
of reigning distributions of merit and worth.

The problem, however, is that any commitment to cultural integrity and to
the self-determination rights of other communities is too general and abstract
to provide any help in answering the inevitable issues involved in identifying
culture and distinguishing cultural integrity from cultural domination, even if
one thought that was the best way to think of racial justice. There is no formal
or determinate way to give ideas like "the Black community" meaning separate

from the way whites participate inevitably in its construction. Understanding that culture is historical and constructed, rather than given and essential, means there is no canonical way to represent the "authentic" mores of that community. Given that a "culture" develops in history, over time and in space, with the terms of community life constantly contested in various ways, whites should not reflexively accept authoritarian or sexist representations of the culture of minority communities as simply an authentic, unchallengeable given. Deferring to sexist authoritarian representations of African American culture, like those promulgated by the Nation of Islam or Orlando Patterson, means actively disempowering Black feminist and other cultural insurgents.

From the perspective of contemporary multicultural sensibility, it is apparent that *Brown* represented a coercive cultural intervention into Southern life. Parts of that intervention were, to my mind, colonialist and oppressive. There was little gained and much lost when white Southern culture was repudiated *in toto* as irrational and parochial because the antiseptic New South culture of technocracy is, in its own way, alienating and hierarchical. In contrast to the self-understanding of liberal integrationists, the coercive regulation of the South was not justified on the ground that a neutral rationality would replace cultural backwardness; in retrospect, it is clear that the ideologies and institutional practices of transformed Southern schools are not acultural and universal, but specifically Northeastern. However, saying that there was no acultural or transcultural ground for the regulation of the South is not to say it was groundless. Rather, the coercive overthrow of Southern apartheid was right and often heroic, even if its terms were imperfect. It helped (partially) topple a racial regime that was oppressive and unjust; it helped (partially) empower Southern insurgents, Black and white, whose struggle might have failed but for "external" assistance and legitimation.

However, the ground for concluding that intervention was warranted cannot be a universal, transcultural set of principles because that does not exist, just as the idea of respecting "difference" could not, at the time, have provided a neutral basis for refusing to intervene. The issue was about power, not propriety. Respecting difference could have meant privileging the rule of Old South leaders, rather than vindicating the interests of Blacks. Instead, the justification for the exercise of power over the Old South and for the assistance provided to Southern insurgents was historical, existential, and necessarily partial. As I argue in the next chapter, that is all we ever ultimately have.

CHAPTER 7
IDENTITY, IMPURITY, AND POSTMODERNITY

Racism's characteristic catch-22 insists on racial difference and then punishes it as deviance. Integration/assimilation is a reaction against the insistence on racial difference, but in its more uncompromising manifestations it underwrites the punishment of any group solidarity as a form of deviance. Difference discourse does precisely the opposite: in reacting against the punishment of difference, it reinforces the insistence that racial differences are intrinsic and real.[1]

This is more than the recognition of group identification born as a collective response to social prejudice. It is the production of identity as a lifestyle, a way of being ... an easy solidarity, a V.I.P. pass to belonging.... The necessary correlative to this unearned solidarity is an unwarranted presumption about the entailments of group membership.... This political correctness requires and duly produces opprobrium for people who miss their cue: we encounter "Oreos"—Blacks on the outside who don't "act black" and therefore presumably aren't black on the inside.... These figures of scorn imply that there is a particular type of behavior that is appropriate to a given race, and thereby censures deviation from it. This message not only provides ready justification for continued bigotry ... it also encourages group members to emphasize their difference from outsiders.... The idea that minorities should hew to "their" cultural traditions is just as hegemonic as the idea that they should assimilate to a mythical white-bread mainstream.[2]

Richard Ford, 2005

In the first six chapters of this book, I posed the Black nationalist tradition as an alternative to the universalist, rationalist assumptions of liberal integrationism, and I argued that the nationalist tradition provided a better way to understand racial justice. I described how integrationism nevertheless became the official ideology of American racial enlightenment and has remained so, at least for the public sphere of law and the legitimate exercise of state power, since *Brown*. My main purpose there was to impugn the claim of liberal integrationism to represent a rational and principled, rather than political and ideological, approach to racial justice.

In contrasting the universalism of liberal integrationism with Black nationalism as it was articulated by left nationalists in the 1960s, I referred to different manifestations the nationalist tradition has taken historically, which I described on an axis, running from the fundamentalism of the Nation of Islam and Afrocentrism advocates to the revolutionary historicism of the 1960s nationalism articulated by Malcolm X, the Black Panthers, Harold Cruse, and others.

In Chapter 6, I criticized the dominant ways that, since the 1970s or so, liberal and progressive whites have embraced a type of multiculturalism, with its attendant version of justice consisting of respecting the cultural integrity of all identifiable cultural groups. I argued that African American identities are hybrid and in historical, dialectical relation to the surrounding white culture(s). The images of "respect" and "nonintervention" wrongly posit the Black community as pregiven, with stable and easily identifiable markers. Multiculturalism, seeking an objective, principled stance on race and cultural identity, becomes drawn to fundamentalist/essentialist versions of the group's identity because descriptions of the group that present clear borders are formally realizable and therefore appear objective, and thus liberal multiculturalists can find in fundamentalist representations of identity the borders they are committed to respecting.

But a group's identity is not exhausted by the formal markers presented by its most fundamentalist members; an African American social group *exists* separate from the insistence by the Nation of Islam or Afro-centrists on its essential character, just as the Orthodox and Ultra-Orthodox are marginal, not central, in American Jewish culture.

In this work, my strategy has been to pose an identity-based discourse against the universalist claims of liberal integrationism, but then to deploy the postmodern critique of identity against the multicultural claims of identity fundamentalists.

In this chapter, I seek to develop the implication behind these strategies. The implication is that it is possible to conceive of identities like "the Black community" in a postmodern/historicist way, one that honors "their" contingent, socially constructed, nonessentialist, and performative status while nevertheless asserting an identity presenting a surplus of meaning and multiple tracks of coherence. One could call this a "postmodern nationalism" or, more generally, a "social subjectivity."

My motive, in part, is to respond to some leftist critics of identity politics—as Richard Ford presents himself—who mistake the significance of the postmodern critique of identity for essentialism. The adherents to this current of "liberal postmodernism" treat groups like "African Americans" as not "real" because their identity is socially, historically created. Ford, for example, spends most of two books showing that particular assertions of cultural identity are not essential but contingent, and therefore cannot be objectively demonstrated to be a part of any essential cultural identity (e.g., a white woman can wear cornrows).[3] But, as the above statements indicate, he fails to consider the possibility that identity is no less meaningful even if it is historical, contingent, hybrid, and dialectic, rather than "real and intrinsic."

The tendency of this strand of self-titled postmodernism[4] is to revert to liberal individualism, say, to colorblindness about race because racial culture cannot be objectively identified. Despite the theoretical veneer, Ford posits a traditional modernist subject, a person who is anterior to identity and who chooses identity like a commodity—"a V.I.P. pass"—and who is then subject to opprobrium when the social discipline of the group is imposed. But the critique of such an ahistorical, free-standing subject who chooses between social structures has been the focus of much postmodernism work already.[5]

I think Ford's mistake is to fail to see that the content of the group's identity is one of the terms of struggle *within* groups, between traditionalists and fundamentalists on one hand, who assert a stable, ahistoric, essential group identity, and historicists and revolutionaries on the other, who understand that the terms of group identity are never fixed and always up for grabs, being constantly copied, reproduced, and necessarily changed in every iteration, articulation, and performance. Ford's objection to the policing of identity by "censure" is really an objection to the policing function of any culture, language, or social system for conferring meaning whatsoever. He posits a radically free (liberal) subject on whom the disciplinary apparatus of group identity is imposed after he chooses to align with one group or another. But such a being is an ideal or, more literally, a monad. He does not *exist*. A person's very existence entails being defined (and defining others) in terms of social languages external to himself, but that depend on them for any continued life, that is, on the exercise of "social subjectivity."[6]

Ford's view is an attempt to rationalize as normal the alienation that members of the group may feel once the group no longer experiences "its" identity as a social subjectivity. Instead, like the workers' products in the Marxist version of alienation, group identities can become reified, so that "African American culture" assumes a "phantom objectivity"[7]—a fixed essence separate from what any group member might do or not do. But Ford's evocation of the power of opprobrium and censure to police the identity group's borders treats the disciplinary apparatus as if it had a life separate from its performance by the group's members, and therefore was not subject to struggle and contestation from the inside. In short, he describes being *alienated* from a form of social power because (he claims) he cannot see himself reflected in the construction of the African American community identity and he does not conceive that he could affect its future. He posits a subject, somehow constituted independent of all such social identities, who is censured by an external group that he has lost any hope of influencing, and who is "discriminated against" because he is perceived as "raced" even when he wants to play other roles.

The project of this chapter is to situate the conception of racial identity I am proposing in terms of a more general, postmodern stance toward interpreting and understating the social world as always constructed and articulated. One of the challenges is that postmodernism, in my opinion, "properly" understood, is based on a starting-point denial of the possibility of a stable identity over time or across space. I take it that meaning is infinitely relational, always occurring within a language of signs, and always articulated because any new performance changes the whole and therefore everything in relation to the "system" of signs. So the very fact of being in another moment already changes the thing so that it cannot be "identical" to itself in a prior moment. When in earlier chapters I have described the "nation" that Black nationalism takes as its project, I was purposely vague ("a spiritual complexion") to avoid at the outset the identification of the nationalist project with essentialism—a position in this context more precisely seen as "racialism"—and to place racial identity in history, the field on which all "identity" is born.

I do not think the Black community has a stable, essential identity over time or across space; instead, what it means to be Black in America is constantly articulated and rearticulated through every performance that constitutes that community, from the inside *and* outside. But that just does not mean there *is* no such social group. A multiplicity of meaning is not the same thing as a lack of meaning.

Instead, the African American community *exists* as a group and can be followed through time and space even if the group can never be objectively and determinately defined, even if its borders are continuously contested, and even if its meaning is multiple and indeterminate. It is true that the group's existence is partly constituted by performances like this book, in which the group is produced by being articulated and rearticulated. It is true that the group may be constituted very differently in the future or might not "exist" in the future at all. But, again, that contingency does not make the group less real.

To put this in existential terms, then, I would say that Ford and others are making the converse mistake of traditional metaphysics. Rather than assert that there are essences that precede existence (and of which existence was a deteriorated version of the ideal), Ford treats the *lack* of an essence to social groups as if that meant that they have no existence, either. The picture of "the Black community" I am trying to evoke is the "*critical* race consciousness" of the book's title—an approach that sides with the existentialist tradition that it is coherent to assert the *existence* of African Americans without positing an *essence* to the group, at least until its death.[8]

This chapter proceeds by more fully describing the "postmodernism" that informs the interpretation of the politics of identity nationalism that I am advocating.

The Politics of Representation

> You might be sitting in a history class/listening to the analysis of "what was going on" in the thirties in new york, say/and you hear nothing of shtetls where grandma's generation came from/and the descriptions of sweatshops sound oddly abstract and disembodied, that is, emphatically unsweaty-scientific-full-of-clear-light—spared of the dust of ripped cloth—and quiet so you can hear yourself (someone else) think and the machines' screaming and bobbing has stopped, all put in terms of an analysis of the labor structure of the immigrant population, complete with statistics/and politics sounds like this or that labor policy adopted by this or that administration/not at all what grandma described going to work as/but you came to school to learn/and it feels like an interesting addition to what you already know from family history and hot tea

mornings in kitchens in brooklyn apartments/but it still seems like the viewpoint of other, of the officials giving the official line on what was happening—the politics at the pinochle games just can't be reduced to "labor unrest"/but we're going too fast.

Then it's years later and you wonder again about the shtetls and what you might have lost in the history class/and you focus on some imaginary moment when it happened—when the statistics and the analysis of the labor structure were no longer just interesting additions to the lived experience in new york of grandma and her friends but instead became the reality itself; and grandma's description about why her boss acted like he did was just shtetl superstition, or worse, silly. because at some point the feeling of learning new things was replaced by the idea of learning things the way they really are, free from superstition and prejudice, and stuff might be left out for the sake of time but what was there, presented as knowledge, was knowledge, in a particular form and in a particular language that you recognize as not the way you started out looking at things. but we're for education, after all.

And then you start wondering, what if the language of true knowledge that you learned, the way of talking about things intelligently and dispassionately, was itself a mythology that contained prejudice and superstition; and then that it's not just new york in the thirties, it's the way the whole picture is organized, a whole hierarchy of what counts and what doesn't that might present itself as neutral knowledge but is really just an ideology of power/and the imaginary moment that you crystallized, the moment when the statistics and the analysis began to represent the true and the real against the superstitious, was the moment of self-denial and treachery as you implicitly agreed to a test of truth that would count out most of what you know most deeply. Even if you can't prove it.

Gary Peller, 1987[9]

The moment that I have tried to evoke here, the point at which we begin to believe the dominant Enlightenment teaching about the differences between truth and myth, and between reason and sentiment, and simultaneously begin to suppress our particularity, history, and place in the social world, is central in the creation of social power in our society. Even after the philosophers have abandoned the epistemological project, the attempt to find some firm ground to distinguish truth from myth, and even after the notion that the world can be neatly divided in the Cartesian way between mind and body has been rejected intellectually, these liberal categories for perceiving and talking about the world continue to play powerful roles in our day-to-day lives, in the way we understand ourselves and each other.

The reason is simple. The construction of a realm of knowledge separate from superstition and the identification of a faculty of reason separate from passion was not, after all, simply some mind game played by philosophers and professional intellectuals. These categories have always served political roles in differentiating groups as worthy or unworthy and in justifying particular social hierarchies. They were not merely abstract musings about the ultimate nature of things, but rather part of the everyday texture of the way we construct our world and its possibilities. And a continuing thread of that construction of the world has been the notion that there is a radical distinction between truth (the representation of the way the world really is) and myth (an interpretation of the world that cannot be proven and thus is merely sentimental or poetic). It is this sense, of some grand distinction between truth and myth, that is supposed to distinguish the rational from the emotive, the legal from the political, the scientific from the aesthetic, the civilized from the primitive, the objective from the subjective, the neutral from the interested, the essential from the accidental, and fact from opinion.

From the viewpoint of the postmodern critique of the Enlightenment tradition,[10] however, there is no possibility of a neutral or objective interpretative practice or of merely representing (as opposed to interpreting) the world. When we attempt simply to represent, free from bias or distortion, we must always do so through language, broadly conceived as a socially created way to categorize perception of and communication about the world.

Language necessarily mediates perception and communication by shaping ways of thinking about the world that are themselves not necessary and natural, but social and contingent. When we try to move beyond language and rhetoric, beyond the means of representation, to what is being represented, we find only more language, metaphor, and interpretation. There is no objective reference point, separate from culture and politics, available to distinguish truth from ideology, fact from opinion, or representation from interpretation. And thus, philosophy, science, economics, literary criticism, and the other intellectual "disciplines" can be interpreted according to the same process that has been traditionally reserved for literature and art—they, too, can be read merely as "texts" organizing the thick texture of the world according to their own metaphors. They enjoy no privileged status vis-à-vis the "merely" aesthetic or subjective because they, too, are simply languages, simple ways of carving up what seems similar and what seems different in the world. The "critical theory" tradition I am evoking is "poststructuralist" to the extent it rejects the notion that there is some deeper logic that governs the production of meaning, and thus they include within their critique the grand theories of Sigmund Freud, Claude Lévi-Strauss, Karl Marx, and other structuralists who purport to have found a unified, underlying scheme of social life that itself stands outside the play of rhetoric and metaphor.

This is not, of course, to say that a postmodern critical approach denies that we can and do make decisions about the world. The point is that there is no grand organizing theory or principle with which to justify "our" social choices as neutral and apolitical, as the products of reason and truth rather than of passion or ideology, or even as "ours."

In short, the postmodern stance denies there is a difference between rational, objective representation and interested, biased interpretation. This attitude toward interpretation emerged first in literary criticism and philosophy, and has at least some practitioners in virtually all the fields of the humanities, including sociology, anthropology, history, economics, and law.

As I see it, the deconstructive approach puts at issue what have been the traditional mainstays of the liberal and progressive commitment to Enlightenment culture. Indeed, the whole way that one conceives of liberal progress (overcoming prejudice in the name of truth, seeing through the distortions of ideology to get at reality, and surmounting ignorance and superstition with the acquisition of knowledge) is called into question. Instead, what has been presented in our social-political and intellectual traditions as knowledge, truth, objectivity, and reason are actually merely the *effects* of a particular form of social power, the victory of a particular way of representing the world that then presents itself as beyond mere interpretation, as truth itself. This critical attitude is oriented toward uncovering the ways in which, say, the rational sociology of New York in the 1930s is a cultural and political construct, built on exclusions of other, "less worthy" knowledge—like my grandmother's knowledge of her social situation—or the ways that the identification of "principles" of racial justice in law depend for their "principled" status on an assumed ideology of race.[11]

This approach is controversial to traditionalists because it challenges what they believe their whole task is about. If what separates the rational from the irrational is the claim that the rational approach is able to purify itself of ideology and mere social conventionality, the point is to challenge reason on its own ground and demonstrate that what gets called reason and knowledge is simply a particular way of organizing perception and communication, a way of organizing and categorizing experience that is social and contingent, but whose socially constructed nature and contingency have been suppressed.

I believe the rise of these interpretative approaches in our time marks an important movement toward unmasking the politics of social life. Accordingly, I want to discuss "postmodern deconstruction," with a particular focus on the social and identity implications. And rather than attempt some kind of summary of the "premises" of deconstruction or poststructuralism (a discordant task for an intellectual movement that poses itself against totalizing theories or methods), I will first provide an example of a critical reading of a text.

I have chosen parts of an article from the *Virginia Quarterly Review* written by Nathan Scott, an African American professor of religious studies at the University of Virginia. Because Scott is writing about "the post-Structuralist movement," which he believes has engendered a "crisis in humanistic studies," his article provides a convenient starting point from which we can get an idea of what a postmodern approach might do with a particular text, and at the same time consider the political and social implications of the deconstructive stance through the issues that are raised in interpreting Scott.

Reason and the Mob

> Today, of course, the enterprising anti-humanism of the post-Structuralist movement is in full tide, and it presents us with the greater example in contemporary intellectual life of the new *trahison des clercs*. This phrase forms the title of a once famous book by the French critic Julien Benda which was first published in 1927, and in English the phrase is best rendered as the "betrayal of the intellectuals." [Benda] was moved to advance the rather extravagant charge that the typical intellectuals of the modern period, identifying themselves with class rancor and nationalist sentiment, have abdicated their true calling in the interests of political passion: instead of quelling the mob and beckoning it toward true community, they have joined the mob, concurring in its lust for quick results and adopting its devotion to the pragmatic and the expedient.... And it is his fiercely reproachful term that appears now to be the appropriate epithet for the intellectual insurgency that is currently sowing a profound disorder in the ... humanities.
>
> Nathan Scott, 1986[12]

This paragraph is supposed to form the general context for Scott's warning about the threat of poststructuralism to modern intellectual life. As Scott sees it, the humanist approaches he defends depend for their "cultural authority ...

on what can be claimed for them as disciplines aimed at *knowledge* and *truth*."
The problem with the new critical approach is that it is a form of "nihilism"—as
such, it "radically impugns any truly cognitive dimension of the human endeavor,
it strikes at its most vital nerve—more threateningly than anything else in our
period, since it strikes from within."

Scott identifies the humanist approach with the "intellectuals" and the "post-
Structuralist" approaches with the "mob." But for these associations to constitute
an argument against the new approaches, the reader must first understand what
is bad about the mob and what is good about the intellectuals. Thus, a useful
place to begin unpacking the text would be to determine what the contrast
between the intellectual and the mob means and what conceptions allow us to
make sense of the elevation of the intellectual over the mob.

Scott's rhetoric helps in this analysis because it contains a group of associations
with the intellectuals and with the mob that can assist us in determining its meaning. The distinction between the mob and the intellectuals and the justification
for the superiority of the intellectuals are suggested by the fact that the mob is
characterized by social desire; it is associated with "class rancor," "nationalist
sentiment," "political passion," "lust," "disorder," and "insurgency."

The intellectual, on the other hand, stands in contrast to these features; the
intellectual is supposed to represent order and dispassion rather than "rancor"
and "sentiment"; neutrality as opposed to politics; the "disciplined" search
for "knowledge and truth" rather than the lustful satisfaction of passion and
desire; and the ideal and the long-term as opposed to the "pragmatic and the
expedient."

In short, Scott's argument seems animated by a structure of meaning where
reason and passion are distinguished from each other. Reason is associated with
intellect, knowledge, truth, neutrality, and objectivity; passion is associated with
disorder, politics, sentiment, class rancor, and unthinking nationalism. Finally,
reason is elevated to a superior position vis-à-vis emotion.

Next, we must consider why reason should presumptively enjoy this privileged
status, what it is about the two categories that makes it seem beyond question
that right-thinking and progressive-minded people would "naturally" understand
from the text, both the contrast between the two categories and the superiority
of the rational over the emotive.

To understand the way that Scott succeeds in communicating, to uncover
the manner in which his language resonates with what a reader might already
understand about the world, we might at this point imagine the contrast

between the rationality of the intellectuals and the passion of the mob in terms of individual, rather than social, issues. Here, we recognize the relationship between the mob and the intellectual in the relationship between reason and desire, the mind and the body. Just as the text associates being civilized at the social level with subordinating the mob—social desire—to the intellectual, so we have reference to a cultural language in which being civilized and mature as an individual means subordinating passion to reason, making the mind the ruler of the body, rather than the other way around. In addition, the sense of the temporal relation between the shortsightedness of the mob and the long view of the intellectuals is repeated in the notion that the mind must delay the satisfaction of desire in the civilized individual—the regulative function of reason is temporal, to keep emotion and desire in their proper places at their proper times, to resist the animal urge for immediate satisfaction.

And at this level of the individual, the full force of the superiority of the intellectual and the mob is exposed, for the body represents our natural, animal side, and the mind our human side. Just as the intellectual must "quell" the mob's passion and lust for the humanist position to survive, so the mind must quell the urges of the body if we are to be civilized and escape our animal selves. Our animal passions represent the continuing hold of nature over us, just as the possibility of mob action represents the need for the continuing vigilance of the intellectual, lest social life degenerate to an animal state. To transfer the issues back to the social level, then, Scott's appeal is to a general language of social progress and development—the intellectual is favored over the mob because the mob is, in a sense, less human, closer to nature, and primitive.

In our cultural knowledge, we have concrete historical images that support the reasonableness of the hierarchy of reason over passion. Probably the most powerful single image in the American experience is the Southern lynch mob; there, in the common understanding, the mob, ruled by irrational racism against Blacks, bypassed the orderly, rational, and judicial means of dispensing justice in favor of the "pragmatic and the expedient," simply acting based on their passionate emotions. In this image, reason can play a heroic role and justify its privileged status vis-à-vis passion, by standing against the forces of the mob and speaking from principles, objectivity, and dispassion.

At this point, it seems we have a good hold on the meaning of the text. We are asked to reject the mob in favor of the intellectual, just as we must reject our passions in favor of our reason. In either sphere, the failure to regulate the emotional with the rational would, in a sense, be giving in to our animal urges, opening up the possibility of regression and the end of civilization.

But just as soon as we begin to feel we have a hold on this determinate meaning of Scott's argument, we feel it begin to slip away. If the "reason" for subordinating the mob to the intellectuals is the threat of the mob to coerce with its passion, then it strikes us as initially dissonant that the intellectuals are asked to "quell" the mob. The very ability of intellect to "quell" suggests that in some way the intellectuals are like the mob, possessing coercive power. Yet, it was the potential for the mob to coerce that justified its regulation by the intellectuals.

This power of the intellect to "quell" introduces the possibility that reason is actually a means of discipline, a coercive technology, for the social regulation of passion and emotion. At both the individual and social levels, reason plays the role of standing in the place of desire and deferring it to another time or place. Accordingly, we imagine reason at the individual level deferring desire until the "right" place—for example, in our social mores, reason defers passion to the privacy of the home or perhaps to the marital relation. At the social level, the intellectuals defer the passion of the mob into the courtroom or other "appropriate" places.

But once we see reason as the regulator of passion—as a technology—we also realize that reason is constructed out of social power. The notion of reason regulating desire to "appropriate" times and places exposes the ways that reason embodies social choices about what is appropriate or inappropriate. With respect to sexuality, for example, regulation might occur according to the Victorian notions of propriety or according to "our" modern permissiveness. Reason itself yields no determinate basis that would allow us to choose between the alternatives. Reason does not tell us whether to prefer the nuclear family over the alternatives, or whether the present segregation of reason and desire according to public or private realms is reasonable. Any choice of this or that mode of regulation seems to reflect merely a preference, a desire. Short of some "natural" embodiment of the relationship between reason and desire, any choice looks political, willed, or a reflection of desire itself.

By this strange twist, reason can only "quell" desire on an individual level by the means of desire itself, by becoming the desire to defer desire, and reason can only control desire on a social scale by becoming social desire (the mob). Thus, reason is only desire that has become institutionalized as good sense, has achieved social conventionality, and is no longer recognizable as a mob because it no longer bears the signs of its emotion—the rage that marked the historic efforts to repress the passion of the other, the infidel, and the heretic. Reason appears as desire that has been frozen in its "appropriate" place, and having achieved its goal, reason can appear free of the violence that is its history. Like the mob, reason promises a coerced social order based on a particular social desire. In contrast to the sharp, qualitative distinction we began with, here reason and passion appear simply as different points on a spectrum; neither concept refers to anything positive and substantial. Reason appears as a social choice about how to regulate passion, but thus it only has meaning as the flipside of passion, as a deferment of passion that is ruled by passion itself. Reason is simply what is not passion, but only social choices tell us in any particular instance which is which.

Moreover, this indeterminacy with respect to the relation between reason and passion, the intellectuals and the mob, extends to what we think of as the "mob." Our earlier model of the irrational, threatening mob was a lynch mob. But when we look again at the ways social history has been constructed, we find a multitude of contexts where there was an attempt to identify a lustful, emotional mob unworthy of power and in need of discipline: the mob of immigrants through Ellis Island, the mob at the Bastille, the mob at the wildcat factory strikes, the mob at the sweatshop sewing machines, the mob in the housing projects and the Polish ghettos, the mob in the March on Washington.

What seems to connect the meanings of "the mob" in these contexts is a consistent pattern of dominant groups justifying their privileged status by associating the "other" with base, animal urges—a pattern extending from Nazi caricatures of Jews, to white racist caricatures of Blacks, to the middle-class vision of the poor, to male visions of femininity, to factory owners' vision of workers, to skyscraper office images of the people on subways. In each class relation, the dominant group projects the other as emotional and primitive, ruled by irrational passion. In this interpretation, the language of the distinction between reason and passion seems to be simply the language by which the powerful and dominant justify their own power on the basis that they are more civilized and human; as such, the very categories of reason and passion, far from giving us a vantage point from which to distinguish politics from truth, seem to be merely one form of the rhetoric of social power. The text's reference to the "mob" is indeterminate. The choice between which group to call "the mob" is a political choice, one that "reason" cannot decide.

Moreover, this indeterminacy about the text's meaning is not even limited by what we earlier assumed was the paradigm of bad group action—the lynch mob. We initially understood the text by identifying the lynch mob with the coercive threat of civilization disintegrating to an animal state. The lynch mob acts irrationally, in a prejudiced fashion against the Black person being lynched, out of passion rather than reason.

But when we look inside the language of the lynch mob itself, we find the same terms used to justify the lynching. What made Blacks threatening and "other," in need of the discipline of the lynch mob, was, from the lynch mob's point of view, the passionate, lustful, sexual nature of Blacks. It was precisely the white group's view of Black lust that made Blacks represent, for the lynch mob, the threat of the insurgency of a primitive, animalistic nature that threatened the civilized social order.

Here, the interpretation seems to be at a crossroads, with no sure way to determine how we are to understand Scott's argument. If it is lust and passion, the animal side, that must be regulated and quelled, then the lynch mob's self-understanding of what it was doing is consistent with Scott's claims. Surely, Scott doesn't mean that—that's not the point here. Rather, what is called into question is the notion that something called "reason" can neutrally and dispassionately dictate how we are to distinguish the bad mobs from the good. What started out as the paradigm of the mob threat to overcome reason with emotion can, from a different point in history and a different place in social life, become the identification of the mob with reason.

Reason and passion can both be associated with the mob; the association of passion with particular groups and the association of reason with other groups are political acts that cannot be determined by reason itself. In this interpretation, reason cannot be the *source of* the intellectual's legitimacy in Scott's text because the content of reason is simply an *effect* of a particular group being in power and therefore being able to categorize others as irrational. Accordingly, in Scott's own terms, reason is actually nothing more than some mob having the social power to define its coercive force as what is necessary to quell the passion of the other.

At this point, Scott's text seems to be at war with itself. Scott seems to suggest that the intellectual is to be favored over the mob because the intellectual would be rational, objective, and neutral, while the mob is passionate, biased, and coercive. But the language of the distinction between reason and passion is indeterminate. Nothing in the concepts or the words determines what is being referred to; determinacy is achieved through a contingent social choice—that is, through politics. Rather than point away from politics and toward reason, the text simply advocates a particular politics, a particular disciplinary discourse of social order. The text's invocation of a place outside politics and passion, a social space outside the mob, seems to be simply one form that the social struggle between groups takes.

This interpretation of Scott's text is an example of one of the many ways a deconstructive, postmodern reading might proceed. At the risk of reductionism, we can at this point articulate some aspects of the approach to Scott's argument that are often present in such readings. First, we were able to show that Scott's text yielded no stable, authoritative meaning; to the contrary, Scott's argument could be read in one way as advocating the elevation of reason over passion. Yet, we were also able to use the text's own terms of analysis to reverse this meaning, to find that there is no qualitative distinction between reason and passion, and that reason is simply a particular form of passion. Second, the reading also demonstrated the active participation of the interpreter in constructing meaning; the interpretation was not neutral and passive, but rather depended on the sense that the reader brought to the text, on the conceptual language that the reader already possessed. Finally, we identified a critical opposition in the text—the contrast between the intellectual and the mob—and showed how the text itself could be read to subvert the good sense of the contrast upon which the argument is built. By reversing the relationship between reason and passion, and thereby showing how reason might be seen as simply the effect of passion rather than its regulator, this critical interpretation showed how the rational, determinate sense of the argument actually depended on an initial, arational association between reason and particular cultural and political visions of social life.

The point of this kind of reading is not that Scott was somehow insufficiently rigorous in constructing his argument—that, had he been more careful, he could have articulated his position in a way that would have made it immune to the kind of interpretation I have pursued. Any text can be read in this manner. Meaning does not somehow reside in a text, to be discovered by an innocent, unbiased reader, and language is not a self-executing, static reference to objects in the world. Meaning is always constructed and always subject to being constructed differently. The attribution of meaning to texts and events is a political process that cannot be determined by the authority of reason. Therefore, it is not that something is bad about Scott's argument because it can be shown to depend on a particular ideology, on a particular language for attributing likeness and difference in the world. The point, rather, is that there is no way to flee from the politics of interpretation to the purity of reason.

I believe that Scott has correctly identified the political nature of the challenge this kind of practice represents to the traditions and institutions he defends. Postmodernism, in Scott's view, poses the threat of the mob coming to power because it subverts the legitimacy of the discourse with which authority commonly justifies social hierarchies, such as the superiority of the intellectuals over the mob. The position and prestige of the intellectual depends, in Scott's view, on laying claim to being rational and apolitical. Reason is not itself supposed to be power, but rather the way that power is tamed to ensure that it is legitimate and appropriate. However, if the category of reason is itself a social construct, and if the mantle of social legitimacy depends on being called reason, then the question of what to call reason is a political question about a contingent exercise of the social power of marginalization and exclusion. It is power all the way through.

The postmodern approach works to politicize the boundaries between knowledge and superstition, truth and myth, reason and passion, fact and opinion. In doing so, it helps to expose the ways that these distinctions are not simply natural and necessary ways to divide the world, but rather form the language for a particular discourse of authority and power. As such, the point of demonstrating that, say, Scott's commitment to reason against the mob actually rests on a particular ideology about the world is not to fault his analysis for being partial or political. The goal is not simply to reverse the hierarchies and thus to favor passion over reason, the mob over the intellectuals, or superstition over knowledge, but to see that these very ways of thinking and talking about social life already embody a particular discourse of power that seeks to legitimize social hierarchy by claiming to have escaped politics, superstition, and the mere conventionality of language.

And that is why, I think, so much controversy has arisen over these projects. By exposing the dependence of supposedly rational or scientific interpretations of the world on language and textuality, on the contingent ways the thick texture of the world might be carved up, the postmodern practice subverts the claims of the Enlightenment tradition to have transcended time and space, to have found through reason or science a place outside historical struggle and beyond the partiality of a particular place in the terrain of social geography. Thus, we can recognize in Scott's argument about reason a particular language for interpreting the world—a language within which it seems natural rather than controversial to divide the world according to the categories of reason and desire, the elite intellectual and the popular mob, knowledge and superstition, principles and politics. But these categories are not, in fact, natural or necessary. Rather, they are social constructions that can be deconstructed to reveal their history, to reveal the excluded voices or "subjugated knowledges"[13] that have been diminished as "primitive," "passionate," or "emotional" in the march of "enlightenment" and "progress." And this language can be deconstructed to reveal its place in the current social geography—in the claims of the powerful that their power is justified by their superior reason or education, or by their civilized nature in sublimating their passion and desire according to middle-class notions of propriety. Or, in the more general cultural tradition marked by fear of passion and sexuality, fear of emotion and keeping proper public appearances.

We can also see in the analysis of Scott's text a particular way that such language or ideology works to, in a sense, cover its tracks, to suppress the constructed nature of its categories. The coherence of Scott's approach depends on believing not only that his categories for interpreting the social world are natural and necessary, but also that they can be applied apolitically because they are not merely words or ideas, but actually refer to something real in the world, something out there somewhere before the mere convention of language that the distinction between reason and desire reflects. The point of showing that reason is simply what is not desire and vice versa is to demonstrate that there is no escape from the contingencies of language. There is nothing in the words or concepts of "reason" and "desire" that dictates they be associated with particular experiences; the two concepts exist only as they are socially constructed within language.

The Nonrationalism of Identity

> What Brian Barry says of religious fanaticism is as true of the quasi-religious commitment to group difference: "few people have ever been converted by a process of 'examining beliefs critically' ... [instead such commitment] is whipped up by nonrational means."
>
> Richard Ford, 2005[14]

The notion that there is no escape from language and politics, no way to represent the social world free of ideology, is not meant simply to correct some intellectual mistake that academics have made in the process of interpreting the world. Rather, it is to oppose the authority of official knowledge on its own terms, to demonstrate that if the justification for certain people being marginalized and excluded from social power is that they view the world through the lenses of myth and superstition, so too do the so-called rational and civilized. The significance of this kind of critical practice is not simply to reveal the constructed nature of what gets taken as fact, knowledge, and truth, as opposed to opinion, superstition, and myth. It is an important practice because, in our social world, these claims to truth have played powerful political roles in the construction of our social relations—in the ways those in power have justified their power and those out of power have been made to feel that their powerlessness is their own fault and the result of their own inadequacy.

Moreover, the practice is significant to the extent that it may help to demystify the ideology of necessity and naturalness, not only in intellectual life, but also in social experience. The notion that we are always perceiving and communicating about the world through language, through socially created and contingent ways of articulating the social space, is relevant not only to "texts" in the sense of written documents, but also to the "text" of our social relations themselves. One aspect of the textuality of experience is reflected in the language of social roles and identities. We approach each other in large part through a social matrix for distributing meaning that influences how the other will be perceived and how we perceive ourselves. Accordingly, social power, represented in the language of social roles and identities, influences every social relation. For example, the relations between men and women proceed largely based on what it means to be a man or a woman within the particular language of social roles. As recent feminist work has powerfully articulated, there is no basis outside social power for the way these roles have been constructed. However, like racial identity, the language of gender roles does not reflect some objective, natural reality. It is a construct with a particular history and place in the social field. So it is with race as well, denoting an identity in flux that gets mistaken as fixed and objective.

As long as identities are taken to reflect something positive and substantial, something that predates language and is merely reflected by language, their social construction is suppressed and assumes a place outside politics, outside history, and beyond the possibilities of social change. That is, as I see it, the situation of alienation—social subjects failing to recognize the social subjectivity of the performances they enact and re-enact, for whom it is experienced as something imposed from the outside, the "censure" of the group against the individuating subject, as Ford described it.

The Enlightenment tradition of contrasting knowledge with ignorance, truth with mythology, and reason with passion beckoned us toward a place of universality where we would meet outside the play of politics and passion, free from the hold of mythology and the particularities of our history. But the most successful form of social power is one that presents itself not as power, but as reason, truth, and objectivity. Rather than continue the liberal quest to find a place that is outside politics and independent of social struggle, racial identity should be understood and recognized as one of the ways social power (the ability to set the terms for the possibility of social meaning) is at stake across the social space—in what gets called "politics" and what gets called "reason," in what gets called "private" choice and what is recognized as public power, in what "identity" African Americans or other social group embrace and project and have projected unto them.

Revelation of the contingency of the dominant forms of knowledge is only the first step of a committed critical practice. Having debunked the dominant form of knowledge because it suppresses its socially created character, we are thrown into the task of creating meaning socially—the task of politics itself.

To some, like Ford or Scott, the assertion that there is no neutral, authoritative, and apolitical interpretation of social life available sounds like a message of hopelessness and nihilism. I think this reaction is rooted in a conviction that the only kind of knowledge worth having is a kind that can be elevated above social life and social history, above passion—one that can be immunized from bias or change. For me, the message of social construction and social contingency is one of hope. It is hopeful because it also suggests there is no objective necessity or rational principle to justify the way things are, to legitimate the hierarchies and status quo distribution of wealth, power, prestige, and freedom. Because our social relations are social products, there is no "reason" they cannot be remade by us, working and struggling and dreaming together.

Notes

Introduction

1. Malcolm X with Alex Haley, *Malcolm X Speaks,* ed. George Breitman (New York: Grove Press, 1965), 31.

2. My thinking about race, law, and politics has been shaped by my engagement with friends in the Conference on Critical Legal Studies and in the Critical Race Theory movement.

On Critical Legal Studies, see Robert Gordon, "New Developments in Legal Theory," in *The Politics of Law: A Progressive Critique,* ed. David Kairys (New York: Basic Books, 1998); James Boyle, ed., *Critical Legal Studies* (New York: NYU Press, 1992); Duncan Kennedy, *Legal Education and the Reproduction of Hierarchy: A Polemic Against the System* (Boston: AFAR, 1983)—updated and republished as Duncan Kennedy, *Legal Education and the Reproduction of Hierarchy: A Polemic Against the System—A Critical Edition* (New York: NYU Press, 2004); Mark Kelman, *A Guide to Critical Legal Studies* (Cambridge, MA: Harvard University Press, 1987); Roberto Mangabeira Unger, *The Critical Legal Studies Movement* (Cambridge, MA: Harvard University Press, 1983). See generally Richard W. Bauman, *Critical Legal Studies: A Guide to the Literature* (Boulder, CO: Westview Press, 1996).

On Critical Race Theory, see Kimberlé Crenshaw, Neil Gotanda, Gary Peller, and Kendall Thomas, eds., *Critical Race Theory: The Key Writings That Formed the Movement* (New York: New Press, 1995); Richard Delgado and Jean Stefancic, eds., *Critical Race Theory: The Cutting Edge,* 2nd ed. (Philadelphia: Temple University Press, 2000); Richard Delgado, *Critical Race Theory: An Introduction* (New York: NYU Press, 2001); Dorothy A. Brown, ed. *Critical Race Theory: Cases, Materials and Problems,* 2nd ed. (Minneapolis: West, 2007); Francisco Valdes, Jerome Culp, and Angela P. Harris, eds., *Crossroads, Directions, and a New Critical Race Theory* (Philadelphia: Temple University Press, 2002); Edward Taylor, David Gillborn, and Gloria Ladson-Billings, eds., *Foundations of Critical Race Theory in Education* (New York: Routledge, 2009); Adrienne

D. Dixson and Celia K. Rousseau, eds., *Critical Race Theory in Education: All God's Children Got a Song* (New York: Routledge, 2006).

3. See e.g. Gary Orfield, Daniel J. Losen, Johanna Wald, and Christopher B. Swanson, eds., *Losing Our Future: How Minority Youth Are Being Left Behind in the Graduation Rate Crisis* (Washington, D.C.: Urban Institute, 2004); Thomas M. Shapiro, *The Hidden Cost of Being African-American: How Wealth Perpetuates Inequality* (New York: Oxford University Press, 2005); Bakari Kitwana, *The Hip-Hop Generation: Young Blacks and the Crisis in African American Culture* (New York: Basic Civitas Books, 2002); Juan Williams, *Enough: The Phony Leaders, Dead-End Movements, and Culture of Failure That Are Undermining Black America, and What We Can Do About It* (New York: Crown, 2006); Robert M. Franklin, *Crisis in the Village: Restoring Hope in African American Communities* (Minneapolis: Fortress Press, 2007); S. Craig Watkins, *Hip Hop Matters: Politics, Pop Culture, and the Struggle for the Soul of a Movement* (Boston: Beacon, 2006); Douglas Massey, *Categorically Unequal: The American Stratification System* (New York: Russell Sage, 2007). The U.S. Department of Justice reports that Blacks are six times more likely to be incarcerated than whites; see U.S. Bureau of Justice Statistics, "Jail Incarceration Rates by Race and Ethnicity, 2000–2009," available at http://bjs.ojp.usdoj.gov/content/pub/pdf/pim09st.pdf.

4. See Michael Eric Dyson, *Is Bill Cosby Right? Or Has the Black Middle Class Lost Its Mind?* (New York: Basic Civitas Books, 2005).

5. The late Senator Daniel Patrick Moynihan (D-NY) used this term in a January 1970 memo to President Richard M. Nixon that recommended strategies for dealing with Black communities, noting that "[t]he time may have come when the issue of race could benefit from a period of 'benign neglect.'" He also said that Americans needed "a period in which Negro progress" continued and "racial rhetoric" faded (Daniel Patrick Moynihan, "Text of the Moynihan Memorandum on the Status of Negroes," *New York Times*, March 1, 1970). It has been called "one of the most famous memoranda in White House History" (Tevi Troy, *Intellectuals and the American Presidency: Philosophers, Jesters, or Technicians* [Lanham, MD: Rowman & Littlefield, 2002], 105–106). See also: John Ehrman, *The Rise of Neo-Conservatism: Intellectuals and Foreign Affairs, 1945–1994* (New Haven, CT: Yale University Press, 1995).

6. There were some exceptions, but they tended to be characterized by "white guilt." See pp. 53, 66, 69.

7. See e.g. *City of Richmond v. Croson*, 488 U.S. 469, 521 (1989) (Scalia, J., concurring) ("only a social emergency rising to the level of life and limb ... can justify an exception to the principle embodied in the Fourteenth Amendment that 'our Constitution is color-blind'") (quoting *Plessy v. Ferguson*, 163 U.S. 537, 559 [1896]) (Harlan, J., dissenting).

8. By "vulgar Black nationalism," I mean to compare these essentialist identity conceptions to the positivist versions of social thought prevalent in the mid-20th century that came to be called, at least on the left, "vulgar Marxism." For a relatively recent usage, see Richard Hudelson, *Marxism and Philosophy in the Twentieth Century: A Defense of Vulgar Marxism* (New York: Praeger, 1990).

Chapter 1

1. Malcolm X, *By Any Means Necessary: Speeches, Interviews and a Letter,* ed. George Breitman (New York: Pathfinder, 1970), 16–17.

2. For examples of opposition to affirmative action among academics, see Alexander Bickel, *The Morality of Consent* (New Haven, CT: Yale University Press, 1975), 133–134 (affirmative action divides society, reduces productivity, and promotes inequality); Thomas Sowell, *Civil Rights: Rhetoric or Reality* (New York: Harper Perennial, 1984), 13–48, 109–116; Morris Abram, "Affirmative Action: Fair Shakers and Social Engineers," *Harvard Law Review* 99(1986): 1312; Richard Posner, "The *DeFunis* Case and the Constitutionality of Preferential Treatment of Racial Minorities," *Supreme Court Review* (1974): 1, reprinted in *Affirmative Action and the Constitution,* Vol. 1, ed. Gabriel Chin (New York: Garland, 1998), 249–280; Shelby Steele, *The Content of Our Character: A New Vision of Race in America* (New York: St. Martin's Press, 1990); Steven M. Cahn, *The Affirmative Action Debate,* 2nd ed. (New York: Routledge, 2002); Terry Eastland, *Ending Affirmative Action: The Case for Colorblind Justice* (New York: Basic Books, 1997); Michael Walzer, *Spheres of Justice* (New York: Basic Books, 1983), 143–154; Glenn Loury, "How to Mend Affirmative Action," *The Public Interest* 127(Spring 1997): 33, http://www.bu.edu/irsd/articles/howtomnd.htm; Stephan Thernstrom and Abigail Thernstrom, *America in Black and White: One Nation, Indivisible* (Cambridge, MA: Harvard University Press, 1998); Dinesh D'Souza, *Illiberal Education: The Politics of Race and Sex on Campus* (New York: Vintage, 1992); Martin Schiff, "Reverse Discrimination Re-Defined as Equal Protection: The Orwellian Nightmare in the Enforcement of Civil Rights Laws," *Harvard Journal of Law and Public Policy* 8(1985): 627; William Van Alstyne, "Rites of Passage: Race, the Supreme Court, and the Constitution," *University of Chicago Law Review* 46(1979): 775.

For examples of academics supporting affirmative action, see Derrick A. Bell, "*Bakke,* Minority Admissions and the Usual Price of Racial Remedies," *California Law Review* 67(1979): 3; Troy Duster, "Individual Fairness, Group Preferences, and the California Strategy," in *Race and Representation: Affirmative Action,* eds. Robert Post and Michael Rogin (New York: Zone Books, 1998); Daniel Sabbagh, *Equality and Transparency: A Strategic Perspective on Affirmative Action in American Law* (New York: Palgrave Macmillan, 2007); Ronald Dworkin, "Affirmative Action: Does It Work?" in *Sovereign Virtue: The Theory and Practice of Equality* (Cambridge, MA: Harvard University Press, 2002); Ronald Dworkin, "Affirmative Action: Is It Fair?" in *Sovereign Virtue: The Theory and Practice of Equality* (Cambridge, MA: Harvard University Press, 2002); Luke C. Harris, "Contesting the Ambivalence and Hostility to Affirmative Action within the Black Community," in *A Companion to African-American Philosophy,* eds. Tommy Lee Lott and John P. Pittman (London: Blackwell Publishing, 2003); Paul Brest, "Foreword: In Defense of the Antidiscrimination Principle," *Harvard Law Review* 90(1976): 1; Richard Delgado, "The Imperial Scholar: Reflections on a Review of Civil Rights Literature," *University of Pennsylvania Law Review* 132(1984): 566–573; John Hart Ely, "The Constitutionality of Reverse Racial Discrimination," *University of Chicago Law Review* 41(1974): 723; Owen

Fiss, "Groups and the Equal Protection Clause," *Philosophy and Public Affairs* 5(1976): 147–170; Alan Freeman, "Racism, Rights and the Quest for Equality of Opportunity: A Critical Legal Essay," *Harvard Civil Rights—Civil Liberties Law Review* 23(1988): 295, 362–385; Kenneth L. Karst and Harold W. Horowitz, "Affirmative Action and Equal Protection," *Virginia Law Review* 60(1974): 955; Randall Kennedy, "Persuasion and Distrust: A Comment on the Affirmative Action Debate," *Harvard Law Review* 99(1986): 1327; Richard A. Wasserstrom, "Racism, Sexism and Preferential Treatment: An Approach to the Topics," *UCLA Law Review* 24(1977): 581.

For examples of the Supreme Court's reactions to affirmative action plans, see *City of Richmond v. Croson*, 488 U.S. 469, 498–499 (1989) (affirmative action by municipality in awarding contracts not justified by general societal discrimination); *Wygant v. Jackson Board of Education*, 476 U.S. 267 (1986) (affirmative action hiring plans in consent decrees cannot impinge on whites' seniority rights for layoff purposes absent showing that the Blacks to be laid off were themselves victims of discrimination). Compare *United Steelworkers v. Weber*, 433 U.S. 193 (1979) (broad statistical disparity between workforce and population sufficient predicate for affirmative action provision in collective bargaining agreement); *Regents of the University of California v. Bakke*, 438 U.S. 265, 311–317 (1978) (race as a factor in an admissions plan may be upheld based on medical school interest in diversity); *Ricci v. DeStefano*, 557 U.S.—, 129 S. Ct. 2658, 2677 (2009) (before an employer can engage in race-conscious discrimination to remedy an unintentional disparate impact, the employer must have a strong basis in evidence to believe it will be subject to disparate-impact liability if it does not take race-conscious action); *Parents Involved in Community Schools vs. Seattle School District No. 1*, 551 U.S. 701, 723–724 (2007) (an allegedly compelling interest of diversity in higher education could not justify a school district's use of racial classifications in student assignment plans); *Grutter v. Bollinger*, 539 U.S. 306, 334 (2003) (law school's race-conscious admissions program was narrowly tailored to serve its compelling interest); *Gratz v. Bollinger*, 539 U.S. 244 (2003) (university's policy of automatically granting extra consideration to all "underrepresented minority" applicants solely because of race was not narrowly tailored).

3. Compare *Wards Cove Packing Co. v. Atonio*, 490 U.S. 642 (1989) (plaintiffs in Title VII suits must demonstrate how particular invidious employment practices caused discriminatory results to shift burden of production to the defendants) and *Washington v. Davis*, 426 U.S. 229 (1976) (holding that a "racially discriminatory purpose" must be proved to make out a claim under the Equal Protection Clause), with *Griggs v. Duke Power Co.*, 401 U.S. 424 (1971) (disparate impact of facially neutral employment practices makes out a *prima facie* Title VII claim, subject to showing of "business necessity") and *White v. Register*, 412 U.S. 755 (1973) (inhibiting effect of redistricting on minority political participation sufficient for *prima facie* violation of Equal Protection Clause).

Academic defenses of at least some form of the intent requirement include: Paul Brest, "*Palmer v. Thompson*: An Approach to the Problem of Unconstitutional Legislative Motivation," *Supreme Court Review* (1971): 95; John Hart Ely, "Legislative and Administrative Motivation in Constitutional Law," *Yale Law Journal* 79(1970): 1205; Jorge

Garcia, "The Heart of Racism," *Journal of Social Philosophy* 27(1996): 5–46; Richard Ford, *Racial Culture: A Critique* (Princeton, NJ: Princeton University Press, 2005).

Criticisms of the doctrine include: Fiss, supra note 2; Charles Lawrence, "The Id, the Ego and Equal Protection: Reckoning with Unconscious Racism," *Stanford Law Review* 39(1987): 317; David Strauss, "Discriminatory Intent and the Taming of *Brown*," *University of Chicago Law Review* 56(1989): 935; Pamela S. Karlan, "Discriminatory Purpose and Mens Rea: The Tortured Argument of Invidious Intent," *Yale Law Journal* 93(1983): 111. See generally Alan Freeman, "Legitimating Racial Discrimination through Antidiscrimination Law: A Critical Review of Supreme Court Doctrine," *Minnesota Law Review* 62(1978): 1049 (arguing that the intent/impact controversy is one element of a more general ideological struggle between "victim" and "perpetrator" perspectives within antidiscrimination law); Gertrude Ezorsky, "Overt and Institutional Racism," in *Racism and Justice: The Case for Affirmative Action* (Ithaca, NY: Cornell University Press, 1991), Ch. 1; Alfred Blumrosen, "Strangers in Paradise: *Griggs v. Duke Power Co.* and the Concept of Employment Discrimination," *Michigan Law Review* 71(1972): 59 (gratuitous burden unfair).

For general discussions of the constitutional issues, see Brest, supra note 2; Theodore Eisenberg, "Disproportionate Impact and Illicit Motive: Theories of Constitutional Adjudication," *New York University Law Review* 52(1977): 36; Gary Peller, "A Subversive Strand of the Warren Court," *Washington & Lee Law Review* 59(2002): 1141.

4. There is now a substantial body of work describing the early years of the "direct action" civil rights movement. I have found most useful: Rhoda L. Blumberg, *Civil Rights: The 1960s Freedom Struggle* (Boston: Twayne Publishers, 1984); Taylor Branch, *At Canaan's Edge: America in the King Years, 1965–1968* (New York: Simon & Schuster, 2006); Taylor Branch, *Parting the Waters: America in the King Years, 1954–1963* (New York: Simon & Schuster, 1988); Taylor Branch, *Pillar of Fire: America in the King Years, 1963–1965* (New York: Simon & Schuster, 1998) (focusing on King and the Southern Christian Legal Conference); Robert Brisbane, *Black Activism: Racial Revolution in the United States, 1954–1970* (Valley Forge, PA: Judson Press, 1974); Thomas R. Brooks, *Walls Come Tumbling Down: A History of the Civil Rights Movement, 1940–1970* (Englewood Cliffs, NJ: Prentice Hall, 1974); Clayborne Carson, *In Struggle: SNCC and the Black Awakening of the 1960s* (Cambridge, MA: Harvard University Press, 1981); James A. Colaiaco, "Martin Luther King, Jr., and the Paradox of Nonviolent Direct Action," *Phylon* 47(1986): 16; David J. Garrow, *Bearing the Cross: Martin Luther King, Jr., and the Southern Christian Leadership Conference* (New York: William Morrow & Co., 1986); August Meier and Elliot Rudwick, *CORE: A Study in the Civil Rights Movement, 1942–1968* (New York: Oxford University Press, 1973); Aldon D. Morris, *The Origins of the Civil Rights Movement: Black Communities Organizing for Change* (New York: The Free Press, 1984); Benjamin Muse, *The American Negro Revolution: From Nonviolence to Black Power* (Bloomington: Indiana University Press, 1968); Charles M. Payne, *I've Got the Light of Freedom: The Organizing Tradition and the Mississippi Freedom Struggle* (Berkeley: University of California Press, 2007); Harvard Sitkoff, *The Struggle for Black Equality, 1954–1980* (New York: Hill & Wang, 1981); Emily Stoper,

The Student Non-Violent Coordinating Committee: The Growth of Radicalism in a Civil Rights Organization (New York: Carlson, 1989); Jeanne Theoharis and Komozi Woodard, *Freedom North: Black Freedom Struggles Outside the South, 1940–1980* (New York: Palgrave Macmillan, 2003); Robert Weisbrot, *Freedom Bound: A History of America's Civil Rights Movement* (New York: W. W. Norton & Co., 1990); Howard Zinn, *SNCC: The New Abolitionists* (Boston: Beacon Press, 1965); Raymond Arsenault, *Freedom Riders: 1961 and the Struggle for Racial Justice* (New York: Oxford University Press, 2006); Catherine A. Barnes, *Journey from Jim Crow: The Desegregation of Southern Transit* (New York: Columbia University Press, 1983); Martha Biondi, *To Stand and Fight: The Struggle for Civil Rights in New York City* (Cambridge, MA: Harvard University Press, 2003); Robert Self, *American Babylon: Race and the Struggle for Postwar Oakland* (Princeton, NJ: Princeton University Press, 2003); Jason Sokol, *There Goes My Everything: White Southerners in the Age of Civil Rights, 1945–1975* (New York: Knopf, 2006); Thomas J. Sugrue, *Sweet Land of Liberty: The Forgotten Struggle for Civil Rights in the North* (New York: Random House, 2008); John Dittmer, *Local People: The Struggle for Civil Rights in Mississippi* (Urbana: University of Illinois Press, 1994); Patricia Sullivan, *Lift Every Voice: The NAACP and the Making of the Civil Rights Movement* (New York: New Press, 2009).

5. The classic text embodying this perspective is: Gary Allport, *The Nature of Prejudice* (New York: Perseus Books, 1954). The comprehension of racism as embodied in the idea of prejudice has had wide influence in academic study. See Robert Blauner, *Racial Oppression in America* (New York: Harper Collins College, 1972), 19. ("The analysis of race by social scientists has been shaped by an underlying assumption that the concern with color in human society is ultimately irrational or nonrational.") For works employing this concept of prejudice, see Oliver Cox, *Race Relations: Elements and Social Dynamics* (Detroit: Wayne State University Press, 1976), 21–40, 226–241; Theodore Cross, *The Black Power Imperative: Racial Inequality and the Politics of Nonviolence* (New York: Faulkner, 1984), 83–136; Roger Daniels and Harry H. L. Kitano, *American Racism: Exploration of the Nature of Prejudice* (Englewood Cliffs, NJ, Prentice Hall, 1970); James M. Jones, *Prejudice and Racism* (Reading, MA: Addison-Wesley Publishers, 1972); Gunnar Myrdal, *An American Dilemma: The Negro Problem and Modern Democracy* (New York: Harper & Bros., 1944), 106–112; Robert Park, *Race and Culture* (Glencoe, IL: The Free Press, 1950), 231–243; Herbert Blumer, "Race Prejudice as a Sense of Group Position," *Pacific Sociological Review* 1 (Spring 1958): 1; Louis Lusky, "The Stereotype: The Hard Core of Racism," *Buffalo Law Review* 13(1964): 450; Charles Stangor, ed., *Stereotypes and Prejudice: Essential Readings* (Levittown, PA: Psychology Press, 2001); George Simpson and J. Milton Yinger, *Racial and Cultural Minorities: An Analysis of Prejudice and Discrimination*, 5th ed. (New York: Plenum, 1985); Debra Van Ausdale and Joe R. Feagin, *The First R: How Children Learn Race and Racism* (Lanham, MD: Rowman & Littlefield, 2001); Samuel L. Gaertner and John F. Dovidio, "The Aversive Form of Racism," in *Prejudice, Discrimination, and Racism*, eds. John F. Dovidio and Samuel L. Gaertner (Orlando, FL: Academic, 1986), 61–89; Andrew Karpinski and James Hilton, "Attitudes and

the Implicit Association Test," *Journal of Personality and Social Psychology* 81(2001): 744–788; Laurie A. Rudman, Richard D. Ashmore, and Melvin L. Gary, "'Unlearning' Automatic Biases: The Malleability of Implicit Prejudice and Stereotypes," *Journal of Personality & Social Psychology* 81(2001): 856 (diversity in education can reduce racial prejudice and stereotypes); Glenn Loury, *The Anatomy of Racial Inequality* (Cambridge, MA: Harvard University Press, 2002) (prejudice/stereotype).

This view of racism as based in prejudice was embodied in the *Report of the National Advisory Commission on Civil Disorders* (New York: Bantam, 1968). For criticisms of this report, see Gary T. Marx, "Two Cheers for the National Riot Commission," in *Black America*, ed. John F. Szwed (New York: Basic Books, 1970), 78; William K. Tabb, "Race Relations Models and Social Change," *Social Problems* 18(1971): 431–434. For general critiques of the way social scientists have comprehended race through the images of ir-rationality and bias, see Lerone Bennett, *The Challenge of Blackness* (Chicago: Johnson Publishing Co., 1972), 121 (discussing the vision of racism as a mental error); Blauner, supra, at 2–11; William J. Wilson, *Power, Racism, and Privilege: Race Relations in Theo-retical and Sociohistorical Perspectives* (New York: Macmillan, 1973), 29–68.

6. See Michael Cassity, *Legacy of Fear: American Race Relations to 1900* (West-port, CT: Greenwood Press, 1985), 32–63; St. Clair Drake, *Black Folk, Here and There* (Los Angeles: University of California Press, 1987), 28–30 (explaining the origin and perpetuation of the stereotype of "the Negro"); George M. Fredrickson: *The Black Im-age in the White Mind: The Debate in Afro-American Character and Destiny, 1817–1914* (New York: Harper & Row, 1972), 53–58, 275–282; Reginald Horsman, *Race and Manifest Destiny: The Origins of American Racial Anglo-Saxonism* (Cambridge, MA: Harvard University Press, 1981), 43–61, 116–157; Winthrop D. Jordan, *White over Black: American Attitudes toward the Negro, 1550–1812* (Chapel Hill, NC: University of North Carolina Press, 1968); Idus A. Newby, *Jim Crow's Defense: Anti-Negro Thought in America, 1900–1930* (Westport, CT: Greenwood Press, 1968); C. Vann Woodward, *The Strange Career of Jim Crow* (New York: Oxford University Press, 1958), 56–95; Kimberlé Crenshaw, "Race, Reform, and Retrenchment: Transformation and Legitima-tion in Antidiscrimination Law," *Harvard Law Review* 101(1988): 1373–1376.

7. See George M. Fredrickson, *White Supremacy* (New York: Oxford University Press, 1981); Woodward, supra note 6. The classic study is: John Dollard, *Caste and Class in a Southern Town* (New York: Doubleday, 1949). See generally Abd-l Hakimu Ibn Alkalimat, "The Ideology of Black Social Science," in *The Death of White Sociol-ogy*, ed. Joyce Ladner (New York: Random House, 1973), 173–174 (linking prejudice, discrimination, and segregation as key elements of restrictive "white" ideology about racism).

8. According to Fein, "the central tenet of liberals, when dealing with race, has been to assert its irrelevance. The argument has been that color is an accidental charac-teristic, which, in the truly rational, liberated, social order, ceases to have any empirical correlates.... The main thrust of the civil rights movement has been, therefore, in the direction of persuading white America to become color-blind. The corollary of the liberal ethic that white people ought not to pay attention to the blackness of Negroes was the

proposition that Negroes ought not to pay attention to their own blackness." Leonard Fein, "Community Schools and Social Theory: The Limits of Universalism," in *Community Control of Schools*, ed. Henry M. Levin (Washington, DC: Brookings Institution Press, 1970), 76, 91.

The continuing strength of this idea is reflected in Spencer J. Salend, *Creating Inclusive Classrooms: Effecting and Reflective Practices*, 4th ed. (Upper Saddle River, NJ: Merrill, 2001); Walter G. Stephan and James A. Banks, *Reducing Prejudice and Stereotyping in Schools* (New York: Teachers College Press, 1999); Cedric Cullingford, *Prejudice: From Individual Identity to Nationalism in Young People* (London: Kogan Page Ltd., 2000); Harold D. Fishbein, *Peer Prejudice and Discrimination: The Origins of Prejudice*, 2nd ed. (Mahwah, NJ: Erlbaum, 2002); John Duckitt, "Reducing Prejudice: An Historical and Multi-Level Approach," in *Understanding Prejudice, Racism, and Social* Conflict, eds. Martha Augoustinos and Katherine Reynolds (London: Sage, 2001); Glenn Loury, supra note 5.

James Farmer tells a story indicating the extreme manifestation of the colorblindness affliction, at least among some whites. A 20-year-old white CORE worker was mugged in her apartment. She described the assailant with great detail to the police, including height, weight, eyes, teeth, and clothing, but she didn't mention that fact that he was Black "for fear of indicating prejudice" (James Farmer, *Freedom, When?* [New York: Random House, 1965], 85).

As Farmer makes clear, this analysis of racism and prejudice was extremely individualistic; the error of prejudice was taken to be reaching conclusions about people based on any group association at all. See also Blauner, supra note 5, at 2–50 (describing the focus of sociologists of race on prejudice, stereotype, and assimilation and linking such a frame with individualist norms); Harold Cruse, *The Crisis of the Negro Intellectual* (New York: William Morrow & Co., 1967); Loren Miller, "Farewell to Liberals," in *Black Protest Thought in the Twentieth Century*, eds. August Meier and Elliot Rudwick (Indianapolis, IN: Bobbs-Merrill Co, 1971), 379 (liberals individualize racism and look toward the elimination of all race distinction, failing to recognize race as a group status).

9. The equality of opportunity or formal equality ideology underlying this basic vision of racism is discussed in: Crenshaw, supra note 6, at 1336–1349; Richard H. Fallon, "To Each According to His Ability, from None According to His Race: The Concept of Merit in the Law of Antidiscrimination," *Boston University Law Review* 60(1980): 815; Freeman, "Legitimating Racial Discrimination through Antidiscrimination Law," supra note 3, at 354–385; Patricia Williams, "The Obliging Shell: An Informal Essay on Formal Equal Opportunity," *Michigan Law Review* 87(1989): 2128. See also Malcolm X and James Farmer, "Separation or Integration: A Debate," *Dialogue* (May 1962): 14, reprinted in *Black Protest Thought in the Twentieth Century*, eds. Meier and Rudwick, supra note 8, 387, 404 (according to Farmer, integration means "each individual [is to be] accepted on the basis of his individual merit and not on the basis of his color"); Bayard Rustin, "Separate Is Not Equal," in *Black Protest Thought in the Twentieth Century*, eds. Meier and Rudwick, supra note 8, 622 ("after graduation [Black students] will have to engage in free and open competition for jobs in a marketplace where standards are universal");

Weisbrot, supra note 4, at xiii ("A basic assumption of liberalism in the 1960s was that equal protection of constitutional rights would afford all Americans, regardless of color, an equal chance to amass wealth, influence, and stature."); Stephan Thernstrom and Abigail Thernstrom, *America in Black and White: One Nation, Indivisible* (Cambridge, MA: Harvard University Press, 1998); Thomas Sowell, *Race and Culture: A World View* (New York: Basic Books, 1994).

10. See Cross, supra note 5, at 609–610. According to Cross, "[i]ntegration is indispensable to shattering racial stereotypes. . . . Only in day-to-day contact with blacks will whites learn that blacks are not less intelligent, less honest, or less human than whites. Through time, integrated living and integrated education are the most forceful weapons for breaking the stubborn and enduring mental habit of defining people's traits according to their race."

See also Alkalimat, supra note 7, at 177 (investing in education is a major integrationist policy because racism is seen to be based in ignorance); Malcolm X and Farmer, supra note 9, at 17 (According to Farmer, "it is segregation that produces prejudice, as much as prejudice produces segregation."); Fein, supra note 8, at 90 ("liberals have seen the public schools as society's best hope for achieving comprehensive integration"); Rudman, Ashmore, and Gary, supra note 5, at 856 (diversity in education can reduce racial prejudice and stereotypes).

The roots of the idea that overcoming racism would mean integration, understood as assimilation, can be found in academic thought in the widely influential study by Robert Park. See Park, supra note 5 (describing a structure of race relations based on distinct stages of contact, competition, accommodation, and assimilation). Louis Wirth somewhat refined Park's basic model (Louis Wirth, "The Problem of Minority Groups," in *The Science of Man in the World Crisis,* ed. Ralph Linton [New York: Columbia University Press, 1945], 347). See also Nathan Glazer and Daniel Patrick Moynihan, *Beyond the Melting Pot* (Boston: MIT Press, 1963); Milton M. Gordon, *Assimilation in American Life: The Role of Race, Religion, and National Origins* (New York: Oxford University Press, 1964) (discussing Park's definition of assimilation). For discussions of the influence of Park's basic model, see Blauner, supra note 5, at 5–12; Alkalimat, supra note 7, at 173–181. For a description of this perspective at the level of everyday culture among civil rights activists in the 1950s and early 1960s, see Farmer, supra note 9, at 53–128; Edgar G. Epps, "The Integrationists," in *Through Different Eyes: Black and White Perspectives on American Race Relations,* eds. Peter I. Rose, Stanley Rothman, and William J. Wilson (New York: Oxford University Press, 1973).

11. See Blauner, supra note 5, at 266–268; Alkalimat, supra note 7, at 177–182; Farmer, supra note 9, at 85–86; Fein, supra note 8, at 89–93.

Although integrationism rejected the essentialism of white supremacy ideology, it constituted its own form of essentialism by assuming that the categories of description themselves were outside the social economy of race—that is, the assumption that the division of the world between the rational and the emotional, or the pious and the lustful, was not itself part and parcel of a rhetoric of domination. According to integrationists, racism consists only in the failure to recognize the distribution of these characteristics across racial lines, rather than in the ideological structure that conceives of the mind and the body, reason and desire, and intelligence and ignorance as the natural categories to organize social perception. See infra Chapter 2, notes 60–70 and accompanying text.

12. Tamotsu Shibutani and Kian M. Kwan, *Ethnic Stratification: A Comparative Approach* (New York: Macmillan, 1965), 589. Shibutani and Kwan argue that "[h]uman beings throughout the world are fundamentally alike.... Hence, whenever social distance is reduced, individuals recognize their resemblances. The basic differences between ethnic groups are cultural, and conventional norms serve as masks to cover the similarities. Whenever men interact informally, the common human nature comes through. It would appear, then, that it is only a matter of time before a more enlightened citizenry will realize this. Then, there will be a realignment of group loyalties, and ethnic identity will become a thing of the past."

13. See Fein, supra note 8, at 87–94 (describing the centrality of the idea of universalism to liberal integrationists). For other writers linking integrationism with a commitment to universalism, see Blauner, supra note 5, at 266–267; Bennett, supra note 5, at 35–36; Robert Staples, *Introduction to Black Sociology* (New York: McGraw-Hill, 1976), 260–261; Alkalimat, supra note 7, at 188.

14. See Blauner, supra note 5, at 266–267 ("The liberal wants to judge a man in terms of his individual uniqueness and his universal humanity, not in terms of 'accidental' features like skin color. Universalism thus goes hand in hand with individualism, and in the area of race the two join in the ideal of 'color blindness.'"). For descriptions of the centrality of these distinctions to Enlightenment thought generally, see Max Horkheimer and Theodor W. Adorno, *Dialectic of Enlightenment,* trans. John Cumming (New York: Continuum International, 1972); Herbert Marcuse, *Reason and Revolution: Hegel and the Rise of Social Theory* (London: Routledge, 1955).

15. See Fein, supra note 8, at 87 ("The liberal commitment, in education as in other spheres, is to universalism. We approach liberal salvation as we move from the sacred to the secular ... from tradition through charisma to rational bureaucracy.").

16. Robert Nisbet, *Community and Power* (New York: Oxford University Press, 1962). Nisbet describes the liberal vision of progress as a move toward increasing secularization: "The demands of freedom appeared to be in the direction of the release of large numbers of individuals from the statuses and identities that had been forged in them by the dead hand of the past. A free society would be one in which individuals were morally and socially as well as politically free, free from groups and classes.... Freedom would arise from the individual's release from all the inherited personal interdependencies of traditional community, and from his existence in an impersonal, natural, economic order" (Nisbet at 22). For other discussions of the general secularization associated with liberal visions of progress, see generally Horkheimer and Adorno, supra note 14; Roberto Mangabeira Unger, *Law in Modern Society: Toward a Criticism of Social Theory* (New York: The Free Press, 1976).

17. See Blauner, supra note 14.

18. See Blauner, supra note 5, at 19–21 (linking repudiation of race consciousness with similar images of religiosity and other forms of "primordial" belief).

19. Nisbet, supra note 16, at 214. The link between images of universalism and progress in liberal ideology are well summarized by Nisbet: "To regard all evil as a persistence or revival of the past has been a favorite conceit of liberals nourished by the idea of Progress…. Present evils could safely be regarded as regrettable evidences of incomplete emancipation from the past—from tribalism, from agrarianism, religion, localism, and the like. In one form or another, the theory of cultural lag has been the secular approach to the problem of evil."

20. See Christopher Jencks, *Inequality: A Reassessment of the Effect of Family and Schooling in America* (New York: Basic Books, 1972), 253–265; Fiss, supra note 2, at 154–155.

The "cultural deprivation" analysis was especially prevalent in the 1960s. See e.g. Glazer and Moynihan, supra note 10, at 53 (arguing that lower-class problems are so great and the line dividing lower from middle class is so thin that the "middle-class Negro" cannot deal with them); Elliot Liebow, *Tally's Corner: A Study of Negro Streetcorner Men* (Lanham, MD: Rowman & Littlefield, 1966), 208–222 (concluding that Black male street culture is not distinct from white culture, but merely a shadow system of values); Charles E. Silberman, *Crisis in Black and White* (New York: Random House, 1964), 249–307 (arguing that an "overall poverty of environment" accounts for the problems in slum schools and the poor educational performance of Black children). Silberman later repudiated the position (Charles E. Silberman, *Crisis in the Classroom: The Remaking of American Education* [New York: Random House, 1970], 81). For one of many criticisms of the "cultural deprivation" approach as racist, see Kenneth B. Clark, *Dark Ghetto: Dilemmas of Social Power* (New York: Harper & Row, 1965), 129–153; Michael Rosenfeld, *Affirmative Action and Justice* (New Haven, CT: Yale University Press, 1991); Troy Duster, "Individual Fairness, Group Preferences, and the California Strategy," in *Race and Representation: Affirmative Action,* eds. Robert Post and Michael Rogin (New York: Zone Books, 1998), 111–133; Gertrude Ezorsky, *Racism and Justice: The Case for Affirmative Action* (Ithaca, NY: Cornell University Press, 1991).

21. See *Regents of the University of California v. Bakke,* 438 U.S. 265, 311–315 (1978) (finding the goal of a diverse student body to be a compelling justification for affirmative action admissions); Ronald Dworkin, *A Matter of Principle* (Cambridge, MA: Harvard University Press, 1985), 301–303 ("Places in medical schools are scarce resources and must be used to provide what … society most needs…. Racial justice is now a special need."); Robert Lack, "Letter to the Editors," *New York Times,* March 9, 1981 (defending affirmative action plan for *Harvard Law Review* based on "the need for diversity"); Scott Page, *The Difference: How the Power of Diversity Creates Better Groups, Firms, Schools, and Societies,* new ed. (Princeton, NJ: Princeton University Press, 2008); Robert Post, "Introduction: After *Bakke,*" in *Race and Representation: Affirmative Action,* eds. Robert Post and Michael Rogin (New York: Zone Books, 1998), 13–27; Cynthia Estlund, *Working Together: How Workplace Bonds Strengthen a Diverse Democracy* (Oxford: Oxford University Press, 2005); Elizabeth Anderson, "Racial Integration as a Compelling Interest," *Constitutional Commentary* 21(2004): 101–127; Martha Nussbaum, *Cultivating Humanity: A Classical Defense of Reform in Liberal Education*

(Cambridge, MA: Harvard University Press, 1997); Elizabeth Anderson, "Integration, Affirmative Action, and Strict Scrutiny," *New York University Law Review* 77(2002): 1195–1271.

22. I do not mean to suggest that the ideology of merit has never been questioned within the mainstream discourse. See e.g. Fallon, supra note 9 (merit is but one value that competes and conflicts with other values); Wasserstrom, supra note 2, at 619 (arguing that no normative justification can be found for meritocracy). Conventional discourse, however, has contained the critique of meritocracy to low-level, blue-collar positions; the assumption has been that higher-level jobs are truly based on merit. See Elizabeth Bartholet, "Application of Title VII to Jobs in High Places," *Harvard Law Review* 95(1982): 945. For a particularly telling example of this elitism, see the sharp reaction that the usually "liberal" *New York Times* editors expressed in opposing the adoption of an affirmative action program for membership on the *Harvard Law Review* ("Drawing Distinctions at Harvard Law," *New York Times*, March 3, 1981) (characterizing selection procedures as "a fixed standard of [absolute] merit"). For an extended analysis of the link between the ideology of meritocracy and issues of race, see Freeman, supra note 3, at 295, 362–385.

23. Peter Wallenstein, "Black Southerners and Nonblack Universities: The Process of Desegregating Southern Higher Education, 1935–1965," in *Higher Education and the Civil Rights Movement: White Supremacy, Black Southerners, and College Campuses,* ed. Peter Wallenstein (Gainesville: University Press of Florida, 2007).

24. Robbins L. Gates, *The Making of Massive Resistance: Virginia's Politics of Public School Desegregation, 1954–1956* (Chapel Hill: University of North Carolina Press, 1962); Benjamin Muse, *Virginia's Massive Resistance* (Bloomington: Indiana University Press, 1961); J. Harvie Wilkinson III, *From* Brown *to* Bakke*: The Supreme Court and School Integration: 1954–1978* (Oxford: Oxford University Press, 1979).

25. See Wallenstein, supra note 23.

26. See U.S. Census Bureau, 1980 Census of Population, Chapter D, Part 48, Section 1, Table 194, http://www.census.gov/prod/www/abs/decennial/1980cenpopv1.html#va.

27. On the racial culture of elite law schools, see Wendy Leo Moore, *Reproducing Racism: White Space, Elite Law Schools, and Racial Inequality* (Lanham, MD: Rowman & Littlefield, 2008).

28. See Staples, supra note 13, at 260–261. Staples linked the origin of the theory that whites and Blacks are identical to the ideology of universalism: "The theory that no important differences exist between Blacks and Whites in America—either biologically or culturally—is of recent origin. It gained prominence at precisely the time when Blacks began to insist they did have distinctive attitudes, values, and lifestyles and began to question the validity and relevance of White culture. At the same time that Whites wanted to be color-blind, Blacks were demanding separate admissions standards to schools and jobs. Thus the ideology of universalism must be viewed in proper context. It is mostly an attempt by Whites to maintain institutional arrangements which embody the residual results of past overt racism."

29. See *Abington School Dist. v. Schempp*, 374 U.S. 203, 223–225 (1963) (prohibiting public school children from reciting verses of the Bible and the Lord's Prayer does not establish a "religion of secularism," but instead allows the government to maintain strict neutrality vis-à-vis religion); *Engel v. Vitale*, 370 U.S. 421 (1962) (declaring unconstitutional state-sponsored, nondenominational prayer in schools).

30. See Blauner, supra note 5, at 19 (linking social-science view of religious beliefs as irrational with similar view about race consciousness).

31. The link between integration and the ban on school prayer was made explicit by both George Wallace and Martin Luther King, Jr. See Martin Luther King, Jr., *A Testament of Hope: The Essential Writings of Martin Luther King, Jr.*, ed. James M. Washington (New York: HaperCollins, 1986), 374. See also Fein, supra note 8, at 87 (linking secularism and integrationism).

32. See Freeman, supra note 3, at 375–385. For a general description of the cultural and political clash reflected in the reform of Southern schools, see Gary Peller, "Creation, Evolution and the New South," *Tikkun* 2 (November–December 1987): 72.

33. Myron Lieberman, *The Future of Public Education* (Chicago: University of Chicago Press, 1960), 60.

34. Id. at 38. For a more general discussion of the link between professionalism, centralism, and progress in liberal attitudes toward public education, see Fein, supra note 8, at 87.

35. Lieberman, supra note 33, at 34.

Chapter 2

1. Robert S. Browne, "A Case for Separation," in *Separatism or Integration, Which Way for America: A Dialogue*, eds. Robert S. Browne and Bayard Rustin (New York: A. Philip Randolph Educational Fund, 1968), 7–15. Browne, then a professor of economics at Fairleigh Dickinson University, advocated "partitioning the United States into two separate and independent nations" at the Conference on Black Power held in Newark, New Jersey, in July 1967 (Theodore Draper, *The Rediscovery of Black Nationalism* [New York: Viking, 1969], 136–137). See Robert S. Browne, "The Case for Black Separatism," *Ramparts* 6 (December 1967): 50.

2. For the best general histories of black nationalism, see Robert Allen, *A Guide to Black Power in America: An Historical Analysis* (London: Gollancz, 1970); Rodney P. Carlisle, *The Roots of Black Nationalism* (Port Washington, NY: Kennikat Press, 1975); Harold Cruse, *The Crisis of the Negro Intellectual* (New York: William Morrow & Co., 1967), 6–8 (describing integrationist link to individualist mythology of merit); Loren Miller, "Farewell to Liberals," in *Black Protest Thought in the Twentieth Century*, eds. August Meier and Elliot Rudwick (Indianapolis, IN: Bobbs-Merrill Co., 1971), 379 (liberals individualize racism and look toward the elimination of all race distinction, failing to recognize race as a group status); Harold Cruse, *Rebellion or Revolution?* (New York: William Morrow, 1968), 48–97, 193–258; Draper, supra note 1; Wilson J. Moses, *The*

Golden Age of Black Nationalism, 1850–1925 (New York: Oxford University Press, 1978); Alphonso Pinkney, *Red, Black, and Green: Black Nationalism in the United States* (New York: Cambridge University Press, 1976); John Bracey, Jr., August Meier, and Elliot Rudwick, eds., *Black Nationalism in America* (Indianapolis, IN: Bobbs-Merrill Co., 1970) (a documentary history). Although I utilize different frames of reference, my analysis of competing African American traditions has been influenced by Cornel West's excellent study; see Cornel West, *Prophesy Deliverance! An Afro-American Revolutionary Christianity* (Louisville, KY: Westminster John Knox Press, 2002); Jeremiah Moses Wilson, ed., *Classical Black Nationalism: From the American Revolution to Marcus Garvey* (New York: NYU Press, 1996); William L. Van DeBurg, ed., *Modern Black Nationalism: From Marcus Garvey to Louis Farrakhan* (New York: NYU Press, 1997); Dean E. Robinson, *Black Nationalism in American Politics and Thought* (New York: Cambridge University Press, 2001); Tommy Shelby, *We Who Are Dark: The Philosophical Foundations of Black Solidarity* (Cambridge, MA: Verso, 2005); Roderick Bush, *We Are Not What We Seem: Black Nationalism and Class Struggle in the American Century* (New York: NYU Press, 1999); Komozi Woodard, *A Nation within a Nation: Amiri Baraka (LeRoi Jones) & Black Power Politics* (Chapel Hill: University of North Carolina Press, 1999).

3. For Delany's views of American race relations, see Martin R. Delany, *The Condition, Elevation, Emigration and Destiny of the Colored People of the United States* (Baltimore: Black Classic Press, 1993), 159–173 ("[T]hat there are circumstances under which emigration is absolutely necessary to [our] political elevation cannot be disputed.... We desire the civilization and enlightenment of Africa."). Recently, a body of scholarly work has considered Delany's significance in terms of the Black nationalist tradition. See Draper, supra note 1, at 21–41; Cyril E. Griffith, *The African Dream: Martin R. Delany and the Emergence of Pan-African Thought* (University Park: Pennsylvania State University Press, 1975); Pinkney, supra note 2, at 23–27; Victor Ullman, *Martin R. Delany: The Beginnings of Black Nationalism* (Boston: Beacon Press, 1971); Robert S. Levine, *Martin Delany, Frederick Douglass, and the Politics of Representative Identity* (Chapel Hill: University of North Carolina Press, 1997).

Prior to Delany, Paul Cuffe had called for repatriation of Blacks to Africa, petitioned Congress for assistance in 1814, and actually resettled 38 Blacks to Sierra Leone in 1815. See also Sheldon H. Harris, *Paul Cuffe: Black American and the African Return* (New York: Simon & Schuster, 1972), 62–65; William Alexander, ed., *Memoir of Captain Paul Cuffe, A Man of Colour* (York, PA, 1811). Congress funded the American Colonization Society, founded by whites to resettle free Blacks to Africa, in 1819. The society purchased land on the west coast of Africa and began what became, in 1847, the country of Liberia. The society had an explicit white supremacist ideology and was opposed by most African Americans, although it claimed to have resettled 13,000 blacks before the Civil War. Delany, among other Black leaders, refused to cooperate with the society, denouncing its leaders as "arrant hypocrites" (Edwin S. Redkey, *Black Exodus* [New Haven, CT: Yale University Press, 1969], 18–21). See Carlisle, supra note 2 (summaries of antebellum emigration proposals and efforts); Draper, supra note 1, at 14–33; Pinkney, supra note 2, at 19–23. Delany's nationalism was explicitly opposed to the ideology of constitutional civil rights, and he and Frederick Douglass had public disagreements. See Martin Delany, "I Have No Hopes in This Country," quoted in Thomas Wagstaff, *Black Power: The Radical Response to White America* (Glencoe, IL: Glencoe Press, 1969), 43.

An important advocate of emigration to Africa during the late 19th and early 20th centuries was Bishop Henry Turner. See Draper, supra note 1, at 43–47; Pinkney, supra note 2, at 28–36; Mungo M. Ponton, *The Life and Times of Henry M. Turner* (New York: Negro Universities Press, 1970).

4. According to Harold Cruse, Booker T. Washington is a central figure in the tradition of Black nationalism in the United States. "Black Power is militant Booker T.-ism" (Cruse, *Rebellion or Revolution,* supra note 2, at 201). For Washington's analysis of racial progress, including his philosophy of economic self-improvement, see Booker T. Washington, *The Future of the American Negro* (Boston: Small, Maynard & Co., 1900); Booker T. Washington, *Up from Slavery* (New York: Doubleday, Page & Co. 1901). See also August Meier, *Negro Thought in America, 1880–1915: Racial Ideologies in the Age of Booker T. Washington* (Ann Arbor: University of Michigan Press, 1963). The leading biography of Washington is the two-volume work by Louis Harlan: Louis R. Harlan, *Booker T. Washington: The Making of a Black Leader, 1865–1901* (New York: Oxford University Press, 1972); Louis R. Harlan, *Booker T. Washington: The Wizard of Tuskegee, 1901–1915* (New York: Oxford University Press, 1983). Documents concerning Washington are exhaustively collected in Louis R. Harlan and Raymond W. Smock, eds., *The Booker T. Washington Papers* (Urbana: University of Illinois Press, 1972–1989) (14 vols.). See also Robert J. Norrell, *Up from History: The Life of Booker T. Washington* (Boston: Harvard University Press, 2009); Raymond W. Smock, *Booker T. Washington: Black Leadership in the Age of Jim Crow* (Chicago: Ivan R. Dee, 2009).

5. The most effective early-20th-century Black nationalist leader, Garvey (a Jamaican immigrant to the United States), founded the Universal Negro Improvement Association (UNIA). The UNIA advocated Black unity, a mass migration to Africa, and the liberation and unification of Africa as a homeland for all Black people. Garvey urged the immediate organization of all-Black businesses and established UNIA-operated cooperatives, including the Black Star Line steamship company. Garvey also started *Negro World.* Critical of the NAACP's focus on politics and civil rights and disparaging of its intellectual leader, Du Bois, Garvey attacked NAACP activists as race traitors. The UNIA attracted a half-million people at its height in the 1920s, almost entirely from the poor of the urban ghettoes, with chapters in cities across the United States and abroad. For the best studies of Garvey, see E. David Cronon, *Black Moses: The Story of Marcus Garvey and the Universal Negro Improvement Association* (Madison: University of Wisconsin Press, 1955) (focusing on Garvey's shortcomings as a leader); Amy J. Garvey, *Garvey and Garveyism* (New York: Collier, 1970) (a description of Garvey and the movement by his widow); Tony Martin, *Race First: The Ideological and Organizational Struggle of Marcus Garvey and the Universal Negro Improvement Association* (Westport, CT: Greenwood Press, 1976) (arguing that Garvey was a revolutionary and the greatest Black figure of the century); Theodore Vincent, *Black Power and the Garvey Movement* (Berkeley, CA:

Ramparts Press, 1971) (contending that Garvey was the direct forerunner of 1960s nationalists). The religious component of Garveyism is analyzed in Randall K. Burkett, *Garveyism as a Religious Movement: The Institutionalization of a Black Civil Religion* (Metuchen, NJ: Scarecrow Press, 1978). For a collection of Garvey's pre-1925 views, see Amy J. Garvey, ed., *The Philosophy and Opinions of Marcus Garvey* (New York: Atheneum, 1969) (two vols.). See also Robert A. Hill, ed., *The Marcus Garvey and Universal Negro Improvement Association Papers* (Berkeley: University of California Press, 1983) (ongoing, 10 vols.) (collection of documents relating to the Garvey movement); Colin Grant, *Negro with a Hat: The Rise and Fall of Marcus Garvey and His Dream of Mother Africa* (New York: Oxford University Press, 2008).

   6.   For diverse views of the Muslims, see Essien Udosen Essien-Udom, *Black Nationalism: A Search for Identity in America* (Chicago: University of Chicago Press, 1962); Charles E. Lincoln, *The Black Muslims in America* (Boston: Beacon Press, 1961); Elijah Muhammad, *Message to the Blackman in America* (Chicago: Muhammad Mosque of Islam No. 2, 1965); Pinkney, supra note 2, at 155–164; Mattias Gardell, *In the Name of Elijah Muhammad: Louis Farrakhan and the Nation of Islam* (Durham, NC: Duke University Press, 1996).

For an analysis that connects the Nation of Islam to Booker T. Washington, see Cruse, *Rebellion or Revolution*, supra note 2, at 211. Cruse writes that "[the] Nation of Islam was nothing but a form of Booker T. Washington's economic self-help, black unity, bourgeois hard work, law abiding, vocational training, stay-out-of-the-civil-rights-struggle agitation, separate-from-the-white-man, etc., etc., morality. The only difference was that Elijah Muhammad added the potent factor of the Muslim religion to a race, economic, and social philosophy of which the first prophet was none other than Booker T. Washington. Elijah also added an element of 'hate Whitey' ideology which Washington, of course, would never have accepted."

   7.   See W. E. B. Du Bois, "Postscript: The N.A.A.C.P. and Race Segregation," *The Crisis* 41(1934): 52–53; W. E. B. Du Bois, "Does the Negro Need Separate Schools?" *Journal of Negro Education* (July 1935): 328–335; W. E. B. Du Bois, *Dusk of Dawn* (New York: Harcourt, Brace & World, 1940). For a discussion of the significance of Du Bois' shift in ideology, see Harold Cruse, *Plural but Equal: A Critical Study of Black and Minorities and America's Plural Society* (New York: William Morrow, 1987); Cruse, *The Crisis of the Negro Intellectual*, supra note 2, at 175–177, 330–336, 558–565; Manning Marable, *W. E. B. Du Bois: Black Radical Democrat* (Boston: Twayne, 1986), 140–142; John White, *Black Leadership in America, 1895–1968* (London: Longman, 1985), 52–61.

   8.   See Malcolm X, *The Autobiography of Malcolm X*, ed. Alex Haley (New York: Grove Press, 1965); Malcolm X, *By Any Means Necessary: Speeches, Interviews, and a Letter*, ed. George Breitman (New York: Pathfinder Press, 1970), 16–17; Malcom X, *Malcolm X Speaks: Selected Speeches and Statements*, ed. George Breitman (New York: Grove Press, 1965); Peter Goldman, *The Death and Life of Malcolm X* (Champaign: University of Illinois Press, 1979); Michael E. Dyson, *Making Malcolm: The Myth and Meaning of Malcolm X* (New York: Oxford University Press, 1995); William W. Sales,

From Civil Rights to Black Liberation: Malcolm X and the Organization of Afro-American Unity (Boston: South End Press, 1994); Robert Terrill, *Malcolm X: Inventing Radical Judgment* (Lansing: Michigan State University Press, 2004).

9. See Eldridge Cleaver, *Eldridge Cleaver: Post-Prison Writings and Speeches,* ed. Robert Scheer (New York: Random House, 1969); Eldridge Cleaver, *Soul on Ice* (New York: Laurel, 1968).

10. See Stokely Carmichael and Charles V. Hamilton, *Black Power: The Politics of Liberation in America* (New York: Random House, 1967) (Carmichael, a former chairperson of SNCC, is now known as Kwame Ture).

11. See Amiri Baraka, "The Pan-African Party and the Black Nation," *Black Scholar* (March 1971): 24; Amiri Baraka, *Raise, Race, Rays, Raze* (New York: Random House, 1971).

12. See Cruse, *The Crisis of the Negro Intellectual,* supra note 2; Cruse, *Rebellion or Revolution,* supra note 2.

13. See Phillip S. Foner, ed., *The Black Panthers Speak* (New York: HarperCollins, 1969); H. Rap Brown, *Die Nigger Die! A Political Autobiography* (Chicago: Lawrence Hill Books, 1969); George Jackson, *Soledad Brother: The Prison Letters of George Jackson* (New York: Bantam, 1970); Gene Marine, *The Black Panthers* (New York: New American Library, 1969); Huey P. Newton, *To Die for the People: The Writings of Huey P. Newton* (New York: Random House, 1972). "The Black Panther Party Platform and Program," the founding platform and program of the Black Panther Party, is reprinted in Edward Greer, ed., *Black Liberation Politics: A Reader* (Boston: Allyn and Bacon, 1971), 380–382.

14. See Clayborne Carson, *In Struggle: SNCC and the Black Awakening of the 1960s* (Cambridge, MA: Harvard University Press, 1981); August Meier and Elliot Rudwick, *CORE: A Study in the Civil Rights Movement: 1942–1968* (New York: Oxford University Press, 1973), 431 (describing the nationalist turn within CORE).

For general histories of Black nationalism in the 1960s, see Allen, supra note 2, at 18–74, 108–239; Draper, supra note 1, at 86–167; Herbert H. Haines, *Black Radicals and the Civil Rights Mainstream, 1954–1970* (Knoxville: University of Tennessee Press, 1988), 57–76; Pinkney, supra note 2, at 76–219; Robert Weisbrot, *Freedom Bound: A History of America's Civil Rights Movement* (New York: W. W. Norton & Co., 1990), 222–261; James Turner, "Black Nationalism: The Inevitable Response," *Black World* (January 1971): 4.

15. The March Against Fear was begun as a solitary march across Mississippi by James Meredith to protest the slaying of Medgar Evers. After a would-be assassin shot Meredith, the leaders of the SCLC, SNCC, CORE, NAACP, and Urban League got together in Memphis to plan to continue the march symbolically on Meredith's behalf. The Urban League and NAACP eventually refused to participate in opposition to the manner in which the March's manifesto sharply criticized the slow pace of civil rights reform of the federal government. See David J. Garrow, *Bearing the Cross: Martin Luther King, Jr., and the Southern Christian Leadership Conference* (New York: William Morrow & Co., 1986), at 475–497; Vincent Harding, *The Other American Revolution* (Berkeley:

University of California Press, 1980), 185–187; Weisbrot, supra note 14, at 193–221; White, supra note 7, at 139–143.

16. Richard Wright, *Black Power: A Record of Reactions in a Land of Pathos* (New York, Harper, 1954).

17. See Cruse, *Rebellion or Revolution*, supra note 2, at 207.

18. See Carson, supra note 14, at 56–65, 83–95; Aldon D. Morris, *The Origins of the Civil Rights Movement: Black Communities Organizing for Change* (New York: The Free Press, 1984), 239–250; Weisbrot, supra note 14, at 30–38, 130–143.

19. See Allen, supra note 2, at 20–21; Taylor Branch, *Parting the Waters: America in the King Years, 1954–1963* (New York: Simon & Schuster, 1988), 869–870, 873–874, 878–880 (focusing on King and the SCLC); Garrow, supra note 15, at 281–283; Weisbrot, supra note 14, at 76–83.

20. For descriptions of this context of the march, see Carson, supra note 14, at 209–210; Garrow, supra note 15, at 475–497; Martin Luther King, Jr., *Where Do We Go from Here: Chaos or Community?* (Boston: Beacon Press, 1968), 31–32; Weisbrot, supra note 14, at 193–221.

21. For examples of the substantial writing from this time devoted to defining and evaluating Black Power, see Carmichael and Hamilton, supra note 10; Edward Peeks, *The Long Struggle for Black Power* (New York: Charles Scribner's Sons, 1971); Robert L. Scott and Wayne Brockriede, eds., *The Rhetoric of Black Power* (New York: Harper & Row, 1969); Nathan Wright, *Black Power and Urban Unrest: Creative Possibilities* (New York, Hawthorn Books, 1967); Floyd Barbour, ed., *The Black Power Revolt* (Boston: Sargent, 1968); Lerone Bennett, Jr., "Of Time, Space, and Revolution," *Ebony* (August 1969): 24, 31–44; Norman Mailer, "Black Power: A Discussion," *Partisan Review* 35 (Spring 1968): 195 (symposium); Carl Bloice, "Black Labor Is Black Power," *Black Scholar* 2 (October 1970): 2; Christopher Lasch, "The Trouble with Black Power," *New York Review of Books* (February 29, 1968): 10; P. Chike Onwuachi, "Identity and Black Power," *Negro Digest* 16 (March 1967): 16; Harold C. Relyea, "Black Power as an Urban Ideology," *Education Digest* 35 (February 1970): 35, 46–49; "Symposium on Black Power," *New South* (Summer 1966).

For general commentaries on the Black Power controversy, see Allen supra note 2; Draper, supra note 1, at 118–131; Haines, supra note 14, at 57–70; Harding, supra note 15, at 177–200; Benjamin Muse, *The American Negro Revolution: From Nonviolence to Black Power* (Bloomington: Indiana University Press, 1968), 243–244; Fred Powledge, *Black Power, White Resistance: Notes on the New Civil War* (Cleveland: World Publishing Co., 1967); Hettie V. Williams, *We Shall Overcome to We Shall Overrun: The Collapse of the Civil Rights Movement and the Black Power Revolt (1962–1968)* (Lanham, MD: University Press of America, 2009); William L. Van DeBurg, *New Day in Babylon: The Black Power Movement and American Culture, 1965–1975* (Chicago: The University of Chicago Press, 1992); John T. McCartney, *Black Power Ideologies: An Essay in African-American Political Thought* (Philadelphia: Temple University Press, 1992); Peniel E. Joseph, *Waiting 'Til the Midnight Hour: A Narrative History of Black Power in America* (New York: Henry Holt and Company, 2006); Jeffrey C. Ogbar, *Black Power: Radical Politics and African American Identity* (Baltimore: Johns Hopkins University Press, 2004).

22. See Allen, supra note 2, at 132–161; Harding, supra note 15, at 194–195; Chuck Stone, "The National Conference on Black Power," in *The Black Power Revolt*, ed. Floyd B. Barbour (Boston: Sargent, 1968), 189. Further evidence of the elasticity of the slogan is provided by a more recent book by Theodore Cross, *The Black Power Imperative: Racial Inequality and the Politics of Nonviolence* (New York: Faulkner, 1984). Cross uses the concept of Black Power as an organizing idea for a clearly integrationist-oriented, antinationalist argument.

23. See Pinkney, supra note 2, at 64 ("The introduction of the concept of Black power was the beginning of the current spread of nationalist sentiment among Afro-Americans, and signaled the decline of integration as the dominant thrust of the Black movement."); Wagstaff, supra note 3, 103 ("The Black Power Movement is a conscious attempt to harness the emotional power of Black Nationalism to a practical program for the elimination of racial oppression in America."); Weisbrot, supra note 14, at 169–170, 236–256.

24. For discussions of the mainstream reactions to the slogan "Black Power" from which these examples are drawn and from which my analysis proceeds, see Allen, supra note 2, at 66–67; Carson, supra note 14, at 153–243; Manning Marable, "Black Nationalism in the 1970s: Through the Prism of Race and Class," *Socialist Review* 10 (March–June 1980): 66–72. For empirical research on white and Black reactions to the term "Black Power," see Joel D. Aberbach and Jack L. Walker, "The Meanings of Black Power: A Comparison of White and Black Interpretations of a Political Slogan," *American Political Science Review* 64(1970): 367, 370 (interviewed 855 whites and Blacks in Detroit asking, "What do the words 'Black power' mean to you?"; the largest percentage of whites said that the words meant "Black rules white," while about 65% of Blacks said the words meant "nothing," "a fair share for Black people," or "racial unity"). For discussions of the reactions to "Black Power" as reverse racism, see Martin Duberman, "Black Power in America," *Partisan Review* (Winter 1968): 34–48 (ambiguity in the phrase "Black Power" derives from a failure in clarity or frankness on the part of its advocates; the dangers of Black racism in "Black Power" are real and not the invention of frightened white liberals); Paul Feldman, "How the Cry for 'Black Power' Began," *Dissent* 13(1966): 472 (reactions to Black Power include thoughts of racial war, "racism in reverse," and actual withdrawal of support from the civil rights movement). See also Charles E. Fager, *White Reflections on Black Power* (Grand Rapids, MI: W. B. Eerdmans Publishing Company, 1967), 41–63, 83–96; Powledge, supra note 21; Scott and Brockreide, "The Rhetoric of Black Power: Order and Disorder in the Future," in *Rhetoric,* supra note 21, at 194, 204.

25. Address by Hubert Humphrey, 57th Annual NAACP Convention (July 6, 1966), reprinted in *Rhetoric,* supra note 21, at 65, 71.

26. Roy Wilkins, "Whither 'Black Power?'" *The Crisis* 73(1966): 353–354, reprinted

in *Black Protest Thought in the Twentieth Century*, eds. Meier and Rudwick, supra note 2 (excerpts from keynote address delivered at the 57th NAACP Annual Convention, July 5, 1966).

27. Carson, supra note 14, at 22.

28. Editorial, "The Black Neo-Segregationists," *The Crisis* 74(1967): 439–40 (editorial), reprinted in *Black Protest Thought in the Twentieth Century*, eds. Meier and Rudwick, supra note 2, 598–604.

29. For further examples of writers identifying Black Power as racism, see Oliver Cox, *Race Relations: Elements and Social Dynamics* (Detroit: Wayne State University Press, 1976), 210–218, 298–302; Samuel D. Cook, "The Tragic Myth of Black Power," *New South* 21 (Summer 1966): 58 ("[T]he slogan 'Black Power' does have, when words, context, shorn of pretensions, hypocrisy and intellectual dishonesty and program are combined, a generic or core meaning, and that meaning is racist."); Herbert Wechsler, "Killers of the Dream," *Progressive* (December 1966): 12. For a more complicated association of Black Power with racial domination that locates Black Power proponents on the dominated side of the relationship, see *Report of the National Advisory Commission on Civil Disorders* (New York: Bantam, 1968), 235 ("Black Power advocates ... function as an accommodation to white racism ... reminiscent of Booker T. Washington.") Several "moderate" Black leaders, including Roy Wilkins, Whitney Young, Jr., Bayard Rustin, Bishop Carey Gibbs (leader of the AME Church), Dorothy Height (president of the National Council of Negro Women), and Marion Bryant (president of the National Association of Negro Business and Professional Women's Clubs) issued a statement that appeared in an advertisement in the *New York Times* and Black-owned newspapers across the country, denouncing "any strategies of violence, reprisal or vigilantism" and rejecting "the way of separatism, either moral or spatial." The statement declared that Blacks fighting and dying in Vietnam were more representative of the Black community than those Blacks who were rioting in the streets (advertisement published in *New York Times* [October 14, 1966], 35, col. 3, reprinted in "Crisis and Commitment," *Crisis* 73[1966]: 474). See also Thomas A. Johnson, "Negro Leaders Issue a Statement of Principles Repudiating 'Black Power' Concepts," *New York Times* (October 14, 1966), 27, col. 2. Interestingly, King's response was more ambiguous. To the extent the "Black Power" slogan was associated with a renunciation of the principle of nonviolence or with separatism and withdrawal from the struggle for equality, he was clearly opposed. However, he saw positive aspects to the concept in terms of building race pride and solidarity in political and economic struggles. See King, supra note 16, at 23–66. See also Garrow, supra note 15, at 475–574; Scott, "Black Power Bends Martin Luther King," in *Rhetoric*, supra note 21, at 166 (describing King's utilization of Black Power imagery in speech to Tenth Anniversary Convention of the SCLC shortly before he was assassinated).

For a critique of the Black Power/nationalist turn from the viewpoint of a Black socialist who saw the issue as fundamentally strategic, see Bayard Rustin, "'Black Power' and Coalition Politics," *Commentary* (September 1966): 35.

30. Carmichael and Hamilton, supra note 10, at 54.

31. Browne, supra note 1, at 7.

32. See supra notes 3 and 5 and infra note 33.

33. This program characterized the early colonization efforts, as well as Garvey's Back to Africa movement and the Black Muslims' program. See supra note 5. See also the "Republic of New Africa" movement's proposal that the states of Mississippi, Louisiana, Alabama, Georgia, and South Carolina be ceded by the U.S. government for the creation of an independent Black nation, along with the payment of $200 billion in reparations. See Robert Brisbane, *Black Activism: Racial Revolution in the United States, 1954–1970* (Valley Forge, PA: Judson Press, 1974), 183–185; Pinkney, supra note 2, at 125–126; Robert Sherrill, "Birth of a (Black) Nation," *Esquire* (January 1969): 70, 72.

34. Draper complains that a nationalist ideology is incoherent without geographic separation rooted in sovereignty over land. Draper, supra note 1, at 120–125, 131–147, 168–181. I believe that Draper has an overly formalistic and traditional view of nationhood and sovereignty. All that Draper proves is that the language of "nationhood" does not precisely match the way that "nations" were recognized in a particular world order that, at least in the 1960s, was explicitly linked to the African American situation through an analysis centering around the concept of "colonialism." See infra text accompanying Chapter 4 notes 25–27. See e.g. Allen, supra note 2, at 1–14; Carmichael and Hamilton, supra note 10, at 3–32 (discussing the "colonial situation" in America under which policies are based on subordinating a racial group and maintaining control); Pinkney, supra note 2, at 3–13; Robert Staples, *Introduction to Black Sociology* (New York: McGraw-Hill, 1976), 13–14, 300–310.

35. The phrase originated with Delany (Delany, supra note 3, at 203). Delany has been called "the first major Negro nationalist." See Lerone Bennett, Jr., *Before the Mayflower: A History of the Negro in America, 1619–1966* (Chicago: Johnson Publishing Co., 1966), 137. However, Draper argues that "Delany's Black nationalism was based on unrequited love on rejection by whites" (Draper, supra note 1, at 24). For more inspiring views of Delany, see Carlisle, supra note 2, at 67–84; Pinkney, supra note 2, at 23.

36. "[T]he central significance of Black Nationalism is the emergence of Black group-consciousness, self-assertion and cultural identity" (Turner, supra note 14, at 8).

37. The idea that African Americans have created a distinct culture that is not reducible to class or Americanism has been a controversial notion in the fields of sociology and anthropology. For example, it was long the dominant view that African Americans have no ethnic culture, but instead "the Negro is only an American and nothing else. He has no values and culture to guard and protect" (Nathan Glazer and Daniel Patrick Moynihan, *Beyond the Melting Pot* [Boston: MIT Press, 1963], 53). For other writers articulating the same idea, see E. Franklin Frazier, *The Negro Family in the United States*, rev. ed. (Chicago: University of Chicago Press, 1957), 680–681; Gunnar Myrdal, *An American Dilemma: The Negro Problem and Modern Democracy* (New York: Harper & Bros., 1944), 928 ("In practically all of its divergencies American Negro culture is not something independent of general American culture. It is a distorted development, or a pathological condition of American culture."); Robert Park, *Race and Culture* (Glencoe, IL: The Free Press, 1950), 231–243; Kenneth M. Stampp, *The Peculiar Institution:*

Slavery in the Antebellum South (New York: Vintage, 1956), vii ("[S]laves were merely ordinary human beings.... [I]nnately Negroes *are*, after all, only white men with black skins, nothing more, nothing less").

For criticism of this tradition in social science, see Robert Blauner, *Racial Oppression in America* (New York: HarperCollins College, 1972), 124–155; Ralph Ellison, "An American Dilemma: A Review," in *Shadow and Act* (New York: Random House, 1964); Staples, supra note 34, at 6–9; William J. Wilson, *Power, Racism, and Privilege: Race Relations in Theoretical and Sociohistorical Perspectives* (New York: Macmillan, 1973), 143; Abd-l Hakimu Ibn Alkalimat, "The Ideology of Black Social Science," in *The Death of White Sociology*, ed. Joyce Ladner (New York: Random House, 1973) (linking prejudice, discrimination, and segregation as key elements of restrictive "white" ideology about racism), at xxiii.

For discussions of the need to analyze a unique African American culture, see Lerone Bennett, Jr., *The Challenge of Blackness* (Chicago: Johnson Publishing Co., 1972) (discussing the vision of racism as a mental error), at 1–43, 293–312; Addison Gayle, ed., *The Black Aesthetic* (New York: Doubleday, 1971); Henry L. Gates, ed., *Black Literature and Literary Theory* (London: Methuen & Co., 1984); James E. Blackwell, *The Black Community: Diversity and Unity* (New York: Harper & Row, 1985); Janice E. Hale-Benson, *Black Children: Their Roots, Culture, and Learning Styles* (Salt Lake City: Brigham Young University Press, 1982); Charles Keil, *Urban Blues* (Chicago: University of Chicago Press, 1966); Thomas Kochman, *Black and White Styles in Conflict* (Chicago: University of Chicago Press, 1982); Joyce A. Ladner, *Tomorrow's Tomorrow: The Black Woman* (New York: Doubleday, 1971); Alphonso Pinkney, *Black Americans* (Englewood Cliffs, NJ: Prentice Hall, 1969); Staples, supra note 34; Amiri Baraka, "A Black Value System," *Black Scholar* 1 (November 1969): 54–60; Badi Foster, "Toward a Definition of Black Referents," in *Beyond Black and White: An Alternative America*, eds. Vernon J. Nixon and Badi Foster (Boston: Little, Brown & Co., 1971); LeRoi Jones, "The Need for a Cultural Base to Civil Rites & Bpower Mooments," in *The Black Power Revolt*, ed. Floyd B. Barbour (Boston: Sargent, 1968), 119; Kwasi B. Konadu, *A View from the East: Black Cultural Nationalism and Education in New York City* (Syracuse, NY: Syracuse University Press, 2009).

Black nationalist descriptions of the character of African American culture have roughly divided between an emphasis on African roots in the Pan-Africanism tradition (see e.g. Baraka, supra) and the description of a unique Afro-American culture and community (see e.g. Cruse, *Rebellion or Revolution*, supra note 2, at 48–138). See generally Norman E. Whitten and John F. Szwed, eds., *Afro-American Anthropology: Contemporary Perspectives* (New York: The Free Press, 1970); Pinkney, supra note 2, at 127–150; Jennifer Jordan, "Cultural Nationalism in the 1960s: Politics and Poetry," in *Race, Politics, and Culture: Critical Essays on the Radicalism of the 1960s*, ed. Adolph Reed, Jr. (Westport, CT: Greenwood Press, 1986), 29–60; Yvonne V. Jones, "African American Cultural Nationalism," in *Cultural Portrayals of African Americans: Creating An Ethnic/Racial Identity*, ed. Janis F. Hutchinson (Westport, CT: Greenwood, 1997); Scott Brown, *Fighting for US: Maulana Karenga, the US Organization, and Black Cultural Nationalism*

(New York: NYU Press, 2003); Dana Williams and Sandra Shannon, eds., *August Wilson and Black Aesthetics* (New York: Palgrave Macmillan, 2004).

38. Turner, supra note 14, at 7–8 (quoting an address by Clarence Munford, "Black National Revolution in America," Utah State University, May 1970).

39. Liberals typically associate the phenomenon of nationalism in general with irrationality, danger, and regression. The invocation of organic communities is identified with status-based feudalism and group irrationality; emotional "patriotism" to country is the mark of backwardness.

40. Along with Clarence Munford and James Turner, Cruse's conception of Black nationalism exemplifies the historicist perspective I believe marked the intellectual and theoretical advances made in the Black nationalist position in the 1960s. See Cruse, *The Crisis of the Negro Intellectual,* supra note 2, at 20–44, 544–565; Cruse, *Rebellion or Revolution,* supra note 2, at 48–138, 193–258; Harold Cruse, "The Fire This Time?" *New York Review of Books* (May 8, 1969): 13–18.

41. Carmichael and Hamilton, supra note 10, at 54–55.

42. See Cruse, *Plural but Equal,* supra note 7, at 1–52, 192–202, 244–260; Cruse, *Rebellion or Revolution,* supra note 2, at 51–65.

43. Carmichael and Hamilton, supra note 10, at 55.

44. Browne, supra note 1. See also Frazier, supra note 37.

45. Cruse, *The Crisis of the Negro Intellectual,* supra note 2, at 283.

46. Id. at 234. For further examples of the association of integration with assimilation to white norms, see Derrick Bell, *And We Are Not Saved: The Elusive Quest for Racial Justice* (New York: Basic Books, 1987), 110, discussing Ray C. Rist, *The Invisible Children: School Integration in American Society* (Cambridge, MA: Harvard University Press, 1978) and stating that "Rist … followed … a group of young Black children bused to an upper class, mainly white school. The principal's policy was to 'treat all the kids just alike.' This evenhanded policy meant—in practice—that the handful of Black children from the ghetto were expected to perform and behave no differently than did the white children from comfortable suburbs in this mainly white school where the curriculum, texts, and teaching approaches were designed for the middle-class white kids. As you can imagine, the results of this evenhanded integration were disastrous."

See also Cruse, *Rebellion or Revolution,* supra note 2, at 48–125; Cruse, *The Crisis of the Negro Intellectual,* supra note 2, at 7–9, 64–95, 240–252. See e.g. Allen, supra note 2, at 101; Staples, supra note 34, at 35–36, 251–254, 301 (public schools are an important site for the transmission of the white majority's worldview); Alkalimat, supra note 37, at 175–183; Browne, supra note 1; Robert Chrisman, "The Formation of a Revolutionary Black Culture," *Black Scholar* 1 (June 1970): 2 (analyzes integrationism as the co-optation of the Black middle class to white culture accomplished through the clash between race and class interests); Ladner, Introduction, supra note 37, at xxiii (Blacks "have been considered to be a deviation from an ambiguous white middle-class model"); Alvin F. Poussaint, "The Negro American: His Self-Image and Integration," *Journal of the National Medical Association* 58(1966): 419.

47. See Cruse, *The Crisis of the Negro Intellectual,* supra note 2, at 64–95; John O.

Calmore, "Fair Housing vs. Fair Housing: The Problems with Providing Increased Housing Opportunities through Spatial Deconcentration," *Clearinghouse Review* 14(May 1980): 7 (discussing impact of integrationist housing policy on African American communities).

48. Stokely Carmichael, *Stokely Speaks: Black Power Back to Pan-Africanism* (New York: Random House, 1971), 39. See also Cruse, *Rebellion or Revolution*, supra note 2, at 72 (the trend toward integrationism has "favored the eradication of the Negro community as a symbol of segregation"); id. at 33–67 (criticizing integrationism in the arts as entailing destruction of African American cultural forms in favor of an already despiritualized and deadened European tradition).

49. See Derrick Bell, "The Chronicle of the Sacrificed Black Schoolchildren," in Bell, *And We Are Not Saved*, supra note 46, 102, 109 (citing *amicus curiae* brief for the National Educational Association, *United States v. Georgia*, 445 F.2d 303 [5th Cir. 1971]) (for empirical data on burden borne by Black teachers, administrators, and students by school integration); Cruse, *Plural but Equal*, supra note 7, at 20–24 (public school integration resulted in loss of traditional Black educator class); Blackwell, supra note 37, at 107–110 (same); Adam Fairclough, *A Class of Their Own: Black Teachers in the Segregated South* (Cambridge, MA: Harvard University Press, 2007).

50. See e.g. Kimberlé W. Crenshaw, "Foreword: Toward a Race-Conscious Pedagogy in Legal Education," *National Black Law Journal* 11(1989): 1, 2–6 (describing typical law school classes as assuming white perspective under the guise of "perspectivelessness"); Douglas Davidson, "The Furious Passage of the Black Graduate Student," in *The Death of White Sociology*, ed. Joyce Ladner (New York: Random House, 1973), 23 (describing graduate education as based on white norms); Charles V. Hamilton, "An Advocate of Black Power Defines It," in *Rhetoric*, supra note 21, at 190–191 (discussing ways that Black-controlled schools would be reorganized to reflect the culture of the Black community); Miller, supra note 2 (describing the cultural alienation of Black students from predominantly white colleges); Jason Sokol, *There Goes My Everything: White Southerners in the Age of Civil Rights, 1945–1975* (New York: Knopf, 2006).

For more general discussions of the idea that dominant images of neutrality and objectivity reflect white, European culture, see Jones, *The Need for a Cultural Base*, supra note 37; Chrisman, supra note 46, at 2–6; Milton M. Gordon, *Assimilation in American Life: The Role of Race, Religion and National Origins* (New York: Oxford University Press, 1964), 9 (the central images of American culture are the expressions of white Anglo-Saxon Protestant ethnic consciousness).

This concept is aptly illustrated by the Black Intelligence Test of Cultural Homogeneity, or BITCH test—a test oriented toward the language, attitudes, and lifestyles of African Americans. White students perform poorly on this test in comparison to Blacks, suggesting the existence of important dissimilarities in the cultural and educational backgrounds of Blacks and whites (Robert L. Williams, "The BITCH-100: A Culture-Specific Test," presented at the American Psychological Association Annual Convention, Honolulu, HI, September 1972, available at http://www.eric.ed.gov:80/PDFS/ED070799.pdf).

51. For discussions of the racial impact of student classification schemes, see Cross,

supra note 22, at 488–495, 668; Jeannie Oakes, *Keeping Track: How Schools Structure Inequality*, (New Haven, CT: Yale University Press, 2005); David L. Kirp, "Schools as Sorters: The Constitutional and Policy Implications of Student Classifications," *University of Pennsylvania Law Review* 121(1973): 705; Tom Loveless, *The Tracking Wars: State Reform Meets School Policy* (Washington, DC: Brookings Institution Press, 1999); Kevin Welner and Carol Corbett Burris, "Alternative Approaches to the Politics of Detracking," *Theory into Practice* 45(2006): 90–99.

52. See Staples, supra note 34, at 36–38 (poverty has come to replace race as explanation for disparate Black performance in schools); Gary Peller, "Creation, Evolution and the New South," *Tikkun* (November–December 1987): 74–75 (same).

53. Cruse, *The Crisis of the Negro Intellectual*, supra note 2, at 283.

54. See Blauner, supra note 37, at 288–294 (discussing white liberal faculty opposition to African American studies programs); Naomi Levine and Richard Cohen, *Ocean Hill-Brownsville: Schools in Crisis* (New York: Popular Press, 1969), 39, 56 (describing liberal opposition to community control movements as implemented by the New York Board of Education).

55. The most well-known movement for community control occurred in the Ocean Hill-Brownsville area of Brooklyn, New York, where the City agreed to the establishment of an experimental school district over which local parents would have authority. When the local committee requested the transfer of several teachers to schools outside their neighborhood, the teachers' union went on strike citywide, and relations in New York, in particular between Jews and African Americans, reached high levels of hostility. For an account of the Ocean Hill-Brownsville movement, see Martin Mayer, "The Full and Sometimes Very Surprising Story of Ocean Hill, the Teachers' Union and the Teacher Strikes of 1968," *New York Times Magazine* (February 2, 1969): 18. See also Cruse, *Plural but Equal*, supra note 7, at 246–248; Levine and Cohen, supra note 54; Maurice R. Berube and Marilyn Gittell, eds., *Confrontation at Ocean Hill-Brownsville: The New York School Strikes of 1968* (New York: Praeger, 1969); Robert Bendiner, *The Politics of Schools: A Crisis in Self-Government* (New York: Harper & Row, 1969); Cox, supra note 29, at 182–188; Tom Brooks, "Tragedy at Ocean Hill," *Dissent* 16(1969): 28; Leonard Fein, "Community Schools and Social Theory: The Limits of Universalism," in *Community Control of Schools*, ed. Henry M. Levin (Washington, DC: Brookings Institution Press, 1970); Robert Maynard, "Black Nationalism and Community Schools," in *Community Control of Schools*, ed. Henry M. Levin (Washington, DC.: Brookings Institution Press, 1970); Rhody A. McCoy, "The Formation of a Community-Controlled School District," in *Community Control of Schools*, ed. Henry M. Levin (Washington, DC.: Brookings Institution Press, 1970).

The Ocean Hill-Brownsville movement was the best known of several community-control-of-schools movements influenced by the Black Power movement. For accounts of other movements, see also Paul Lauter, "The Short, Happy Life of the Adams-Morgan Community School Project," *Harvard Educational Review* 38(1968): 235 (detailing the origin of the Adams-Morgan project in Washington, D.C. and the ensuing difficulties inherent in such projects); Jason Epstein, "The Politics of School Decentralization,"

New York Review of Books (June 1968): 26–32 (describing movements in Washington, D.C., and East Harlem).

On the movement for the creation of African American Studies, see Allen, supra note 2, at 215–220; Pinkney, supra note 30, at 177–198; Roger A. Fischer, "Ghetto and Gown: The Birth of Black Studies," *Current History* 57(1969): 290; Stephen Lythcott, "The Case for Black Studies," *Antioch Review* 29(1969): 149; James Turner, "Black Students and Their Changing Perspective," *Ebony* (August 1969): 135. See also Alan B. Ballard, *The Education of Black Folk: The Afro-American Struggle for Knowledge in White America* (New York: Harper, 1974); Armstead L. Robinson, Craig C. Foster, and Donald H. Ogilvie, *Black Studies in the University* (New Haven, CT: Yale University Press, 1969); James McEvoy and Abraham H. Miller, eds., *Black Power and Student Rebellion* (Berkeley, CA: Wadsworth Publishing, 1969); Harry Edwards, *Black Students* (New York: The Free Press, 1970). The most notorious episode in the movement for African American Studies curricula occurred at Cornell University in 1968–1969, when African American students demanded an autonomous Afro-American Studies Department and separate living quarters. During the course of the movement, there were several confrontations, including the seizure of the student union building during Parents' Weekend in April 1969. After several attempts by white students to evict them, the African American students acquired guns, and when they finally gave up the occupation, they left in military formation, bearing arms—a scene that was plastered on the front page of newspapers across the country. For various descriptions, see Allan Bloom, *The Closing of the American Mind* (New York: Simon & Schuster, 1987), 91–97, 315–318, 347–356; Cushing Strout and David I. Grossvogel, eds., *Divided We Stand: Reflections on the Crisis at Cornell* (New York: Doubleday, 1970); Draper, supra note 1, at 151–162; Edwards, supra note 55, at 158–183; Pinkney, supra note 37, at 182–183; Thomas Sowell, *Black Education: Myths and Tragedies* (New York: David McKay Co., 1972), 112–118, 192-99; William H. Friedland and Harry Edwards, "Confrontation at Cornell," *Trans-Action* (June 1969): 29.

See generally Delores P. Aldridge, "Status of Africana/Black Studies in Higher Education in the U.S.," in *Out of the Revolution: The Development of Africana Studies*, eds. Delores P. Aldridge and Carlene Young (Lanham, MD: Lexington Books, 2000); William H. Exum, *Paradoxes of Protest: Black Student Activism in a White University* (Philadelphia: Temple University Press, 1985); Robert Harris, Jr., "The Intellectual and Institutional Development of Africana Studies," in *Three Essays: Black Studies in the United States*, eds. Robert L. Harris, Jr., Darlene Clark Hine, and Nellie McKay (New York: The Ford Foundation, 1990); Fabio Rojas, *From Black Power to Black Studies: How a Radical Social Movement Became an Academic Discipline* (Baltimore: Johns Hopkins University Press, 2007).

56. Fein, supra note 55, at 92.

57. Id. at 94.

58. See Blauner, supra note 37, at 267 ("The liberal is uncomfortable with the consciousness of color. Again, unlike the conservative, particularly the Southern breed, the liberal does not like to think of himself as white ..."); Joseph Sobran, "Book Review:

Plural but Equal: Blacks and Minorities in America's Plural Society," *National Review* (September 11, 1987): 64 ("For most [whites,] liberal or conservative, race is an embarrassing residual category, something we should have gotten beyond by now.").

59. See Staples, supra note 34, at 260–261; Richard Delgado, "The Imperial Scholar: Reflections on a Review of Civil Rights Literature," *University of Pennsylvania Law Review* 132(1984): 561, 566–573.

60. Bennett, supra note 35, at 35–36.

61. See Alkalimat, supra note 37, at 188 (criticizing conventional social-science assumption that "society evolves to a higher level based on more universalistic rational standards of operation"); Davidson, supra note 43, at 27–42; Nathan Hare, "The Challenge of a Black Scholar," in *The Death of White Sociology,* ed. Joyce Ladner (New York: Random House, 1973), 67–78; Dennis Forsythe, "Radical Sociology and Blacks," in *The Death of White Sociology,* ed. Joyce Ladner (New York: Random House, 1973), 213 (criticizing mainstream sociology's "ideology of objectivity"). See also Harold Cruse, "Black and White: Outlines of the Next Stage," *Black World* (January 1971): 19 (emphasizing the centrality of culture as a unifying concept for African American studies and arguing that African American studies should mean the construction of new interpretative paradigms related to Black culture, rather than simply focusing existing scholarly assumptions on Black subjects); Harold Cruse, "Part 2: Black and White: Outlines of the Next Stage," *Black World* (March 1971): 4, 13 (criticizing the "liberal consensus" of mainstream scholarship for "reflecting a 'universalist' stance in interpretation").

62. Hare, supra note 61, at 68–69, citing Thorstein Veblen, *The Theory of the Leisure Class* (New York: The Modern Library, 1934).

63. See Joyce Ladner, "Tomorrow's Tomorrow: The Black Woman," in *The Death of White Sociology,* ed. Joyce Ladner (New York: Random House, 1973), 414, 420–421. Ladner writes that "the relationship between the researcher and his subjects ... resembles that of the oppressor and the oppressed, because it is the oppressor who defines the problem, the nature of the research, and to some extent, the quality of the interaction between him and his subjects.... [White sociologists'] inability to understand the nature and effects of neo-colonialism in the same manner as black people is rooted in the inherent bias of the social sciences. The basic concepts and tools of white Western society are permeated by this partiality to the conceptual framework of the oppressor.... Simply put, the slave and his master do not view and respond to the world in the same way.... 'George Washington and George Washington's slaves lived different realities. And if we extend that insight to all the dimensions of white American history we will realize that blacks lived at a different time and a different reality in this country. And the terrifying implications of all this is that there is another time, another reality, another America.'" Id. (quoting Bennett, supra note 30, at 39).

For more general discussions of the links between epistemology and power, see Jürgen Habermas, *Knowledge and Human Interests,* trans. Jeremy J. Shapiro (Boston: Beacon Press, 1971); Karl Mannheim, *Ideology and Utopia: An Introduction to the Sociology of Knowledge,* trans. Louis Wirth and Edward Shils (New York: Harcourt, Brace & Co., 1936); Michel Foucault, "Truth and Power," in *Power/Knowledge: Selected Interviews and Other Writings, 1972–1977,* ed. Colin Gordon (New York: Pantheon, 1980); Alvin W. Gouldner, "Anti-Minotaur: The Myth of a Value-Free Sociology," *Social Problems* 9(Winter 1962).

64. Albert Murray, "White Norms, Black Deviation," in *The Death of White Sociology,* ed. Ladner, supra note 63, 96.

65. Alkalimat, supra note 37, at 175–181.

66. Cleaver, *Soul on Ice,* supra note 9, at 145–173. See also Stanley Pacion, "Still Soul on Ice," *Dissent* 15(1969): 310, 313–315 (discussing Cleaver's mind/body and sexual frame for analyzing racial relations); Norman Mailer, in "Black Power: A Discussion," supra note 21, at 218 (discussing challenge of Black Power as a critique of dominant white culture marked by the elevation of the head and the repression of the body); Gary Peller, "Reason and the Mob: The Politics of Representation," *Tikkun* (July–August 1987): 28 (arguing that the reason/desire dichotomy is the language of a particular technique of power and subordination).

67. Cleaver, *Soul on Ice,* supra note 9, at 145–173.

68. Id.

69. Hare, supra note 61, at 74. Hare concluded that the Black scholar has a different mission than that of the white scholar. The challenge facing the Black scholar "is to cleanse his mind—and the minds of his people—of the white colonial attitudes toward scholarship and people as well. This includes the icons of objectivity, amoral knowledge and its methodology, and the total demolition of the antisocial attitudes of Ivory-Towerism." Id. at 78. See also Robert Staples, "What Is Black Sociology? Toward a Sociology of Black Liberation," in *The Death of White Sociology,* ed. Ladner, supra note 63, 163–168. Staples argues that prevalent "structuralist-functionalist" model of sociological inquiry is oriented toward the assumption of stability in social structure, whereas Black sociologists should be oriented toward the transformation of the social order. "[I]f white sociology is the science of oppression, Black sociology must be the science of liberation." Id. at 168.

For a general exposition of the idea that social position structures perception and experience of the world so that there can be no universal category of "knowledge," see Georg Lukács, "Reification and the Consciousness of the Proletariat," in *History and Class Consciousness: Studies in Marxist Dialectics,* trans. Rodney Livingstone (London: The Merlin Press Ltd., 1971) (focusing on economic class).

70. See Staples, supra note 34.

71. See Cruse, *Plural but Equal,* supra note 7, at 53–58, 280–286, 362–370 (criticizing the conjunction of racial status with gender, immigrant, and minority status).

72. For descriptions of the movements for reparations in the late 1960s and 1970s, see Robert S. Lecky and H. Elliot Wright, eds., *Black Manifesto: Religion, Racism, and Reparations* (New York: Sheed & Ward, 1969) (collection of views from the religious community on the reparations controversy); Bell, supra note 46, at 123–139 (hypothetical discussion of the broad social changes that serious racial reparations might have effected); Brisbane, supra note 33, at 186–190 (discussing James Forman's Black Manifesto movement for reparations). For a more recent work linking race consciousness and a program

of reparations, see Mari J. Matsuda, "Looking to the Bottom: Critical Legal Studies and Reparations," *Harvard Civil Rights–Civil Liberties Law Review* 22(1987): 323. For analyses of the legal dimensions of Black nationalist demands for reparations, see Boris I. Bittker, *The Case for Black Reparations* (Boston: Beacon Press, 1973); Graham Hughes, "Reparations for Blacks?" *New York University Law Review* 43(1968): 1063. The literature on reparations has grown dramatically. See e.g. William Kweku Asare, *Slavery Reparations in Perspective* (Victoria, BC: Trafford, 2002); William L. Banks, *The Case against Black Reparations* (Haverford, PA: Infinity Publishing, 2001); Alfred L. Brophy, *Reconstructing the Dreamland: The Tulsa Riot of 1921—Race, Reparation, and Reconciliation* (New York: Oxford University Press, 2002); J. Angelo Corlett, *Race, Racism, & Reparations* (Ithaca, NY: Cornell University Press, 2003); Joe L. Feagin, *Racist America: Roots, Current Realities, and Future Reparations* (New York: Routledge, 2000); David Horowitz, *Uncivil Wars: The Controversy over Reparations for Slavery* (San Francisco: Encounter Books, 2002); Clarence J. Munford, *Race and Reparations: A Black Perspective for the 21st Century* (Trenton, NJ: Africa World Press, 1996); Randall Robinson, *The Debt: What America Owes to Blacks* (New York: Dutton, 2000); Raymond A. Winbush, ed., *Should America Pay? Slavery and the Raging Debate over Reparations* (New York: Amistad, 2003).

73. Cruse, *The Crisis of the Negro Intellectual,* supra note 2, at 91.

74. The term was first used in a comprehensive analysis of the situation of African Americans by Harold Cruse, "Revolutionary Nationalism and the Afro-American," *Studies on the Left* 2(1962): 12–13. See also Harold Cruse, "An Afro-American's Cultural Views," in *Rebellion or Revolution*, supra note 2, at 48–67 (first published in *Presence Africaine*, December 1957–January 1958, at 31); Harold Cruse, "Negro Nationalism's New Wave," *New Leader* (March 19, 1962): 16. By the mid-1960s, the neocolonial analogy was widely used by Black nationalists. See e.g. Alkalimat, supra note 37, at 183–188; Robert Allen, *Black Awakening in Capitalist America: An Analytic History* (New York: Doubleday, 1969), 5–17; Blackwell, supra note 37, at 12–14; James Boggs and Grace L. Boggs, *Revolution and Evolution in the Twentieth Century* (New York: Monthly Review Press, 1974); Carmichael and Hamilton, supra note 10, at 2–56; Cleaver, *Eldridge Cleaver: Post-Prison Writings and Speeches,* supra note 9, at 57–72; Huey Newton, *Essays from the Minister of Defense Huey Newton* (1968), 2–10; Pinkney, supra note 2, at 8–13; Staples, supra note 34, at 13–14; William K. Tabb, *The Political Economy of the Black Ghetto* (New York: W. W. Norton & Co., 1970); "The Black Panther Party Platform and Program," in *Black Liberation Politics,* supra note 13. See also Jack O'Dell, "A Special Variety of Colonialism," *Freedomways* (Winter 1967): 1. Blauner summarizes the analysis of Black communities through the colonialist metaphor by focusing on four elements of colonization: (1) the colonized subjects enter the system involuntarily; (2) the subjects' indigenous culture is transformed or destroyed; (3) the subjects are managed or controlled by those outside their own ethnic status; and (4) racism prevails or the group is oppressed psychologically and socially by an outside group that conceives of itself as superior. Black communities are an example of the colonization process in that they are controlled politically, economically, and administratively from the outside,

distinguishing them from the voluntary ethnic business and social communities of the Poles, Jews, Italians, and Irish (Blauner, supra note 37, at 83–89).

75. Cruse, *Rebellion or Revolution,* supra note 2, at 76.

76. Cleaver, *Eldridge Cleaver: Post-Prison Writings and Speeches,* supra note 9, at 57–72.

77. See Chrisman, supra note 46; Cruse, *Rebellion or Revolution,* supra note 2. Nationalists speaking in terms of "colonialism" tended to cite Frantz Fanon, *Studies in a Dying Colonialism,* trans. Constance Farrington (New York: Monthly Review Press, 1965); Frantz Fanon, *The Wretched of the Earth,* trans. Constance Farrington (New York: Grove Press, 1965); Frantz Fanon, *Black Skin, White Masks,* trans. Charles L. Markmann (New York: Grove Press, 1967); Albert Memmi, *The Colonizer and the Colonized,* trans. Howard Greenfield (New York: Orion Press, 1967).

78. Carmichael and Hamilton, supra note 10, at 86–87.

79. Cruse, *The Crisis of the Negro Intellectual,* supra note 2, at 91. See also Staples, supra note 34, at 205. Staples notes the structurally different interests of the Black middle class and predicts that "the emergence of a class of Black petty bourgeoisie who will undertake the exploitation of the Black masses that is now done directly by the White colonial power structure. Hence, we shall witness large numbers of Blacks being elected to public office, programs created to develop a Black capitalist class, and Black functionaries replacing Whites in the role of colonial mediating positions such as teachers, social workers, policemen, etc." Id. (citing Eldridge Cleaver, "The Crisis of the Black Bourgeoisie," *Black Scholar* [January 1973], 2–11).

Chapter 3

1. Kwsasi B. Konadu, *A View from the East: Black Cultural Nationalism and Education in New York City* (Syracuse, NY: Syracuse University Press, 2009) (detailing overlap of civil rights and Black Power proponents in concrete community education projects).

2. See generally Townsend Davis, *Weary Feet, Rested Souls: A Guided History of the Civil Rights Movement* (New York: W. W. Norton & Company, 1998); Taylor Branch, *At Canaan's Edge: America in the King Years, 1965–1968* (New York: Simon & Schuster, 2006); Taylor Branch, *Parting the Waters: America in the King Years, 1954–1963* (New York: Simon & Schuster, 1988); Taylor Branch, *Pillar of Fire: America in the King Years, 1963–1965* (New York: Simon & Schuster, 1998); Adam Fairclough, *To Redeem the Soul of America: The Southern Christian Leadership Conference & Martin Luther King* (Athens: University of Georgia Press, 1987); Eric Doner and Joshua Brown, *Forever Free: The Story of Emancipation and Reconstruction* (New York: Knopf, 2005); David J. Garrow, *Bearing the Cross: Martin Luther King and the Southern Christian Leadership Conference* (New York: Morrow, 1986); Clayborne Carson, *In Struggle: SNCC and the Black Awakening of the 1960s* (Cambridge, MA: Harvard University Press, 1981); Clayborne Carson, David J. Garrow, Bill Kovach, and Carol Polsgrove, eds., *Reporting Civil Rights: American Journalism 1941–1963* (New York: Library of America, 2003); Clayborne

Carson, David J. Garrow, Bill Kovach, and Carol Polsgrove, eds., *Reporting Civil Rights: American Journalism 1963–1973* (New York: Library of America, 2003); Juan Williams, *Eyes on the Prize: America's Civil Rights Years, 1954–1965* (New York: Penguin Books, 1987); Aldon D. Morris, *The Origins of the Civil Rights Movement: Black Communities Organizing for Change* (New York: The Free Press, 1984); Manning Marable, *Race, Reform and Rebellion: The Second Reconstruction in Black America, 1945–1982* (Biloxi: University Press of Mississippi, 1984); Ralph David Abernathy, *And the Walls Came Tumbling Down* (New York: Harper & Row, 1989); Mary Aickin, *A Case of Black and White: Northern Volunteers and Southern Freedom Summers, 1964–65* (Westport, CT: Greenwood Press, 1982); Johnny E. Williams, *African American Religion and the Civil Rights Movement in Arkansas* (Biloxi: University Press of Mississippi, 2003).

3. Martin Luther King, Jr., *Where Do We Go from Here: Chaos or Community?* (Boston: Beacon Press, 1968), 9.

4. The term appears in "An Experiment in Love," a sermon King delivered in 1958. Reproduced in Martin Luther King, Jr., *A Testament of Hope: The Essential Writings and Speeches of Martin Luther King, Jr.,* ed. James M. Washington (New York: HarperCollins, 1986), 16. See Charles Marsh, *The Beloved Community: How Faith Shapes Social Justice from the Civil Rights Movement to Today* (New York: Basic Books, 2005); Richard W. Wills, *Martin Luther King, Jr., and the Image of God* (New York: Oxford University Press, 2009), Chapter 6 (tracing roots of the Beloved community concept in Christianity and liberalism). For most white integrationists and many Black ones as well, the connection between the civil rights movement and Black churches was a source of background dissonance because it clashed with their comprehension of religion as representing irrationality and backwardness. Secular liberals soon came up with mediations for this incongruity. They attempted to translate the Christian character of King's discourse into a secular ethic, and to explain the prevalence of ministers among Black civil rights leaders and the central role of the Black church in the movement as merely a functional result of the lack of other organized Black institutions.

Perhaps the best-known testament to the integrationist vision is King's "I Have a Dream" speech: "I have a dream that one day on the red hills of Georgia, sons of former slaves and sons of former slave owners will be able to sit down together at the table of brotherhood .... I have a dream my four little children will one day live in a nation where they will not be judged by the color of their skin but by the content of their character." See Martin Luther King, Jr., "I Have a Dream," in King, *A Testament of Hope* (cited above), 219.

5. King himself attempted to explain the goal of the movement as the achievement of "Black Power" (Martin Luther King, Jr., "Black Power Defined," in King, *A Testament of Hope,* supra note 4, 303–312). See Michael Dyson, *I May Not Get There with You: The True Martin Luther King, Jr.* (New York: Touchstone, 2000); Marsh, supra note 4.

6. For a more general discussion about the cautionary attitude of many Black leaders toward direct-action protest, see Louis E. Lomax, *The Negro Revolt* (New York: New American Library, 1962), 167–168, 209; Robert Weisbrot, *Freedom Bound: A History of America's Civil Rights Movement* (W. W. Norton & Co., 1990), 30–44. See generally

Aldon D. Morris, *The Origins of the Civil Rights Movement: Black Communities Organizing for Change* (New York: The Free Press, 1984).

7. See Bertram Wilbur Doyle, *The Etiquette of Race Relations in the South: A Study in Social Control* (Chicago: University of Chicago Press, 1937) (describing the way that the social protocol developed during slavery continued during segregation); Sarah Patton Boyle, "Inside a Segregationist," in *White on Black: The Views of Twenty-Two White Americans on the Negro*, eds. E. B. Thompson and H. Nipson (Chicago: Johnson Publishing Co., 1963), 48 ("Good Negroes" and "Bad Negroes" distinguished by the former's "good humor," "cheerfulness," "contentment," and "gratitude," with the latter conceived as "dangerous" and "sub-human"); Lewis M. Killian, "White Southerners," in *Through Different Eyes: Black and White Perspectives on American Race Relations*, eds. Peter I. Rose, Stanley Rothman, and William J. Wilson (New York: Oxford University Press, 1973), 89, 96–101 (describing the Southern image of the "courteous, patient domestics ... so willing, so loving and so happy.... The worst indignity inflicted on black Southerners was that they were forced to act as accomplices in preserving the indifference of their oppressors."); Olive W. Quinn, "The Transmission of Racial Attitudes among White Southerners," *Social Forces* 33(1954) (discussing the subtle and pervasive way that the social protocol of race relations was transmitted among whites so that issues of race never reached the level of conscious choice or decision); Ariela Gross, *What Blood Won't Tell: A History of Race on Trial in America* (Cambridge, MA: Harvard University Press, 2008); William H. Chafe, *Civilities and Civil Rights: Greensboro, North Carolina, and the Black Struggle for Freedom* (New York: Oxford University Press, 1980). See also Tamotsu Shibutani and Kian M. Kwan, *Ethnic Stratification: A Comparative Approach* (New York: Macmillan, 1965), 318–321, 589 (describing symbolic social rituals signifying hierarchies between Blacks and whites in Southern society); Calvin Hernton, *Sex and Racism in America* (New York: Grove Press, 1965), 127–129 (describing white sexual exploitation of Black women and taboos on contact between Black men and white women); Jason Sokol, *There Goes My Everything: White Southerners in the Age of Civil Rights, 1945–1975* (New York: Knopf, 2006); cf. Paul B. Sheatsley, "White Attitudes toward the Negro," in *The Negro American*, eds. Talcott Parsons and Kenneth B. Clark (Boston: Houghton Mifflin, 1966), 303, 317 (concluding that survey data of the civil rights movement demonstrates that white attitudes have changed to recognize that integration is correct).

8. Sokol, supra note 7, at 12, 38, 57, 69–83, 98–102, 109–111, 224, 241, 291, 296.

9. See Branch, *Parting the Waters*, supra note 1, 190 (describing Marshall's hostility to the idea of utilizing tactics developed in the Montgomery Bus Boycott to achieve school integration).

10. See generally Morris, supra note 2.

11. See Herbert H. Haines, *Black Radicals and the Civil Rights Mainstream, 1954–1970* (Knoxville: University of Tennessee Press, 1988), 29–41 (describing King-led direct-action integrationism as a radical and disruptive force in the context of the late 1950s and early 1960s); Vincent Harding, *The Other American Revolution* (Los Angeles:

Center for Afro-American Studies, University of California, 1980), 194–195 (describing King's view of protest as not counting "on government goodwill but serv[ing] instead to compel unwilling authorities [sic.] to yield to the mandates of justice"); Morris, supra note 2 (describing the direct-action activities of the SCLC as confrontational as compared with the legalistic strategy of the NAACP); Robert L. Scott, *The Rhetoric of Black Power*, eds. R. L. Scott and W. Brockriede (New York: Harper & Row, 1969), 166–177 (describing King as a Black Power proponent before his death); James A. Colaiaco, "Martin Luther King, Jr., and the Paradox of Nonviolent Direct Action," *Phylon* 47(1986): 16–28 (emphasizing the disruptive quality of direct-action tactics despite their nonviolence); Killian, supra note 7, at 89, 96–102 (describing white Southern sense of a radical disruption of social order in the Montgomery Bus Boycott); id., 69–75, 106–111 (nonviolent direct action was not designed for test cases, but was a strategy to coerce negotiation, a "strategy of power, not persuasion. . . . While the apostles of nonviolence have spoken a language of love and reconciliation, their actions have moved steadily in the direction of a naked display of power."); Martin Luther King, Jr., "The Burning Truth in the South," in King, *A Testament of Hope*, supra note 1, 97 (relating nonviolent tactics to "the necessity of creating discord to alter established community patterns"). See also William J. Wilson, *Power, Racism, and Privilege: Race Relations in Theoretical and Sociohistorical Perspectives* (New York: Macmillan, 1973), 29–68, 131, 137 ("[T]he technique of nonviolence was in reality an aggressive manifestation of pressure.").

12. In this way, the transformation in liberal discourse from a belief in "colorblindness" in the 1960s (see Robert Blauner, *Racial Oppression in America* [New York: Harper & Row, 1972], 267) to a commitment to diversity and pluralism in the 1970s and 1980s can be seen as a partial accommodation to the nationalist position.

13. See Kwame Anthony Appiah, *Cosmopolitanism: Ethics in a World of Strangers* (New York: W. W. Norton & Co., 2006); Paul Gilroy, *After Empire: Multiculture or Postcolonial Melancholia* (New York: Columbia University Press, 2005); Amartya Sen, *Identity and Violence: The Illusion of Destiny* (New York: W. W. Norton & Co., 2006); Martha Nussbaum, *For Love of Country: Debating the Limits of Patriotism* (Boston: Beacon Press, 1996); Duncan Kennedy, "Radical Intellectuals in American Culture and Politics, or My Talk at the Gramsci Institute," *Rethinking Marxism* 1(1988): 121 (describing such a "creole" culture as a utopian possibility immanent in American life). For Duncan Kennedy's description of a liberating form of cultural pluralism, see Duncan Kennedy, "A Cultural Pluralist Case for Affirmative Action in Legal Academia," *Duke Law Journal* 4(1990): 705.

14. Adolph Reed, "All for One and None for All, Part 2," *The Nation* (January 28, 1991): 86–88, 90–92. See also Kendall Thomas, "'Ain't Nothin' Like the Real Thing': Black Masculinity, Gay Sexuality, and the Jargon of Authenticity," in *Traps: African American Men on Gender and Sexuality*, eds. Rudolph P. Byrd and Beverly Guy-Sheftall (Bloomington: Indiana University Press, 2001).

15. Cornel West, *Race Matters* (New York: Basic Books, 1993).

16. See pp. 24–26.

17. See Marimba Ani, *Yurugu: An African-Centered Critique of European Thought*

and Behavior (Trenton, NJ: Africa World Press, 1994); Molefi Kete Asante, *Afrocentricity* (Trenton, NJ: Africa World Press, 1998); Clarence E. Walker, *We Can't Go Home Again: An Argument about Afrocentrism* (London: Oxford University Press, 2000); Stephen Howe, *Afrocentrism: Mythical Pasts and Imagined Homes* (London: Verso, 1998). See also Harold Cruse, *Rebellion or Revolution?* (New York: William Morrow, 1968), 48–49. For the analogous controversy in American feminism, see Catherine MacKinnon, Carol Gilligan, Ellen Du Bois, and Carrie J. Menkel-Meadow, "Feminist Discourse: Moral Values and the Law—A Conversation," *Buffalo Law Review* 34(1985): 73–75.

18. See Harold Cruse, *The Crisis of the Negro Intellectual* (New York: William Morrow, 1967), 333.

19. See, e.g.: Elaine Brown, *A Taste of Power: A Black Woman's Story* (New York: Doubleday, 1992); Patricia Hill Collins, *From Black Power to Hip Hop: Racism, Nationalism, and Feminism* (Philadelphia: Temple University Press, 2006); Kate Dossett, *Bridging Race Divides: Black Nationalism, Feminism, and Integration in the United States, 1896–1935* (Tallahassee: University Press of Florida, 2009); Michael Eric Dyson, *Making Malcolm: The Myth and Meaning of Malcolm X* (New York: Oxford University Press, 1995), 10; Ula Y. Taylor, "Read[ing] Men and Nations: Women in the Black Radical Tradition," *Souls: A Critical Journal of Black Politics, Culture and Society* 1 (Fall 1999); Norm Allen, "Religion and the New African American Intellectuals," *Nature, Society, and Thought* 9(1996): 159–187.

20. That is, the intensity about barring white participation in SNCC (see Clayborne Carson, *In Struggle: SNCC and the Black Awakening of the 1960s* [Cambridge, MA: Harvard University Press, 1981]) or the general "hate whitey" rhetoric of some nationalists might have reflected the attempt to "purify" the Black community from white influences. Harold Cruse and Eldridge Cleaver argued that such a posture reflected the cultural insecurity of middle-class Black nationalists who had formerly been committed to integrationism (see Cruse, supra note 18, at 363–365; Theodore Draper, *The Rediscovery of Black Nationalism* [New York: Viking Press, 1969], 110).

21. Thomas, supra note 14.

22. For diverse views of the Muslims, see Essien Udosen Essien-Udom, *Black Nationalism: A Search for an Identity in America* (Chicago: University of Chicago Press, 1962); C. Eric Lincoln, *The Black Muslims in America* (Boston: Beacon Press, 1961); Elijah Muhammad, *Message to the Blackman in America* (Chicago: Muhammad Mosque of Islam No. 2, 1965); Alphonso Pinkney, *Red, Black, and Green: Black Nationalism in the United States* (New York: Cambridge University Press, 1976), 155–164. For an analysis that connects the Nation of Islam to Booker T. Washington, see Harold Cruse, supra note 17, 211. Cruse writes that "[the] Nation of Islam was nothing but a form of Booker T. Washington's economic self-help, black unity, bourgeois hard work, law abiding, vocational training, stay-out-of-the-civil-rights-struggle agitation, separate-from-the-white-man, etc., etc., morality. The only difference was that Elijah Muhammad added the potent factor of the Muslim religion to a race, economic, and social philosophy of which the first prophet was none other than Booker T. Washington. Elijah also added an element of 'hate Whitey' ideology which Washington, of course, would never have accepted."

23. For example, my earlier invocations of the "white" culture of the University of Virginia in the 1980s do not really capture the specific cultural location—a kind of upper-middle-class, Southern-Protestant (but light on Baptists) site begins to situate it more accurately. The same is true about "Black" culture, but to a lesser degree. That is, there is a more recognizable "Black" culture that exists regardless of many of the same axes of intracommunity struggle and conflict. There might be reasons for this lack of symmetry—fewer people, slavery and Jim Crow as stronger core experiences binding Blacks, and so on—but this kind of point about lived culture is not susceptible of analytic proof.

24. See Robert L. Allen, *A Guide to Black Power in America: An Historical Analysis,* (London: Gollancz, 1970), 246–250; Pinkney, supra note 22, at 93–97.

25. See Allen, supra note 24, at 212–238; Theodore L. Cross, *The Black Power Imperative: Racial Inequality and the Politics of Nonviolence* (New York: Faulkner Books, 1984), 83–136.

26. See Allen, supra note 24, at 230.

27. Kwame Ture described "Black Power" as entailing "group solidarity [to] operate from a bargaining position of strength in a pluralist society" (Stokely Carmichael and Charles V. Hamilton, *Black Power: The Politics of Liberation in America* [New York: Random House, 1967], 44). This provided the basis for Robert Allen's critique that Stokely Carmichael's Black Power amounted to "reformism" (Allen, supra note 24, at 246–253).

28. According to Judge Robert Carter, this is what the NAACP lawyers thought was being accomplished through the litigation strategy in *Brown v. Board of Education* (Robert Carter, "A Reassessment of *Brown v. Board,*" in *Shades of Brown: New Perspectives on School Desegregation,* ed. Derrick Bell [New York: Teachers College Press, Teachers College, Columbia University, 1980], 21).

Chapter 4

1. For a description of the demise of Black nationalism as an organized community presence, see Alex Poinsett, "Where Are the Revolutionaries?" *Ebony* (February 1976), 84; Manning Marable, "Black Nationalism in the 1970s: Through the Prism of Race and Class," *Socialist Review* 10(March–June 1980): 57–108.

2. But see pp. 36–37.

3. To be contrasted with the unofficial, "private" realm of social life, such as culture, where a multicultural, race-conscious sensibility reigns. See Chapter 5 for a discussion of this division.

4. On this view of the dialectic character of ideologies as "discourses of power," see Michel Foucault, "Truth and Power," in *Power/Knowledge: Selected Interviews and Other Writings, 1972–1977,* ed. Colin Gordon (New York: Pantheon, 1980), 109–133.

5. Harold Cruse, *The Crisis of the Negro Intellectual* (New York: William Morrow & Co., 1967), 6–8. Not surprisingly, there is a historiographic controversy about this

point that correlates with the position of the historian on the integration/nationalism issue. Integrationist-oriented commentators tend to see nationalism as a discontinuous tradition in African American history, arising only as a movement of despair and frustration when hopes for civic equality and integration have been raised and then frustrated. See e.g. August Meier, Elliott Rudwick, and John Bracey, Jr., eds., *Black Nationalism in America* (Indianapolis: Bobbs-Merrill Co., 1970), liii–lvi (arguing that Black nationalism is simply a form of ethnic solidarity akin to that of American Jews and a response to worsening social conditions).

For other writers contending that Black nationalism reflects disappointment with the pace of integration, see James E. Blackwell, *The Black Community: Diversity and Unity* (New York: Harper & Row, 1985), 287 (describing Blacks' efforts during the Vietnam period to make the military more responsive to their needs, such as Black literature at the post exchanges, "rakes" for Afro hair, and barbers who could style Black people's hair); Oliver C. Cox, *Race Relations: Elements and Social Dynamics* (Detroit: Wayne State University Press, 1976), 226–241; Theodore Draper, *The Rediscovery of Black Nationalism* (New York: Viking Press, 1969), 180; Robert Weisbrot, *Freedom Bound: A History of America's Civil Rights Movement* (New York: W. W. Norton & Co., 1990), 223; William J. Wilson, *Power, Racism, and Privilege: Race Relations in Theoretical and Sociohistorical Perspectives* (New York: Macmillan, 1973), 136, 139; *Report of the National Advisory Commission on Civil Disorders* (New York: Bantam, 1968), 206–219.

On the other hand, nationalist-oriented commentators tend to see the nationalist tradition as continuous and roughly independent of the opportunity for integration. See Robert Allen, *A Guide to Black Power in America: An Historical Analysis* (London: Gollancz, 1970), 75–98 ("[N]ationalism, and overt separatism, are ever-present undercurrents in the collective black psyche which ... in times of crisis, rise to the surface to become major themes"; most whites do not notice this ever-present belief because they communicate only with middle-class, college-educated African Americans, who in most historical periods are the least likely to be nationalist in orientation); Meier, Rudwick, and Bracey, Jr., *Black Nationalism in America* (cited above), lvi–lx (Bracey, dissenting from the views of his fellow editors, argues that Black nationalism is an ideology that has been fairly continuous among Blacks throughout American history and has never been regarded as an extremist ideology among American Blacks); Alphonso Pinkney, *Red, Black, and Green: Black Nationalism in the United States* (New York: Cambridge University Press, 1976), 76–219; James Turner, "Black Nationalism: The Inevitable Response," *Black World* (January 1971): 7–8.

6. Cruse, supra note 5, at 4–10.

7. According to Cruse, Booker T. Washington is a central figure in the tradition of Black nationalism in the United States: "Black Power is militant Booker T.-ism" (Harold Cruse, *Rebellion or Revolution?* [New York: William Morrow, 1968], 201). For Washington's analysis of racial progress, including his philosophy of economic self-improvement, see Booker T. Washington, *The Future of the American Negro* (Boston: Small, Maynard & Company, 1899); Booker T. Washington, *Up from Slavery* (New York: Doubleday, Page & Co., 1901). See also August Meier, *Negro Thought in America*,

1880–1915: Racial Ideologies in the Age of Booker T. Washington (Ann Arbor: University of Michigan Press, 1963). The leading biography of Washington is the two-volume work by Louis Harlan (Louis Harlan, *Booker T. Washington: The Making of a Black Leader, 1865–1901* [New York: Oxford University Press, 1972]; Louis Harlan, *Booker T. Washington: The Wizard of Tuskegee, 1901–1915* [New York: Oxford University Press, 1983]). Documents concerning Washington are exhaustively collected in Louis Harlan, ed., *The Booker T. Washington Papers* (Urbana: University of Illinois Press, 1972–1989) (14 volumes).

   8. For descriptions of Du Bois' opposition to Washington and his influence on the Niagara Movement and its successor, the NAACP, see Marable, supra note 1, at 44–57.

   9. See Allen, supra note 5, at 100–101.

   10. Pinkney, supra note 5, at 62. For the view that the nationalist/integrationist split has traditionally had a class dimension in the Black community, see id at 75–98; Lerone Bennett, *The Challenge of Blackness* (Chicago: Johnson Publishing Co., 1972), 57–65; Cruse, supra note 5, at 202–284; Weisbrot, supra note 5, at 165–170.

   11. See W. E. B. Du Bois, *The Souls of Black Folk* (Chicago: A. C. McClurg & Co., 1903), 41–59.

   12. See W. E. B. Du Bois, "A Negro Nation within the Nation," *Current History* (June 1935): 265–270; Herbert Aptheker, *Writings by W. E. B. Du Bois in Periodicals Edited by Others* (Millwood, NY: Kraus-Thomson, 1982), 1–6.

   13. See Milton M. Gordon, *Assimilation in American Life: The Role of Race, Religion, and National Origins* (New York: Oxford University Press, 1964), 113.

   14. For discussion of the centrality of the idea of accommodationism in Black politics, see Robert Chrisman, "The Formation of a Revolutionary Black Culture," *Black Scholar* (June 1970); Gunnar Myrdal, *An American Dilemma: The Negro Problem and Modern Democracy* (New York: Harper & Brothers, 1944), 721–727; Nathan I. Huggins, "Afro-Americans," in *Ethnic Leadership in America,* ed. John Higham (Baltimore: Johns Hopkins University Press, 1978), 93–98; Everett C. Ladd, *Negro Political Leadership in the South* (Ithaca, NY: Cornell University Press, 1966).

   15. Paul Cuffe undertook an early colonization effort in 1815 and arranged for a small expedition of Black colonists to Africa, which inspired the creation of the American Colonization Society, a white-controlled group whose purpose was to relocate free Blacks to Africa because they were "a dangerous and useless part of the community" (Herbert Aptheker, *A Documentary History of the Negro People in the United States,* Vol. 1 [New York: Citadel Press, 1951], 71). See Allen, supra note 5, at 76–77. For a general description of white deportationists and an analysis of the "ideological failure of colonization" focused on its associations with racist whites, see Rodney P. Carlisle, *The Roots of Black Nationalism* (Port Washington, NY: Kennikat Press, 1975), 10–12, 24–30.

   16. In criticizing Washington's famous Atlanta Compromise, where he advocated that "[i]n all things purely social we can be as separate as the five fingers, and yet one as the hand in all things essential to mutual progress" (Du Bois, supra note 11, at 42). Du Bois concluded that "Mr. Washington represents in Negro thought the old attitude

of adjustment and submission … [which] practically accepts the alleged inferiority of the Negro races" (id. at 50). See generally id. at 41–59.

17. See Tony Martin, *Race First: The Ideological and Organizational Struggles of Marcus Garvey and the Universal Negro Improvement Association* (Dover, MA: Majority Press, 1986), 297–299 (describing Du Bois' attempt to link Garvey with the accommodationism of Washington). While this was Du Bois' interpretation of Garveyism, Garvey painted the opposite picture. See John White, *Black Leadership in America, 1895–1968* (London: Longman, 1985), 89–95; Cruse, supra note 7, at 86 ("The rise of Garvey nationalism meant that the NAACP became the accommodationists, and the nationalists became the militants.").

18. See e.g. James W. Johnson, *Negro American, What Now?* (New York: Viking Press, 1934), 35–40 ("[T]he outcome of voluntary isolation would be a permanent secondary status.… I do not believe we should ever be willing to pay such a price for security and peace."); Ralph J. Bunche, "A Critical Analysis of the Tactics and Programs of Minority Groups," *Journal of Negro Education* 4(1935): 308, 312 ("Because of the seeming hopelessness of the fight to win equal rights for many minority racial groups, some of the leadership of such groups has often espoused a 'defeatist' philosophy, which takes the form of racial separatism."); James Farmer, "We Cannot Destroy Segregation with a Weapon of Segregation," *Equality* (November 1944): 2 ("Garveyism [and other nationalisms] … are not liberating the Negro people; they are further enslaving their minds under the yoke of caste."); Walter White, "Segregation: A Symposium," *The Crisis* (March 1934): 80–81 (Responding to Du Bois' calls for voluntary self-segregation, White, then executive secretary of the NAACP, argued that "no Negro who respects himself and his race can accept these segregated systems without at least some inward protest."); Robert Staples, *Introduction to Black Sociology* (New York: McGraw-Hill, 1976), 260–261, 301 ("[Garveyism] was an escapist philosophy"), 302 ("Muslims did not engage in political action and insulated themselves from both the culture and everyday life of the Black community."); Weisbrot, supra note 5, at 31 (direct actionists were advised by elders to be cautious).

19. See Herbert H. Haines, *Black Radicals and the Civil Rights Mainstream: 1954–1970* (Knoxville: University of Tennessee Press, 1988), 30–32, 44, 75.

20. See id. (entire book).

21. See Weisbrot, supra note 5, at 30–38, 132–143, 204–270.

22. The confluence of these two issues—militancy versus accommodation and nationalism versus integration—helps explain what otherwise appears to be confusion on the part of the 1960s nationalists about their historical antecedents and heroes. Cruse criticizes 1960s nationalists for their lack of historical comprehension of the nationalist tradition because they looked to Robert Williams and Frederick Douglass as heroes. Williams was the NAACP chapter head in Monroe, North Carolina, who advocated and began to act upon the use of violence to achieve civil rights. See Robert F. Williams, Martin Luther King, Jr., and Truman Nelson, *Negroes with Guns* (New York: Marzani & Munsell, 1962), 39. For a description of Williams's role in Monroe, his subsequent expulsion from the NAACP, his exile to Cuba and the People's Republic of China, see

Poinsett, supra note 1, at 1 (see Chapter 4, note 1). As Cruse points out, while Williams and Douglass employed militant rhetoric and activism, both were committed to the ideology of integrationism. Similarly, Cruse argues that the ideological confusion of 1960s nationalists was confirmed by their adoption of Garvey as a hero and their failure to recognize Washington as, in many ways, the founder of Black nationalism among African Americans, instead making "Booker T.-ism" a synonym for assimilationism. See Cruse, supra note 5, at 347–401, 544–565 (see Chapter 4, Note 3). However, whatever merit there might be to Cruse's criticism in general, it leaves out of the analysis the fact that the ability of 1960s nationalists to combine Black nationalism with a confrontationalist commitment was an independently significant historical development. They valorized both nationalist and militant integrationist figures because they sought to link nationalism with militancy.

23. The community-organizing militancy of the direct-action factions of the civil rights movement in the 1950s and early 1960s and the later critique of nonviolence as a means to achieve integration can be seen to have reflected a submerged form of nationalist ideology itself, to be made explicit by the mid-1960s when CORE and SNCC adopted formal nationalist programs, and in 1967, when Rap Brown, Carmichael, and James Foreman joined the Black Panthers. See Clayborne Carson, *In Struggle: SNCC and the Black Awakening of the 1960's* (Cambridge, MA: Harvard University Press, 1981), 196–207; Haines, supra note 19, at 57–75; Bracey, Meier, and Rudwick, supra note 5, at 17–18 (see Chapter 4, Note 3).

24. For an analysis of the early years of the civil rights movement centered on the ideological and cultural differences between "legalist" and "direct-action" ideologies, see Aldon D. Morris, *The Origins of the Civil Rights Movement: Black Communities Organizing for Change* (New York: The Free Press, 1984); Haines, supra note 19, at 29–46; Weisbrot, supra note 5, at 30–38; Lewis M. Killian, "White Southerners," in *Through Different Eyes: Black and White Perspectives on America Race Relations,* eds. Peter I. Rose, Stanley Rothman, and William J. Wilson (New York: Oxford University Press, 1973), 69–75.

25. It is ironic that Cruse misses the changed meaning of nationalism symbolized by the colonialism analysis because he was one of the first to set it forth in a comprehensive way. The term was first used in a comprehensive analysis of the situation of African Americans by Cruse, "Revolutionary Nationalism and the Afro-American," *Studies on the Left* 2 (1962): 12–13. See also Cruse, supra note 7, at 48–67 (see Chapter 4, Note 5); Harold Cruse, "Negro Nationalism's New Wave," *New Leader* (March 19, 1962): 16.

26. For a more complete account of Garveyism, see footnote 5 in Chapter 2.

27. See Staples, supra note 18, at 291–293; Turner, supra note 5, at 7–8; Robert L. Scott and Wayne Brockriede, eds., *The Rhetoric of Black Power* (New York: Harper & Row, 1969), 4–5.

28. See Malcolm X, *The Autobiography of Malcolm X,* ed. Alex Haley (New York: Grove Press, 1965), 294. According to Malcolm X, it was precisely the Muslim policy of not engaging in conflict with the white power structure that led to his frustration and eventual break with the Nation of Islam: "[O]ur Nation of Islam could be an even greater

force in the American black man's overall struggle—if we engaged in more action.... [W]e should have amended or relaxed our general non-engagement policy. I felt that, whenever black people committed themselves, in the Little Rocks and Birminghams ... militantly disciplined Muslims should be there also."

29. Staples, supra note 18, at 290–292. Staples explores the simultaneous oppositional and nationalist meaning of Black Power: "Black power ideology ... evolved into different nationalist expressions, but it gave rise to the modern-day Black Nationalist movement.... Millions of Black people were inspired by the concept that they should develop the political power to take control over their political, economic and social fortunes. This new Black consciousness was seen in the ghetto rebellions of the 1960s. It was also expressed in the increased support among Afro-Americans for the liberation struggles in the colonial world, in the protests by Black high school and college students, and in the development of militancy and organization by Black workers and professionals. It probably had more influence on Black cultural change than any other social movement. In the short period of five years it had revolutionized Black cultural lifestyles. It most eloquently symbolizes the idea whose time has arrived."

See also Turner, supra note 5, at 7–8 (nationalism was usually politically conservative until the 1960s). But see Carl Gershman, "Black Nationalism and Conservative Politics," *Dissent* 17(1970): 10–11 (arguing that Black nationalism is a conservative movement); Kenneth B. Clark, *Dark Ghetto: Dilemmas of Power* (New York: Harper & Row, 1965), 612 (Black power is accommodationism); *Report of the National Advisory Commission on Civil Disorders*, supra note 5, at 235 (same).

30. See Harry Edwards, *Black Students* (New York: The Free Press, 1970) (noting that the radicalization of Black students during the 1960s brought collaboration between the Black bourgeoisie and poorer classes). Also, Marable (supra note 1, at 20–21) states that "[b]y the late months of 1966 ... the young nationalists had succeeded in creating a broad based wave of support, touching virtually every segment of the black population.... By the end of the decade the Old Guard seemed to be fighting a losing battle.... It is difficult to find an appropriate parallel to any previous stage of black American struggle.... By 1971, the Old Guard leadership appeared to be thoroughly discredited." See also S. E. Anderson, "The Fragmented Movement," *Black World/Negro Digest* (September 1968).

31. Most (integrationist) commentators have interpreted Black nationalism simply as an ideology of frustration when integration does not seem to work. See supra note 5. However, at least in the 20th century, such a diagnosis at most accounts for the cultural position of a segment of the Black middle class. See Cruse, supra note 5, at 175–248; James Farmer, *Freedom, When?* (New York: Random House, 1965), 92–93; Weisbrot, supra note 5, at 169–170; Martin Kilson, "The New Black Intellectuals," *Dissent* 16(1969): 304. Among poorer African Americans, a nationalist political and cultural stance has had a more continuous presence (Allen, supra note 5, at 75–98).

32. See *Report of the National Advisory Commission on Civil Disorders*, supra note 5, at 205–238 (interpreting the rise of Black Power ideology and the increased militancy of ghetto youth as a reflection of frustration with the slow pace of civil rights reform).

33. See Haines, supra note 19, at 55–76.

34. See Haines, supra note 19, at 46–74; Marable, supra note 1, at 20–21; Pinkney, supra note 5, at ix (in 1970, "there seemed to be little doubt that black nationalism was the dominant ethos of the black movement").

35. See Haines, supra note 19, at 35–36 (noting the rapid shift in SNCC ideology), 46–76 (chronology of the momentum toward Black Power and "black separatism" in the late 1960s, and how the sense of radicalism shifted from direct-action integrationism in the late 1950s and early 1960s to Black nationalism in the mid- to late 1960s).

36. For a description of the sense within the SCLC and on the part of King himself that he was losing support, see David J. Garrow, *Bearing the Cross: Martin Luther King, Jr., and the Southern Christian Leadership Conference* (New York: William Morrow and Co., 1986), 431–547.

37. Cruse, supra note 5, at 364.

38. The repression faced by the Black Panthers is well documented. See e.g. Huey P. Newton, *War against the Panthers: A Study of Repression in America* (Chicago: Black Classic Press, 1996) (Black Panther co-founder Newton's doctoral thesis); Edward Jay Epstein, "The Black Panthers and the Police: A Pattern of Genocide?" *The New Yorker* (February 13, 1971), http://www.edwardjayepstein.com/archived/panthers.htm; U.S. Senate, *Final Report of the Select Committee to Study Governmental Operations with Respect to Intelligence Activities*, Book III (Washington DC: U.S. Government Printing Office, 1976) (the U.S. government's official report on COINTELPRO's [Counter Intelligence Program's] mission to "neutralize" "Black Nationalist Hate Groups").

39. For example, plans by various splinter groups to engage the police in urban guerrilla war, to assassinate political figures, etc. See Poinsett, supra note 1.

40. See Harold Cruse, "The Fire This Time?" *New York Review of Books* (May 8, 1969): 13–18 (criticizing simplistic social theories of 1960s nationalists). See also Cruse, supra note 5, at 347–401 (criticizing as unrealistic and romanticizing the 1960s nationalists' invocation of images of armed revolution).

41. See William J. Wilson, *The Declining Significance of Race: Blacks and Changing American Institutions* (Chicago: University of Chicago Press, 1978), 142–143.

42. I do not want to obscure the role of a vanguard of white radicals who did, in fact, engage Black nationalist radicals and who came to recognize Black nationalism as a progressive ideology. Their efforts, however, tended to be characterized by a great deal of self-abnegation and deference to virtually any demand made by radicals of color. The 1967 National Conference for a New Politics was widely considered a fiasco after white radicals acceded to Black demands that their votes count multiple times more than the white conference participants and to a more general manifesto of nationalism. See Simon Hall, *Peace and Freedom: The Civil Rights and Antiwar Movements in the 1960s* (Philadelphia: University of Pennsylvania Press, 2006), 105–140; Nigel Young, *An Infantile Disorder? The Crisis and Decline of the New Left* (London: Routledge & Kegan Paul, 1977).

43. See Malcolm X, *Autobiography of Malcolm X*, supra note 28.

44. The only significant nondeportationist white support for nationalism as a way to

comprehend race relations prior to the 1960s was the formal position of the American Communist Party. From 1928 to 1959, the Communist Party argued that the "Black belt" in the South should be recognized as a sovereign entity of African Americans. In 1959, the Communists changed their position to a call for immediate integration and an end to racial discrimination; even during the period in which Communists formally supported Black nationalism, their support and understanding were deduced from theoretical postulates of Marxism-Leninism, rather than from any engagement with the Black nationalist tradition in the United States. See William Z. Foster, *The Negro People in American History* (New York: International Publishers, 1954), 461 (including the text of the 1928 resolution). For a full analysis of the Communist Party's position on Black nationalism, see Cruse, supra note 7, at 78–94. For more general analysis of the relation of Marxists to Black nationalism, see id. at 139–155 (analyzing Trotskyist racial ideology); id. at 193–258 (analyzing limitations of Marxist analysis more generally).

In any event, the Communists spent their organizing energies on antidiscrimination efforts and attempts to establish interracial trade union and farm worker organizations. See Allen, supra note 5, at 85–90. In the left more generally, the tendency was to see "the race issue" as subordinate to the more fundamental analytic of economic class; accordingly, the reigning image of racial liberation for most American leftists was the creation of an integrated working-class movement that would overthrow capitalism and thereby remove the "cause" of exploitation of all workers, whether Black or white. The sorry record of organized labor on race issues is a source of great embarrassment for the traditional left. For a brief, technical overview of organized labor and race, see Ray Marshall, "The Negro and Organized Labor," *The Journal of Negro Education* 32(1963): 375–389; Herbert Northrup, "Organized Labor and Negro Workers," *The Journal of Political Economy*(1943): 206–221. See also Michael Keith Honey, *Black Workers Remember: An Oral History of Segregation, Unionism and the Freedom Struggle* (Berkeley: University of California Press, 2000). To be sure, there are many historic examples of courageous leftist support for civil rights, and there have been many occasions in the history of American race relations when white leftists were the only dependable allies of African Americans. The point here is that, in the left tradition, integrationism was "integrated" into the class analysis under the general assumption that the structure of racial domination was subsidiary to and comprehended by the structure of capitalist domination.

45. Charles E. Silberman, *Crisis in Black and White* (New York: Random House, 1964), 212.

46. See Student Nonviolent Coordinating Committee, "Position Paper on Black Power," in *Let Nobody Turn Us Around—An African American Anthology: Voices of Resistance, Reform and Renewal*, 2nd ed., eds. Manning Marable and Leith Mullings (Lanham, MD: Rowman & Littlefield, 2009), 425 (announcing and explaining the expulsion of whites from SNCC). The document is also available online at http://www2.iath.virginia.edu/sixties/HTML_docs/Resources/Primary/Manifestos/SNCC_black_power.html.

The paper was widely circulated at the time. See "Excerpts from Paper on Which the 'Black Power' Philosophy Is Based," *New York Times* (August 5, 1966). See generally

Stokely Carmichael and Charles V. Hamilton, *Black Power: The Politics of Liberation in America* (New York: Random House, 1967), 58–84; Carson, supra note 23, at 229–243; Haines, supra note 19, at 57–70. As Carmichael stated the nationalist position on white participation: "How can you, as the youth in this country, move to start carrying those things out? Move into the white community. We have developed a movement in the black community. The white activist has miserably failed to develop the movement inside of his community. Will white people have the courage to go into white communities and start organizing them? That's the question for the white activist."

47. See Cruse, supra note 5; Fred Powledge, *Black Power, White Resistance: Notes on the New Civil War* (Cleveland: World Publishing Co., 1967); Charles E. Fager, *White Reflections on Black Power* (Grand Rapids, MI: W. B. Eerdmans Publishing Company, 1967), 89–96.

48. See Powledge, supra note 47; Fager, supra note 47.

49. See Draper, supra note 5, at 110.

50. Cruse, supra note 5, at 363–365.

51. Tom Wolfe, *Radical Chic & Mau-Mauing the Flak Catchers* (New York: Farrar, Straus and Giroux, 1970).

52. Of course, this is not the whole story of white radical response to nationalism. Many white activists took seriously the Black nationalist analysis that suggested the need for Black leadership and mass participation in the Black liberation struggle, and that pointed to the reform of the white community as the best role for whites to play. The mass struggle against the Vietnam War soon came to pervade virtually all aspects of politics within the white community, and many such activists were quickly absorbed in antiwar issues. Others went to poor white communities in regions such as Appalachia, where they tended more quickly to experience a sense of being outsiders. See Fager, supra note 47, at 89–91.

53. This dynamic of white cultural identification also manifested itself in small, everyday ways. At the micro-level of social intercourse, the dynamic appeared in the cultural politics of interracial relations. One example was the familiar phenomenon of whites beginning to talk "Black," using what they conceived of as Black vernacular and slang when in the presence of Blacks, or adopting Black musical tastes. The flip side of this cultural phenomenon, reflecting the same discomfort with one's own culture, is the sense of awkwardness that whites sometimes experience in interracial contexts concerning any aspect of their lifestyle that might reflect whiteness: the sense that indications of white culture are signs of bias, leading to the aspiration for a culture of "neutrality" in interracial settings and a corresponding compulsion to integrate social and institutional arenas to demonstrate their aracial character.

Chapter 5

1. Jack M. Balkin, introduction to *What* Brown v. Board of Education *Should Have Said* (New York: NYU Press, 2001), 15, 25.

2. *Brown v. Board of Education of Topeka*, 347 U.S. 483 (1954).

3. See e.g. Gary Orfield and Chungmei Lee, *Brown* at 50: King's Dream or *Plessy's* Nightmare? (Cambridge, MA: Civil Rights Project, Harvard University, 2004), http://civilrightsproject.ucla.edu/research/k-12-education/integration-and-diversity/brown-at-50-king2019s-dream-or-plessy2019s-nightmare/orfield-brown-50-2004.pdf; Jonathan Kozol, "Overcoming Apartheid," *The Nation* (December 19, 2005), http://www.thenation.com/doc/20051219/kozol.

4. Compare *Washington v. Davis*, 426 U.S. 229, 244–245 (1976) (holds that impact, standing alone, is not sufficient to prove racial discrimination violative of the Equal Protection Clause) with *Chance v. Board of Examiners*, 458 F.2d 1167–1176 (2d Cir. 1972) ("Even were we to accept the City's allegation that any discrimination here resulted from thoughtlessness rather than a purposeful scheme, the City may not escape responsibility for placing its Black citizens under a severe disadvantage which it cannot justify.").

5. Compare *Gratz v. Bollinger*, 539 U.S. 244 (2003) (Rehnquist, C. J., for the Court) ("It is by now well established that 'all racial classifications reviewable under the Equal Protection Clause must be strictly scrutinized.' This 'standard of review ... is not dependent on the race of those burdened or benefited by a particular classification.'") with *Gratz* (Stevens, J., dissenting) ("In implementing this equality instruction, as I see it, government decision makers may properly distinguish between policies of exclusion and inclusion. Actions designed to burden groups long denied full citizenship stature are not sensibly ranked with measures taken to hasten the day when entrenched discrimination and its aftereffects have been extirpated.")

6. Two notable exceptions are Owen Fiss, "Groups and the Equal Protection Clause," *Philosophy and Public Affairs* 5(1976): 107; Alan Freeman, "Legitimating Racial Discrimination through Anti-Discrimination Law: A Critical Review of Supreme Court Doctrine," *Minnesota Law Review* 62(1978): 1049.

7. *Plessy v. Ferguson*, 163 U.S. 537, 551 (1897).

8. *Brown v. Board of Education of Topeka*, 347 U.S. 483, 494–495 (1954).

9. See Morton J. Horwitz, *The Transformation of American Law, 1870–1960: The Crisis of Legal Orthodoxy* (New York: Oxford University Press, 1992).

10. See e.g. *Lochner v. New York*, 198 U.S. 45 (1905). For the classic "realist" texts impugning the claims that the judiciary was protecting a private, preregulated market, see Robert Hale, "Coercion and Distribution in a Supposedly Non-Coercive State," *Political Science Quarterly* 38(1923): 470; Morris Cohen, "The Basis of Contract," *Harvard Law Review* 46(1933): 533. For fuller descriptions of the analytic structure and ideological significance of the realist critique, see Horwitz, supra note 9; Duncan Kennedy, "Distributive and Paternalist Motives in Contract and Tort Law, with Special Reference to Compulsory Terms and Unequal Bargaining Power," *Maryland Law Review* 41(1982): 563; Duncan Kennedy and Frank Michelman, "Are Property and Contract Efficient?" *Hofstra Law Review* 8(1980): 711; Gary Peller, "The Metaphysics of American Law," *California Law Review* 73(1985): 1151; Gary Peller, "The Classical Theory of Law," *Cornell Law Review* 73(1988): 300; Joseph Singer, "Legal Realism Now," *California Law Review* 76(1988): 465.

11. Compare *Loving v. Virginia*, 388 U.S. 1, 11 (1967) (holding that anti-miscegenation statute was designed to uphold white supremacy).

12. See *Missouri ex. rel. Gaines v. Canada*, 305 U.S. 337, 344 (1938) (holding that a state must provide substantially equal education to Black and white students, and that the state violated that duty by failing to have a law school for Black students and ignoring questions of prestige of the school); *Sipuel v. Board of Regents of University of Oklahoma*, 332 U.S. 631, 633 (1948) (holding that state must provide a law school for Blacks if it provides one for whites); *Sweatt v. Painter*, 339 U.S. 629, 633–634 (1950) (access to a hastily constructed, second-rate law school did not provide a substantially equal educational experience to the University of Texas Law School): "What is more important, the University of Texas Law School possesses to a far greater degree those qualities which are incapable of objective measurement but which make for greatness in a law school. Such qualities, to name but a few, include reputation of the faculty, experience of the administration, position and influence of the alumni, standing in the community, traditions and prestige. It is difficult to believe that one who had a free choice between these law schools would consider the question close."

See also *McLaurin v. Oklahoma State Regents for Higher Education*, 339 U.S. 637, 639–641 (1950) (forcing a Black student at a nonintegrated institution to sit in an attached room rather than a normal classroom and to sit at a special table in the library and in the cafeteria deprived that student of equal protection of the laws). On the NAACP's litigation strategy, see Mark V. Tushnet, *The NAACP's Legal Strategy against Segregated Education, 1925–1950*, 2nd ed. (Chapel Hill: University of North Carolina Press, 2005).

13. *Sweatt v. Painter*, 339 U.S. 629, 633–634 (1950).

14. *McLaurin v. Oklahoma State Regents for Higher Education*, 339 U.S. 637, 639–641 (1950).

15. *Brown v. Board of Education of Topeka*, 347 U.S. 494 (quoting a "finding" of the court below).

16. Id.

17. See Id. at 494, n.11.

18. Kenneth B. Clark, *Effect of Prejudice and Discrimination on Personality Development* (Midcentury White House Conference on Children and Youth, 1950).

19. *Brown v. Board of Education of Topeka*, 347 U.S. 494 ("Segregation of white and colored children in public schools has a detrimental effect upon the colored children. The impact is greater when it has the sanction of the law; for the policy of separating the races is usually interpreted as denoting the inferiority of the Negro group.")

20. Herbert Wechsler, "Toward Neutral Principles of Constitutional Law," *Harvard Law Review* 73(1959): 33.

21. See Alden Whitman, "Obituary: Earl Warren, 83, Who Led High Court in Time of Vast Social Change, Is Dead," *New York Times* (July 10, 1974), http://www.nytimes.com/learning/general/onthisday/bday/0319.html.

22. See generally James W. Ely, Jr., "Book Review: *The Crisis of Conservative Virginia: The Byrd Organization and the Politics of Massive Resistance*," *The Journal of Southern History* 62(May 1977): 324; Clive Webb, ed., *Massive Resistance: Southern Opposition to the Second Reconstruction* (New York: Oxford University Press, 2005).

23. Learned Hand, *The Bill of Rights (Oliver Wendell Holmes Lectures)* (Cambridge, MA: Harvard University Press, 1962).

24. Wechsler, supra note 20, at 73. See generally Horwitz, supra note 10.

25. Id. at 32–33.

26. Id. at 33.

27. Id. at 34.

28. Id.

29. Tamar Lewin, "Herbert Wechsler, Legal Giant, Is Dead at 90," *New York Times* (April 28, 2000), http://www.nytimes.com/2000/04/28/us/herbert-wechsler-legal-giant-is-dead-at-90.html.

30. See generally Gerald Gunther, *Learned Hand: The Man and the Judge* (New York: Knopf, 1994).

31. *Lochner v. New York*, 198 U.S. 45 (1905).

32. *Adkins v. Children's Hospital*, 261 U.S. 525 (1923).

33. See e.g. *Bailey v. Drexel Furniture Co.*, 259 U.S. 20 (1922); *Coppage v. Kansas*, 236 U.S. 1 (1915).

34. *Muller v. Oregon*, 208 U.S. 412 (1908).

35. *Dennis v. United States*, 341 U.S. 494, 517–561 (Frankfurter, J., concurring).

36. *U.S. v. Dennis*, 183 F.2d 201 (2d Cir. 1950).

37. See generally Henry Hart and Albert Sacks, *The Legal Process: Basic Problems in the Making and Application of Law* (Cambridge, MA: Harvard University Press, 1958); Herbert Wechsler, "Toward Neutral Principles of Constitutional Law," *Harvard Law Review* 73(1959): 1.

38. It is hard to believe Wechsler was actually implying that racial domination was all in the heads of Blacks in the 1950s; instead, by individualizing as choice or psychological reaction the way Blacks and women understood segregation, Wechsler was trying to highlight the contingent and subjective nature of any evaluation of power in society.

39. Gary Peller, "Neutral Principles in the 1950s," *University of Michigan Journal of Law Reform* 21(1988): 561.

40. Alexander Bickel, *The Morality of Consent* (New Haven, CT: Yale University Press, 1975), 16, 133–134.

41. *U.S. v. Carolene Products Co.*, 304 U.S. 144, 153, fn. 4 (*internal citations omitted*).

42. Balkin, supra note 1, at 24–25.

43. *Green v. County School Board of New Kent County*, 391 U.S. 430 (1968), quoting *Bowman v. County School Board*, 382 F.2d 326, 333 (4th Cir. 1967) (Soberloff, J., concurring).

44. *Parents Involved in Community Schools v. Seattle School District No. 1*, 551 U.S. 701, 731.

45. Michael J. Klarman, *From Jim Crow to Civil Rights: The Supreme Court and the Struggle for Racial Equality* (New York: Oxford University Press, 2004).

46. The *Green* result meant that, while a constitutional violation in the public school context in the first instance still required (at least formally) a showing of *de jure* action to

segregate schools, once such a violation was shown, a *de facto* remedial standard would apply. Apparently, as Associate Justice William Rehnquist repeatedly charged, the *de facto* remedy was broader than the *de jure* right because continuing segregation could result from parental choice, housing patterns, and other factors that "are the product not of governmental restrictions," in the words of the *Harris* Court.

47. *Keyes v. Denver School District No. 1*, 413 U.S. 189 (1973).

48. Id. at 224 (Powell, J., concurring).

49. *Washington v. Davis*, 426 U.S. 229, 245–246.

50. *Griggs v. Duke Power Co.*, 401 U.S. 424 (1971).

51. Id. at 431.

52. That is, the performance on the test was related to success in the training program, not to success in the job itself. See 426 U.S. 229, 265–266 (Brennan, J., dissenting).

53. Id. at 242.

54. Id. at 248.

55. The Court hinted at institutional concerns without elaboration: "[I]t involves a more probing judicial review of, and less deference to, the seemingly reasonable acts of administrators and executives than is appropriate under the Constitution where special racial impact, without discriminatory purpose, is claimed" (id. at 247). From the perspective of the scope of judicial review under the *Carolene Products* conception that the judiciary should apply heightened scrutiny to laws burdening Blacks (as the paradigm of a "discrete and insular minority"), the debate between the intent and impact standards exposed the inability of this refined conception of institutional competence theory to solve the circularity of the Hand and Wechsler positions in presuming the democratic legitimacy of the legislature, a legitimacy on which their whole arguments about the evils of judicial activism rest. If the task of the judiciary is to ensure that discrete and insular minorities have not been unfairly burdened in the majoritarian process, the intent standard of *Davis* presumes as a starting point that no such unfair burden exists in the status-quo social field. That is, as long as the government has not acted intentionally and affirmatively with respect to race, then no heightened scrutiny is called for, on the presumption that racial domination does not dominate the social field. However, Blacks might be burdened already, by a series of past policies, say, or by the failure of the government to act. Therefore, disproportionate impact of laws facially neutral to race would seem to call for heightened scrutiny on the part of the judiciary. However, the slippery slope of the *Davis* opinion suggests that the institutional characteristics of the judiciary demand that it reject the impact standard because its application would involve the judiciary in reviewing a "whole range" of laws, a task it is not competent to perform given the "countermajoritarian" difficulty.

In 1989, the Rehnquist Court took this a step further, *invalidating* a law passed by the City of Richmond, Virginia, that set a goal of awarding 30% of municipal contracts to minority-owned businesses (in a city with a 50% Black population). The Court stated: "To accept Richmond's claim that past societal discrimination alone can serve as the basis for rigid racial preferences would be to open the door to competing claims for "remedial relief" for every disadvantaged group. The dream of a Nation of equal citizens in a society where race is irrelevant to personal opportunity and achievement would be lost in a mosaic of shifting preferences based on inherently unmeasurable claims of past wrongs. Courts would be asked to evaluate the extent of the prejudice and consequent harm suffered by various minority groups. Those whose societal injury is thought to exceed some arbitrary level of tolerability then would be entitled to preferential classification." *City of Richmond v. J. A. Croson Co.*, 488 U.S. 469, 505–506.

The Court thus took the slippery slope argument of *Davis* a step further: beyond declaring its own incompetence in determining the magnitude of group harms, it also declared the legislature incapable of making the same assessment. According to this logic, the impact standard is not merely not a constitutionally required remedy, it is actually unconstitutional when applied to explicit race-conscious state action.

56. See Paul Brest, "Forward: In Defense of the Antidiscrimination Principle," *Harvard Law Review* 90(1976): 1, 42 ("The poor nonpreferred white and the black beneficiary of a preferential program are like two children raised as brothers in an impoverished household. It is later discovered that one or the other is probably the heir to a small fortune, which is given to the one with the more likely claim, the other taking nothing. All parties concerned would regard the occurrence as a windfall, and certainly not based on desert. So too is a preference premised on a greater probability that the minority's situation is the result of past injury.").

57. See id. at 11. "[A] presumption prohibiting all decisions that stigmatize or cumulatively disadvantage particular individuals would affect an enormously wide range of practices important to the efficient operation of a complex industrial society. (Furthermore, a general doctrine disfavoring harmful results could not be administered by the judiciary.)"

58. Brest, supra note 56, at 15, 17.

59. See id. at 43 ("[T]he thrust of the preceding discussion is that a general preferential treatment or reparations program moves ... to a point where the distinction between compensatory and distributive justice becomes untenable.").

60. *Washington v. Davis*, 429 U.S. 229, 248 (1976).

61. Brest, supra note 56, at 29.

Chapter 6

1. *Missouri v. Jenkins*, 115 S. Ct. 2038, 2064, 2065 (1995) (Thomas, J., concurring).

2. *Brown v. Board of Education of Topeka*, 347 U.S. 483 (1954).

3. For an excellent "philosophical" treatment of many of the issues considered in this chapter, see John Horton, ed., *Liberalism, Multiculturalism and Toleration* (New York: St. Martin's, 1993).

4. Just as a legal decision like *Brown* is part of a process of ideological struggle over how the social world will be constructed, so "scholarly" commentary is immersed in similar ideological condensation. This is to say that I do not offer the following as an

objective or detached interpretation; my "analysis" proceeds from an impressionistic take on the political and ideological significance of *Brown* and on subsequent developments in American racial dynamics—from my own situation as a full-time, white, Critical Legal Studies–oriented progressive law professor and occasional activist, immersed within the ideological framework that I endeavor to depict.

5.   Of course, this is a loaded term, as are any terms used to describe the issue. For a discussion of the issues presented, see Rogaia Mustafa Abusharaf, *Female Circumcision: Multicultural Perspectives* (Philadelphia: University of Pennsylvania Press, 2007); Sunny Kim, "Gender-Related Persecution: A Legal Analysis of Gender Bias in Asylum Law," *American University Journal of Gender & Law* 2(1990): 107, 125–128; Alison T. Slack, "Female Circumcision: A Critical Appraisal," *Human Rights Quarterly* 10(1988): 439; Abdulmumini A. Oba, "Female Circumcision as Female Genital Mutilation: Human Rights or Cultural Imperialism?" *Global Jurist* 8(2008): 1–38; Obioma Nnaemeka, ed., *Female Circumcision and the Politics of Knowledge: African Women in Imperialist Discourses* (Westport, CT: Praeger, 2005).

6.   Norman Mailer, *The White Negro* (San Francisco: City Lights, 1957).

7.   Orlando Patterson, "Race, Gender, and Liberal Fallacies," *New York Times* (October 20, 1991): sec. 4, 2.

8.   Senate Committee on the Judiciary, *Testimony of Anita F. Hill, Professor of Law, University of Oklahoma, Norman, OK* (Washington, DC: U.S. Government Printing Office, 1991), 37, available at http://www.gpoaccess.gov/congress/senate/judiciary/sh102-1084pt4/36-40.pdf.

9.   For a discussion of the ways that the Patterson intervention in particular and the deployment of race particularism in general worked to split antiracist and feminist forces during the Thomas/Hill confrontation, see Kimberlé Crenshaw, "Whose Story Is It, Anyway? Feminist and Antiracist Appropriations of Anita Hill," *in Race-ing Justice, Engendering Power: Essays on Anita Hill, Clarence Thomas, and the Construction of Social Reality*, ed. Toni Morrison (New York: Pantheon Books, 1992).

10.   See Thomas Edsall and E. J. Dionne, Jr., "Core Democratic Constituencies Split: Support for Nominee Reflects Power of Black Vote in the South," *Washington Post* (October 16, 1991): A1.

11.   I do not mean to assert that progressive white groups gave up after Thomas's invocation of the "high-tech lynching" image in his testimony, because they did not. On the other hand, the race turn in the discourse did tend to be met with silence on the part of whites.

12.   Of course, this issue has particular trajectory within the feminist movement. See bell hooks, *Ain't I a Woman: Black Women and Feminism* (Boston: South End Press, 1981); Crenshaw, supra note 9.

13.   I cannot be sure that I have not completely misjudged the current climate in that white power is still so pervasive and unselfconscious that calling for progressives to exercise more power is irresponsible.

14.   Myron Lieberman, *The Future of Public Education* (Chicago: University of Chicago Press, 1960), 34, 38, 60.

15. For a more detailed description of the connection between the ban on school prayer and the prohibition of school segregation in general transformation of Southern culture in the 1960s and 1970s, see Gary Peller, "Creation, Evolution and the New South," *Tikkun* (November–December 1987): 72.

16. Paul D. Escott, et al., eds., *Major Problems in the History of the American South,* Vol. 2, *The New South,* 2nd ed. (Boston: Houghton Mifflin, 1999).

17. This is, of course, not to say that schools were necessarily integrated, given the dynamics of white flight and resegregation within schools pursuant to ability or achievement tracking and other devices.

18. Malcolm X, *By Any Means Necessary: Speeches, Interviews and a Letter,* ed. George Breitman (New York; Pathfinder Press, 1970), 16–17.

19. *Missouri v. Jenkins,* 115 S. Ct. 2061, 2062 (1995).

20. "I have a dream that one day on the red hills of Georgia, sons of former slaves and former slave owners will be able to sit down together at the table of brotherhood.... I have a dream my four little children will one day live in a nation where they will not be judged by the color of their skin but by the content of their character" (Martin Luther King, Jr., *The Martin Luther King, Jr. Companion: Quotations from the Speeches, Essays, and Books of Martin Luther King, Jr.* [New York: St. Martin's Press, 1968]).

21. The reigning discourse on race simply had no way to come to grips with Malcolm X's conception of race as a potentially liberatory aspect of identity, as an affirming but socially constructed characteristic as opposed to the segregationist/imperialist conception of race as an essentialist, divinely ordained signifier of superiority. See Chapter 4, supra.

22. Within the arena of conventional legal commentary, the Court's opinion was controversial on both grounds. With respect to colorblindness, for example, Herbert Wechsler argued that the idea did not state a *neutral* principle because it improperly privileged those desiring interracial contact over those abhorring it. With respect to the social-science basis, mainstream legal scholars contended that constitutional interpretation could not properly be based on historically contingent empirical data.

23. See *Green v. County School Board,* 391 U.S. 430 (1968) (holding that school districts that were once segregated by law came under a duty to produce actually integrated schools, not simply to stop requiring segregation).

24. See *Lochner v. New York,* 198 U.S. 45 (1905).

25. One way to see this approach as embodying the "victim" perspective is provided in Alan Freeman, "Legitimizing Racial Discrimination through Antidiscrimination Law: A Critical Review of Supreme Court Doctrine," *Minnesota Law Review* 62(1978): 1049.

26. See e.g. Charles Black, Jr., "The Lawfulness of the Segregation Decisions," *Yale Law Journal* 69(1960): 421.

27. Charles Silberman, *Crisis in Black and White* (New York: Random House, 1964), 269–273.

28. Charles Silberman, *Crisis in the Classroom: The Remaking of American Education* (New York: Random House, 1970), 81 n.38.

29. See e.g. Frank Reissman, *The Culturally Deprived Child* (New York: Harper,

1962); John Beck and Richard Saxe, eds., *Teaching the Culturally Disadvantaged Pupil* (Springfield, IL: C. C. Thomas, 1965).

30. See Edgar Zigler and Jeanette Valentine, eds., *Project Head Start: A Legacy of the War on Poverty* (New York: The Free Press, 1979), 477–494; Laura Miller, "Head Start: A Moving Target," *Yale Law & Policy Review* 5(1987): 322.

31. Excerpt from President Lyndon Johnson's commencement address at Howard University on June 4, 1965. Cited in Alan Freeman, "Racism, Rights and the Quest for Equality of Opportunity: A Critical Legal Essay," *Harvard Civil Rights–Civil Liberties Law Review* 23(1988), 295.

32. Richard Herrnstein and Charles Murray, *The Bell Curve: Intelligence and Class Structure in American Life* (New York: The Free Press, 1994).

33. See Derrick Bell, *And We Are Not Saved: The Elusive Quest for Racial Justice* (New York: Basic Books, 1987), 102–109; Harold Cruse, *Plural but Equal: A Critical Study of Blacks and Minorities in America's Plural Society* (New York: William Morrow, 1987), 20–24.

34. Robert S. Browne, "A Case for Separation," in *Separatism or Integration: Which Way for America: A Dialogue*, eds. Robert Browne and Bayard Rustin (New York: A. Philip Randolph Educational Fund, 1968): 7–15.

35. See Silberman, supra note 27; Kenneth Clark, *Dark Ghetto: Dilemmas of Social Power* (New York: Harper & Row, 1965), 129–153.

36. Howard Becker, *Outsiders* (New York: The Free Press, 1963) (generally considered the sociological foundational statement of labeling theory).

37. This analysis generally tracks Duncan Kennedy's argument that paternalism is inevitable in the law's construction of contrast and tort rules because it is analytically impossible simply to defer to the wishes of individuals. See Duncan Kennedy, "Distributive and Paternalist Motives in Contract and Tort Law, with Special Reference to Compulsory Terms and Unequal Bargaining Power," *Maryland Law Review* 41(1982): 563.

38. See generally Morton J. Horwitz, *The Transformation of American Law, 1870–1960: The Crisis of Legal Orthodoxy* (New York: Oxford University Press, 1992).

39. See Paul Gilroy, *The Black Atlantic: Modernity and Double Consciousness* (London: Routledge, 1993) (concept of "hybridity" of reciprocal cultural influence); Andrew Ross, *No Respect: Intellectuals and Popular Culture* (New York: Routledge, 1989), 65–101 (describing the influence of whites on African American rhythm-and-blues tradition that in turn influences mostly white rock-'n'-roll tradition).

Chapter 7

1. Richard Ford, *Racial Culture: A Critique* (Princeton, NJ: Princeton University Press, 2005).

2. Ford, supra note 1, at 39–41.

3. See Ford, supra note 1; Ford, *The Race Card: How Bluffing about Bias Makes Race Relations Worse* (New York: Farrar, Straus & Giroux, 2008).

4. See Ford, *Racial Culture,* supra note 1, at 61–64 (adopting notion of racial identity as a performance, citing noted postmodern theorist Judith Butler's groundbreaking book, *Gender Trouble* [New York: Routledge, 1990]).

5. See Michel Foucault, *The Order of Things: An Archaeology of the Human Sciences* (New York: Pantheon Books, 1971); Herbert L. Dreyfus and Paul Rabinow. *Michel Foucault: Beyond Structuralism and Hermeneutics,* 2nd ed. (Chicago: University of Chicago Press, 1983).

6. Gary Peller, "The Metaphysics of American Law," *California Law Review* 73(1985): 1181 (discussing the category of "social subjectivity" as one categorically eliminated by liberal metaphysics of the subject/object dichotomy).

7. See Karl Marx, "The Fetishism of the Commodity and Its Secret," in *Capital, Volume 1: A Critique of Political Economy* (London: Penguin Books, 1992); Georg Lukács, "Reification and the Consciousness of the Proletariat," in *History and Class Consciousness* (London: The Merlin Press Ltd., 1971).

8. The idea that "existence precedes essence" is a central tenet of existentialist philosophy. The slogan was coined by Jean-Paul Sartre, *Existentialism Is a Humanism* (New Haven, CT: Yale University Press, 2007) (translated by Carol Macomber, introduction by Annie Cohen-Solal, and notes and preface by Arlette Elkaïm-Sartre).

9. Gary Peller, "Reason and the Mob: The Politics of Representation," *Tikkun* (July–August 1987): 28.

10. My description and understanding of "postmodernism" links "it" to "deconstruction" and "poststructuralism." See Jacques Derrida, *Of Grammatology,* trans. Gayatri Chakravorty Spivak (Baltimore: Johns Hopkins University Press, 1976); Jonathan Culler, *On Deconstruction: Theory and Criticism after Structuralism* (Ithaca, NY: Cornell University Press, 1983); Hans Bertens, *The Idea of the Postmodern: A History* (London: Routledge, 1995); Steven Best and Douglas Kellner, *Postmodern Theory* (New York: Guilford Press, 1991); Steven Best and Douglas Kellner, *The Postmodern Turn* (New York: Guilford Press, 1997); Judith Butler, "Contingent Foundations," in *Feminist Contentions: A Philosophical Exchange,* eds. Seyla Benhabib et al. (New York: Routledge, 1995).

11. See Michel Foucault, *Power/Knowledge: Selected Interviews and Other Writings, 1972–1977,* ed. Colin Gordon (New York: Pantheon, 1980).

12. Nathan A. Scott, Jr., "The New *Trahison des Clercs*: Reflections on the Present Crisis in Humanistic Studies," *Virginia Quarterly Review* (Summer 1986).

13. Michel Foucault, *Society Must Be Defended: Lectures at the College de France, 1975–76* (New York: St. Martin's Press, 2003), 7; Foucault, supra note 10.

14. Ford, supra note 1, at 211.

BIBLIOGRAPHY

Aberbach, Joel D., and Jack L. Walker. "The Meanings of Black Power: A Comparison of White and Black Interpretations of a Political Slogan." *American Political Science Review* 64(1970): 367–388.

Abernathy, Ralph David. *And the Walls Came Tumbling Down.* New York: Harper & Row, 1989.

Abram, Morris. "Affirmative Action: Fair Shakers and Social Engineers." *Harvard Law Review* 99 (1986): 1312–1326.

Abusharaf, Rogaia Mustafa. *Female Circumcision: Multicultural Perspectives.* Philadelphia: University of Pennsylvania Press, 2007.

Aickin, Mary. *A Case of Black and White: Northern Volunteers and Southern Freedom Summers 1964–65.* Westport, CT: Greenwood Press, 1982.

Aldridge, Delores P. "Status of Africana/Black Studies in Higher Education in the U.S." In *Out of the Revolution: The Development of Africana Studies,* edited by Delores P. Aldridge and Carlene Young, 519–544. Lanham, MD: Lexington Books, 2000.

Alexander, William, ed. *Memoir of Captain Paul Cuffee, A Man of Colour.* York, PA, 1811.

Alkalimat, Abd-l Hakimu Ibn. "The Ideology of Black Social Science." In *The Death of White Sociology,* edited by Joyce Ladner, 173–189. New York: Random House, 1973.

Allen, Norm. "Religion and the New African American Intellectuals." *Nature, Society, and Thought* 9(1996): 159–187.

Allen, Robert. *Black Awakening in Capitalist America: An Analytic History.* New York: Doubleday, 1969.

———. *A Guide to Black Power in America: An Historical Analysis.* London: Gollancz, 1970.

Allport, Gary. *The Nature of Prejudice.* New York: Perseus Books, 1954.

Anderson, Elizabeth. "Integration, Affirmative Action, and Strict Scrutiny." *New York University Law Review* 77(2002): 1195–1271.

———. "Racial Integration as a Compelling Interest." *Constitutional Commentary* 21(2004): 15–40.

Anderson, S. E. "The Fragmented Movement." *Black World/Negro Digest* (September 1968): 4–10.

Ani, Marimba. *Yurugu: An African-Centered Critique of European Thought and Behavior.* Trenton, NJ: Africa World Press, 1994.

Appiah, Kwame Anthony. *Cosmopolitanism: Ethics in a World of Strangers.* New York: W. W. Norton & Co., 2006.

Aptheker, Herbert. *A Documentary History of the Negro People in the United States.* Vol. 1. New York: Citadel Press, 1951.

———. *Writings by W. E. B. Du Bois in Periodicals Edited by Others.* Millwood, NY: Kraus-Thomson, 1982.

Arsenault, Raymond. *Freedom Riders: 1961 and the Struggle for Racial Justice.* New York: Oxford University Press, 2006.

Asante, Molefi Kete. *Afrocentricity.* Trenton, NJ: Africa World Press, 1998.

Asare, William Kweku. *Slavery Reparations in Perspective.* Victoria, BC: Trafford, 2002.

Balkin, Jack M. "*Brown v. Board of Education*: A Critical Introduction." *What Brown v. Board of Education Should Have Said,* edited by Jack M. Balkin, 1–76. New York: NYU Press, 2001.

Ballard, Alan B. *The Education of Black Folk: The Afro-American Struggle for Knowledge in White America.* New York: Harper, 1974.

Banks, William L. *The Case Against Black Reparation.* Haverford, PA: Infinity Publishing, 2001.

Baraka, Amiri. "A Black Value System." *Black Scholar* 1(November 1969): 54–60.

———. "The Pan-African Party and the Black Nation." *Black Scholar* 2(March 1971): 24–32.

———. *Raise, Race, Rays, Raze.* New York: Random House, 1971.

Barbour, Floyd, ed. *The Black Power Revolt: A Collection of Essays.* Boston: Sargent, 1968.

Barnes, Catherine A. *Journey from Jim Crow: The Desegregation of Southern Transit.* New York: Columbia University Press, 1983.

Bartholet, Elizabeth. "Application of Title VII to Jobs in High Places." *Harvard Law Review* 95(1982): 945–1027.

Bauman, Richard W. *Critical Legal Studies: A Guide to the Literature.* Boulder, CO: Westview Press, 1996.

Beck, John, and Richard Saxe, eds. *Teaching the Culturally Disadvantaged Pupil.* Springfield, IL: C. C. Thomas, 1965.

Becker, Howard. *Outsiders.* New York: The Free Press, 1963.

Bell, Derrick A. *And We Are Not Saved: The Elusive Quest for Racial Justice.* New York: Basic Books, 1987.

———. "*Bakke,* Minority Admissions and the Usual Price of Racial Remedies." *California Law Review* 67(1979): 3–20.

Bendiner, Robert. *The Politics of Schools: A Crisis in Self-Government.* New York: Harper & Row, 1969.

Bennett, Lerone. *Before the Mayflower: A History of the Negro in America, 1619–1966.* 3rd ed. Chicago: Johnson Publishing Co., 1966.

———. *The Challenge of Blackness.* Chicago: Johnson Publishing Co., 1972.

———. "Of Time, Space, and Revolution." *Ebony* (August 1969): 24–44.

Bertens, Hans. *The Idea of the Postmodern: A History.* London: Routledge, 1995.

Berube, Maurice R., and Marilyn Gittell, eds. *Confrontation at Ocean Hill-Brownsville: The New York School Strikes of 1968.* New York: Praeger, 1969.

Best, Steven, and Douglas Kellner. *Postmodern Theory.* New York: Guilford Press, 1991.

———. *The Postmodern Turn.* New York: Guilford Press, 1997.

Bickel, Alexander. *The Morality of Consent.* New Haven, CT: Yale University Press, 1975.

Biondi, Martha. *To Stand and Fight: The Struggle for Civil Rights in New York City.* Cambridge, MA: Harvard University Press, 2003.

Bittker, Boris I. *The Case for Black Reparations.* Boston: Beacon Press, 1973.

Black, Charles, Jr. "The Lawfulness of the Segregation Decisions." *Yale Law Journal* 69(1960): 421–431.

Blackwell, James E. *The Black Community: Diversity and Unity.* New York: Harper & Row, 1985.

Blauner, Robert. *Racial Oppression in America.* New York: Harper & Row, 1972.

Bloice, Carl. "Black Labor Is Black Power." *Black Scholar* 2(October 1970): 29–32.

Bloom, Allan. *The Closing of the American Mind.* New York: Simon & Schuster, 1987.

Blumberg, Rhoda L. *Civil Rights: The 1960s Freedom Struggle.* Boston: Twayne Publishers, 1984.

Blumer, Herbert. "Race Prejudice as a Sense of Group Position." *Pacific Sociological Review* 1(Spring 1958): 3–7.

Blumrosen, Alfred. "Strangers in Paradise: *Griggs v. Duke Power Co.* and the

Concept of Employment Discrimination." *Michigan Law Review* 71(1972): 59–110.

Boggs, James, and Grace L. Boggs. *Revolution and Evolution in the Twentieth Century.* New York: Monthly Review Press, 1974.

Boyle, James, ed. *Critical Legal Studies.* New York: NYU Press, 1992.

Boyle, Sarah Patton. "Inside a Segregationist." In *White on Black: The Views of Twenty-two White Americans on the Negro,* edited by E. B. Thompson and H. Nipson, 48. Chicago: Johnson Publishing Co., 1963.

Bracey, John Jr., August Meier, and Elliot Rudwick, eds. *Black Nationalism in America.* Indianapolis, IN: Bobbs-Merrill Co., 1970.

Branch, Taylor. *At Canaan's Edge: America in the King Years, 1965–1968.* New York: Simon & Schuster, 2006.

———. *Parting the Waters: America in the King Years, 1954–1963.* New York: Simon & Schuster, 1988.

———. *Pillar of Fire: America in the King Years, 1963–1965.* New York: Simon & Schuster, 1998.

Breitman, George, ed. *Malcolm X Speaks: Selected Speeches and Statements.* New York: Merit Publishers, 1965.

Brest, Paul. "Foreword: In Defense of the Antidiscrimination Principle." *Harvard Law Review* 90(1976): 1–54.

———. "*Palmer v. Thompson*: An Approach to the Problem of Unconstitutional Legislative Motivation." *Supreme Court Review* (1971): 95–146.

Brisbane, Robert. *Black Activism: Racial Revolution in the United States, 1954–1970.* Valley Forge, PA: Judson Press, 1974.

Brooks, Tom (Thomas R.). "Tragedy at Ocean Hill." *Dissent* 16(1969): 28–40.

———. *Walls Come Tumbling Down: A History of the Civil Rights Movement, 1940–1970.* Englewood Cliffs, NJ: Prentice Hall, 1974.

Brophy, Alfred L. *Reconstructing the Dreamland: The Tulsa Riot of 1921—Race, Reparations, and Reconciliation.* New York: Oxford University Press, 2002.

Brown, Dorothy A., ed. *Critical Race Theory: Cases, Materials and Problems.* 2nd ed. Minneapolis: West, 2007.

Brown, Elaine. *A Taste of Power: A Black Woman's Story.* New York: Doubleday, 1992.

Brown, H. Rap. *Die, Nigger, Die! A Political Autobiography.* Chicago: Lawrence Hill Books, 1969.

Brown, Scott. *Fighting for US: Maulana Karenga, the US Organization, and Black Cultural Nationalism.* New York: NYU Press, 2003.

Browne, Robert S. "The Case for Black Separatism." *Ramparts* 6(December 1967): 46–51.

————. "A Case for Separation." In *Separatism or Integration, Which Way for America: A Dialogue,* edited by Robert Browne and Bayard Rustin, 7–15. New York: A. Philip Randolph Educational Fund, 1968.

Bunche, Ralph J. "A Critical Analysis of the Tactics and Programs of Minority Groups." *Journal of Negro Education* 4(1935): 308–320.

Burkett, Randall K. *Garveyism as a Religious Movement: The Institutionalization of a Black Civil Religion.* Metuchen, NJ: Scarecrow Press, 1978.

Bush, Roderick. *We Are Not What We Seem: Black Nationalism and Class Struggle in the American Century.* New York: NYU Press, 1999.

Butler, Judith. "Contingent Foundations." In *Feminist Contentions: A Philosophical Exchange,* edited by Seyla Benhabib et al., 35–58. New York: Routledge, 1995.

————. *Gender Trouble.* New York: Routledge, 1990.

Cahn, Steven M. *The Affirmative Action Debate.* 2nd ed. New York: Routledge, 2002.

Calmore, John O. "Fair Housing vs. Fair Housing: The Problems with Providing Increased Housing Opportunities through Spatial Deconcentration." *Clearinghouse Review* 14(May 1980): 7.

Carlisle, Rodney P. *The Roots of Black Nationalism.* Port Washington, NY: Kennikat Press, 1975.

Carmichael, Stokely. *Stokely Speaks: Black Power Back to Pan-Africanism.* New York: Random House, 1971.

Carmichael, Stokely, and Charles V. Hamilton. *Black Power: The Politics of Liberation in America.* New York: Random House, 1967.

Carson, Clayborne. *In Struggle: SNCC and the Black Awakening of the 1960s.* Cambridge, MA: Harvard University Press, 1981.

Carson, Clayborne, David J. Garrow, Bill Kovach, and Carol Polsgrove, compilers. *Reporting Civil Rights: American Journalism 1941–1963.* New York: Library of America, 2003.

————. *Reporting Civil Rights: American Journalism 1963–1973.* New York: Library of America, 2003.

Carter, Robert. "A Reassessment of *Brown v. Board.*" In *Shades of Brown: New Perspectives on School Desegregation,* edited by Derrick Bell, 21–28. New York: Teachers College Press, Teachers College, Columbia University, 1980.

Cassity, Michael. *Legacy of Fear: American Race Relations to 1900.* Westport, CT: Greenwood Press, 1985.

Chafe, William H. *Civilities and Civil Rights: Greensboro, North Carolina, and the Black Struggle for Freedom.* New York: Oxford University Press, 1980.

Chrisman, Robert. "The Formation of a Revolutionary Black Culture." *Black Scholar* 1(June 1970): 2–9.

Clark, Kenneth B. *Dark Ghetto: Dilemmas of Social Power.* New York: Harper & Row, 1965.

———. "Effect of Prejudice and Discrimination on Personality Development." Midcentury White House Conference on Children and Youth, 1950.

Cleaver, Eldridge. "The Crisis of the Black Bourgeoisie." *Black Scholar* 4(1973): 2–11.

———. *Eldridge Cleaver, Post-Prison Writings and Speeches.* Edited by Robert Scheer. New York: Random House, 1969.

———. *Soul on Ice.* New York: Laurel, 1968.

Cohen, Morris. "The Basis of Contract." *Harvard Law Review* 46(1933): 533–592.

Colaiaco, James A. "Martin Luther King, Jr., and the Paradox of Nonviolent Direct Action." *Phylon* 47(1986): 16–28.

Collins, Patricia Hill. *From Black Power to Hip Hop: Racism, Nationalism, and Feminism.* Philadelphia: Temple University Press, 2006.

Cook, Samuel D. "The Tragic Myth of Black Power." *New South* 21(Summer 1966): 58–64.

Corlett, J. Angelo. *Race, Racism, & Reparations.* Ithaca, NY: Cornell University Press, 2003.

Cox, Oliver. *Race Relations: Elements and Social Dynamics.* Detroit: Wayne State University Press, 1976.

Crenshaw, Kimberlé. "Foreword: Toward a Race-Conscious Pedagogy in Legal Education." *National Black Law Journal* 11(1989): 1–14.

———. "Race, Reform, and Retrenchment: Transformation and Legitimation in Antidiscrimination Law." *Harvard Law Review* 101(1988): 1331–1387.

———. "Whose Story Is It, Anyway? Feminist and Antiracist Appropriations of Anita Hill." In *Race-ing Justice, En-gendering Power: Essays on Anita Hill, Clarence Thomas, and the Construction of Social Reality,* edited by Toni Morrison, 402–440. New York: Pantheon Books, 1992.

Crenshaw, Kimberlé, Neil Gotanda, Gary Peller, and Kendall Thomas, eds. *Critical Race Theory: The Key Writings That Formed the Movement.* New York: New Press, 1995.

Cronon, Edmund D. *Black Moses: The Story of Marcus Garvey and the Universal Negro Improvement Association.* Madison: University of Wisconsin Press, 1955.

Cross, Theodore. *The Black Power Imperative: Racial Inequality and the Politics of Nonviolence.* New York: Faulkner, 1984.

Cruse, Harold. "Black and White: Outlines of the Next Stage." *Black World* (January 1971): 19.

———. *The Crisis of the Negro Intellectual.* New York: William Morrow & Co., 1967.

———. "The Fire This Time?" *New York Review of Books* (May 8, 1969): 13–18.

———. "Negro Nationalism's New Wave." *New Leader* (March 19, 1962): 16.

———. *Plural but Equal: A Critical Study of Black and Minorities and America's Plural Society.* New York: William Morrow, 1987.

———. *Rebellion or Revolution?* New York: William Morrow, 1968.

———. "Revolutionary Nationalism and the Afro-American." *Studies on the Left* 2(1962): 12–13.

Culler, Jonathan. *On Deconstruction: Theory and Criticism after Structuralism.* Ithaca, NY: Cornell University Press, 1983.

Cullingford, Cedric. *Prejudice: From Individual Identity to Nationalism in Young People.* London: Kogan Page, 2000.

Daniels, Roger, and Harry H. L. Kitano. *American Racism: Exploration of the Nature of Prejudice.* Englewood Cliffs, NJ: Prentice Hall, 1970.

Davidson, Douglas. "The Furious Passage of the Black Graduate Student." In *The Death of White Sociology,* edited by Joyce Ladner, 23. New York: Random House, 1973.

Davis, Townsend. *Weary Feet, Rested Souls: A Guided History of the Civil Rights Movement.* New York: W. W. Norton & Company, 1998.

Delany, Martin R. *The Condition, Elevation, Emigration and Destiny of the Colored People of the United States,* 159–173. Baltimore: Black Classic Press, 1993.

Delgado, Richard. *Critical Race Theory: An Introduction.* New York: NYU Press, 2001.

———. "The Imperial Scholar: Reflections on a Review of Civil Rights Literature." *University of Pennsylvania Law Review* 132(1984): 561–578.

Delgado, Richard, and Jean Stefancic, eds. *Critical Race Theory: The Cutting Edge.* 2nd ed. Philadelphia: Temple University Press, 2000.

Derrida, Jacques. *Of Grammatology.* Translated by Gayatri Chakravorty Spivak. Baltimore: Johns Hopkins University Press, 1976.

Dittmer, John. *Local People: The Struggle for Civil Rights in Mississippi.* Urbana: University of Illinois Press, 1994.

Dixson, Adrienne D., and Celia K. Rousseau, eds. *Critical Race Theory in Education: All God's Children Got a Song.* New York: Routledge, 2006.

Dollard, John. *Caste and Class in a Southern Town.* New York: Doubleday, 1949.

Doner, Eric, and Joshua Brown. *Forever Free: The Story of Emancipation and Reconstruction.* New York: Knopf, 2005.

Dossett, Kate. *Bridging Race Divides: Black Nationalism, Feminism, and Integration in the United States, 1896–1935.* Tallahassee: University Press of Florida, 2009.

Doyle, Bertram Wilbur. *The Etiquette of Race Relations in the South: A Study in Social Control.* Chicago: University of Chicago Press, 1937.

Drake, St. Clair. *Black Folk, Here and There.* Los Angeles: University of California Press, 1987.

Draper, Theodore. *The Rediscovery of Black Nationalism.* New York: Viking Press, 1969.

Dreyfus, Herbert L., and Paul Rabinow. *Michel Foucault: Beyond Structuralism and Hermeneutics.* 2nd ed. Chicago: University of Chicago Press, 1983.

D'Souza, Dinesh. *Illiberal Education: The Politics of Race and Sex on Campus.* New York: Vintage, 1992.

Duberman, Martin. "Black Power in America." *Partisan Review* (Winter 1968): 34–48.

Du Bois, W. E. B. "Does the Negro Need Separate Schools?" *Journal of Negro Education* 4(July 1935): 328–335.

———. *Dusk of Dawn.* New York: Harcourt, Brace & World, 1940.

———. "A Negro Nation within the Nation." *Current History* 42(June 1935): 265–270.

———. "Postscript: The N.A.A.C.P. and Race Segregation." *The Crisis* 41(April 1934): 53.

———. *The Souls of Black Folk.* Chicago: A. C. McClurg & Co., 1903.

Duckitt, John. "Reducing Prejudice: An Historical and Multi-Level Approach." In *Understanding Prejudice, Racism, and Social Conflict,* edited by Martha Augoustinos and Katherine Reynolds, 253–272. London: Sage, 2001.

Duster, Troy. "Individual Fairness, Group Preferences, and the California Strategy." In *Race and Representation: Affirmative Action,* edited by Robert Post and Michael Rogin, 111–134. New York: Zone Books, 1998.

Dworkin, Ronald. "Affirmative Action: Does It Work? In *Sovereign Virtue: The Theory and Practice of Equality,* 386–408. Cambridge, MA: Harvard University Press, 2002.

———. "Affirmative Action: Is It Fair?" In *Sovereign Virtue: The Theory and Practice of Equality,* 409–426. Cambridge, MA: Harvard University Press, 2002.

———. *Is Bill Cosby Right? Or Has the Black Middle Class Lost Its Mind?* New York: Basic Civitas Books, 2005.

———. *A Matter of Principle.* Cambridge, MA: Harvard University Press, 1985.

Dyson, Michael E. *I May Not Get There with You: The True Martin Luther King, Jr.* New York: Touchstone, 2000.

————. *Making Malcolm: The Myth and Meaning of Malcolm X.* New York: Oxford University Press, 1995.

Eastland, Terry. *Ending Affirmative Action: The Case for Colorblind Justice.* New York: Basic Books, 1997.

Edsall, Thomas, and E. J. Dionne, Jr. "Core Democratic Constituencies Split: Support for Nominee Reflects Power of Black Vote in the South." *Washington Post* (October 16, 1991).

Edwards, Harry. *Black Students.* New York: The Free Press, 1970.

Ehrman, John. *The Rise of Neo-Conservatism: Intellectuals and Foreign Affairs, 1945–1994.* New Haven, CT: Yale University Press, 1995.

Eisenberg, Theodore. "Disproportionate Impact and Illicit Motive: Theories of Constitutional Adjudication." *New York University Law Review* 52(1977): 36–172.

Ellison, Ralph. "An American Dilemma: A Review." In *Shadow and Act.* New York: Random House, 1964.

Ely, James W., Jr. "Book Review: *The Crisis of Conservative Virginia—The Byrd Organization and the Politics of Massive Resistance.*" *The Journal of Southern History* 62(May 1977): 324.

Ely, John Hart. "The Constitutionality of Reverse Racial Discrimination." *University of Chicago Law Review* 41(1974): 723–741.

————. "Legislative and Administrative Motivation in Constitutional Law." *Yale Law Journal* 79(1970): 1205–1342.

Epps, Edgar G. "The Integrationists." In *Through Different Eyes: Black and White Perspectives on American Race Relations,* edited by Peter I. Rose, Stanley Rothman, and William J. Wilson, 62–71. New York: Oxford University Press, 1973.

Epstein, Edward Jay. "The Black Panthers and the Police: A Pattern of Genocide?" *The New Yorker* (February 13, 1971).

Epstein, Jason. "The Politics of School Decentralization." *New York Review of Books* (June 1968): 26–32.

Escott, Paul D., et al., eds. *Major Problems in the History of the American South.* 2nd ed. Vol. 2, *The New South.* Boston: Houghton Mifflin, 1999.

Essien-Udom, Essien Udosen. *Black Nationalism: A Search for an Identity in America.* Chicago: University of Chicago Press, 1962.

Estlund, Cynthia. *Working Together: How Workplace Bonds Strengthen a Diverse Democracy.* Oxford: Oxford University Press, 2005.

"Excerpts from Paper on Which the 'Black Power' Philosophy Is Based." *New York Times* (August 5, 1966).

Exum, William H. *Paradoxes of Protest: Black Student Activism in a White University.* Philadelphia: Temple University Press, 1985.

Ezorsky, Gertrude. *Racism and Justice: The Case for Affirmative Action*. Ithaca, NY: Cornell University Press, 1991.

Fager, Charles E. *White Reflections on Black Power*. Grand Rapids, MI: W. B. Eerdmans Publishing Company, 1967.

Fairclough, Adam. *A Class of Their Own: Black Teachers in the Segregated South*. Cambridge, MA: Harvard University Press, 2007.

———. *To Redeem the Soul of America: The Southern Christian Leadership Conference & Martin Luther King*. Athens: University of Georgia Press, 1987.

Fallon, Richard H. "To Each According to His Ability, from None According to His Race: The Concept of Merit in the Law of Antidiscrimination." *Boston University Law Review* 60(1980): 815–878.

Fanon, Frantz. *Black Skin, White Masks*. Translated by Charles L. Markmann. New York: Grove Press, 1967.

———. *Studies in a Dying Colonialism*. Translated by Constance Farrington. New York: Monthly Review Press, 1965.

———. *The Wretched of the Earth*. Translated by Constance Farrington. New York: Grove Press, 1965.

Farmer, James. *Freedom, When?* New York: Random House, 1965.

———. "We Cannot Destroy Segregation with a Weapon of Segregation." *Equality* (November 1944): 2.

Feagin, Joe L. *Racist America: Roots, Current Realities, and Future Reparations*. New York: Routledge, 2000.

Fein, Leonard. "Community Schools and Social Theory: The Limits of Universalism." In *Community Control of Schools*, edited by Henry M. Levin, 76–99. Washington, DC: Brookings Institution Press, 1970.

Feldman, Paul. "How the Cry for 'Black Power' Began." *Dissent* 13(1966): 472.

Fischer, Roger A. "Ghetto and Gown: The Birth of Black Studies." *Current History* 57(1969).

Fishbein, Harold D. *Peer Prejudice and Discrimination: The Origins of Prejudice*. 2nd ed. Mahwah, NJ: Erlbaum, 2002.

Fiss, Owen. "Groups and the Equal Protection Clause." *Philosophy and Public Affairs* 5(1976): 107–177.

Foner, Philip S., ed. *The Black Panthers Speak*. New York: HarperCollins, 1969.

Ford, Richard. *The Race Card: How Bluffing about Bias Makes Race Relations Worse*. New York: Farrar, Straus & Giroux, 2008.

———. *Racial Culture: A Critique*. Princeton, NJ: Princeton University Press, 2005.

Forsythe, Dennis. "Radical Sociology and Blacks." In *The Death of White Sociology*, edited by Joyce Ladner, 213. New York: Random House, 1973.

Foster, Badi. "Toward a Definition of Black Referents." In *Beyond Black and White: An Alternative America*, edited by Vernon J. Nixon and Badi Foster, 7–22. Boston: Little, Brown & Co., 1971.

Foster, William Z. *The Negro People in American History.* New York: International Publishers, 1954.

Foucault, Michel. *The Order of Things: An Archaeology of the Human Sciences.* New York: Pantheon Books, 1971.

———. *Society Must Be Defended: Lectures at the College de France, 1975–76.* New York: St. Martin's Press, 2003.

———. "Truth and Power." In *Power/Knowledge: Selected Interviews and Other Writings, 1972–1977*, edited by Colin Gordon. New York: Pantheon Books, 1980.

Franklin, Robert M. *Crisis in the Village: Restoring Hope in African American Communities.* Minneapolis: Fortress Press, 2007.

Frazier, E. Franklin. *The Negro Family in the United States.* Rev. ed. Chicago: University of Chicago Press, 1957.

Fredrickson, George M. *The Black Image in the White Mind: The Debate in Afro-American Character and Destiny, 1817–1914.* New York: Harper & Row, 1972.

———. *White Supremacy.* New York: Oxford University Press, 1981.

Freeman, Alan. "Legitimating Racial Discrimination through Antidiscrimination Law: A Critical Review of Supreme Court Doctrine." *Minnesota Law Review* 62(1978): 1049–1120.

———. "Racism, Rights and the Quest for Equality of Opportunity: A Critical Legal Essay." *Harvard Civil Rights–Civil Liberties Law Review* 23(1988): 295–392.

Friedland, William, and Harry Edwards. "Confrontation at Cornell." *Trans-Action* (June 1969): 29.

Gaertner, Samuel L., and John F. Dovidio. "The Aversive Form of Racism." In *Prejudice, Discrimination, and Racism*, edited by John F. Dovidio and Samuel L. Gaertner, 61–89. Orlando, FL: Academic, 1986.

Garcia, Jorge. "The Heart of Racism." *Journal of Social Philosophy* 27(1996): 5–46.

Gardell, Mattias. *In the Name of Elijah Muhammad: Louis Farrakhan and the Nation of Islam.* Durham, NC: Duke University Press, 1996.

Garrow, David J. *Bearing the Cross: Martin Luther King, Jr., and the Southern Christian Leadership Conference.* New York: William Morrow & Co., 1986.

Garvey, Amy J. *Garvey and Garveyism.* New York: Collier, 1970.

Garvey, Amy J., ed. *The Philosophy and Opinions of Marcus Garvey*. 2 vols. New York: Atheneum, 1969.

Gates, Henry L., ed. *Black Literature and Literary Theory*. London: Methuen & Co., 1984.

Gates, Robbins L. *The Making of Massive Resistance: Virginia's Politics of Public School Desegregation, 1954–1956*. Chapel Hill: University of North Carolina Press, 1962.

Gayle, Addison, ed. *The Black Aesthetic*. New York: Doubleday, 1971.

Gershman, Carl. "Black Nationalism and Conservative Politics." *Dissent* 17(1970): 10–12.

Gilroy, Paul. *After Empire: Multiculture or Postcolonial Melancholia*. New York: Columbia University Press, 2005.

———. *The Black Atlantic: Modernity and Double Consciousness*. London: Routledge, 1993.

Glazer, Nathan, and Daniel Patrick Moynihan. *Beyond the Melting Pot*. Boston: MIT Press, 1963.

Goldman, Peter. *The Death and Life of Malcolm X*. Champaign: University of Illinois Press, 1979.

Gordon, Milton M. *Assimilation in American Life: The Role of Race, Religion, and National Origins*. New York: Oxford University Press, 1964.

Gordon, Robert. "New Developments in Legal Theory." In *The Politics of Law: A Progressive Critique*, edited by David Kairys. New York: Basic Books, 1998.

Gouldner, Alvin W. "Anti-Minotaur: The Myth of a Value-Free Sociology." *Social Problems* 9(Winter 1962): 199–213.

Grant, Colin. *Negro with a Hat: The Rise and Fall of Marcus Garvey and His Dream of Mother Africa*. New York: Oxford University Press, 2008.

Greer, Edward, ed. *Black Liberation Politics: A Reader*. Boston: Allyn and Bacon, 1971.

Griffith, Cyril E. *The African Dream: Martin R. Delany and the Emergence of Pan-African Thought*. University Park: Pennsylvania State University Press, 1975.

Gross, Ariela. *What Blood Won't Tell: A History of Race on Trial in America*. Cambridge, MA: Harvard University Press, 2008.

Gunther, Gerald. *Learned Hand: The Man and the Judge*. New York: Knopf, 1994.

Habermas, Jürgen. *Knowledge and Human Interests*. Translated by Jeremy J. Shapiro. Boston: Beacon Press, 1971.

Haines, Herbert H. *Black Radicals and the Civil Rights Mainstream, 1954–1970*. Knoxville: University of Tennessee Press, 1988.

Hale, Robert. "Coercion and Distribution in a Supposedly Non-Coercive State." *Political Science Quarterly* 38(1923): 470–494.

Hale-Benson, Janice E. *Black Children: Their Roots, Culture, and Learning Styles.* Salt Lake City: Brigham Young University Press, 1982.

Haley, Alex, ed. *The Autobiography of Malcolm X.* New York: Grove Press, 1965.

Hall, Simon. *Peace and Freedom: The Civil Rights and Antiwar Movements in the 1960s.* Philadelphia: University of Pennsylvania Press, 2006.

Hand, Learned. *The Bill of Rights (Oliver Wendell Holmes Lectures).* Cambridge, MA: Harvard University Press, 1962.

Harding, Vincent. *The Other American Revolution.* Los Angeles: Center for Afro-American Studies, University of California, 1980.

Hare, Nathan. "The Challenge of a Black Scholar." In *The Death of White Sociology,* edited by Joyce A. Ladner, 67–78. New York: Random House, 1973.

Harlan, Louis R. *Booker T. Washington: The Making of a Black Leader, 1865–1901.* New York: Oxford University Press, 1972.

———. *Booker T. Washington: The Wizard of Tuskegee, 1901–1915.* New York: Oxford University Press, 1983.

Harlan, Louis R., and Raymond W. Smock, eds. *The Booker T. Washington Papers.* 14 vols. Urbana: University of Illinois Press, 1972–1989.

Harris, Luke C. "Contesting the Ambivalence and Hostility to Affirmative Action within the Black Community." In *A Companion to African-American Philosophy,* edited by Tommy Lee Lott and John P. Pittman, 324–333. London: Blackwell Publishing, 2003.

Harris, Robert, Jr. "The Intellectual and Institutional Development of Africana Studies." In *Black Studies in the United States: Three Essays,* edited by Darlene Clark Hine, Robert L. Harris Jr., and Nellie McKay. New York: The Ford Foundation, 1990.

Harris, Sheldon H. *Paul Cuffe: Black American and the African Return.* New York: Simon & Schuster, 1972.

Hart, Henry, and Albert Sacks. *The Legal Process: Basic Problems in the Making and Application of Law.* Cambridge, MA: Harvard University Press, 1958.

Hernton, Calvin. *Sex and Racism in America.* New York: Grove Press, 1965.

Herrnstein, Richard, and Charles Murray. *The Bell Curve: Intelligence and Class Structure in American Life.* New York: The Free Press, 1994.

Hill, Robert A., ed. *Marcus Garvey and Universal Negro Improvement Association Papers.* 10 vols. Berkeley: University of California Press, 1983.

Honey, Michael Keith. *Black Workers Remember: An Oral History of Segregation, Unionisim and the Freedom Struggle.* Berkeley: University of California Press, 2000.

hooks, bell. *Ain't I a Woman: Black Women and Feminism.* Boston: South End Press, 1981.

Horkheimer, Max, and Theodor W. Adorno. *Dialectic of Enlightenment.* Translated by John Cumming. New York: Continuum International, 1972.

Horowitz, David. *Uncivil Wars: The Controversy over Reparations for Slavery.* San Francisco: Encounter Books, 2002.

Horsman, Reginald. *Race and Manifest Destiny: The Origins of American Racial Anglo-Saxonism.* Cambridge, MA: Harvard University Press, 1981.

Horton, John, ed. *Liberalism, Multiculturalism and Toleration.* New York: St. Martin's Press, 1993.

Horwitz, Morton J. *The Transformation of American Law, 1870–1960: The Crisis of Legal Orthodoxy.* New York: Oxford University Press, 1992.

Howe, Stephen. *Afrocentrism: Mythical Pasts and Imagined Homes.* London: Verso, 1998.

Hudelson, Richard. *Marxism and Philosophy in the Twentieth Century: A Defense of Vulgar Marxism.* New York: Praeger, 1990.

Huggins, Nathan I. "Afro-Americans." In *Ethnic Leadership in America,* edited by John Higham, 91–118. Baltimore: Johns Hopkins University Press, 1978.

Hughes, Graham. "Reparations for Blacks?" *New York University Law Review* 43(1968): 1063–1074.

Humphrey, Hubert. "Address at the NAACP Convention (July 6, 1966)." In *The Rhetoric of Black Power,* edited by Robert L. Scott and Wayne Brockriede, 65. New York: Harper & Row, 1969.

Jackson, George. *Soledad Brother: The Prison Letters of George Jackson.* New York: Bantam, 1970.

Jencks, Christopher. *Inequality: A Reassessment of the Effect of Family and Schooling in America.* New York: Basic Books, 1972.

Johnson, James W. *Negro American, What Now?* New York: Viking Press, 1934.

Jones, James M. *Prejudice and Racism.* Reading, MA: Addison-Wesley Publishers, 1972.

Jones, LeRoi. "The Need for a Cultural Base to Civil Rites & Bpower Mooments." In *The Black Power Revolt,* edited by Floyd B. Barbour, 123–126. Boston: Sargent, 1968.

Jones, Yvonne V. "African American Cultural Nationalism." In *Cultural Portrayals of African Americans: Creating an Ethnic/Racial Identity,* edited by Janis F. Hutchinson, 113–138. Westport, CT: Greenwood, 1997.

Jordan, Jennifer. "Cultural Nationalism in the 1960s: Politics and Poetry." In *Race, Politics, and Culture: Critical Essays on the Radicalism of the 1960s,* edited by Adolph Reed, Jr., 29–60. Westport, CT: Greenwood Press, 1986.

Jordan, Winthrop D. *White over Black: American Attitudes toward the Negro, 1550–1812*. Chapel Hill: University of North Carolina Press, 1968.

Joseph, Peniel E. *Waiting 'Til the Midnight Hour: A Narrative History of Black Power in America.* New York: Henry Holt and Company, 2006.

Karlan, Pamela S. "Discriminatory Purpose and Mens Rea: The Tortured Argument of Invidious Intent." *Yale Law Journal* 93(1983): 111–134.

Karpinski, Andrew, and James Hilton. "Attitudes and the Implicit Association Test." *Journal of Personality and Social Psychology* 81(2001): 774–788.

Karst, Kenneth L., and Harold W. Horowitz. "Affirmative Action and Equal Protection." *Virginia Law Review* 60(1974): 955–974.

Keil, Charles. *Urban Blues.* Chicago: University of Chicago Press, 1966.

Kelman, Mark. *A Guide to Critical Legal Studies.* Cambridge, MA: Harvard University Press, 1987.

Kennedy, Duncan. "A Cultural Pluralist Case for Affirmative Action in Legal Academia." *Duke Law Journal* (1990): 705–757.

———. "Distributive and Paternalist Motives in Contract and Tort Law, with Special Reference to Compulsory Terms and Unequal Bargaining Power." *Maryland Law Review* 41(1982): 563–658.

———. *Legal Education and the Reproduction of Hierarchy: A Polemic Against the System—A Critical Edition.* New York: NYU Press, 2004.

———. "Radical Intellectuals in American Culture and Politics, or My Talk at the Gramsci Institute." *Rethinking Marxism* 1(1988): 121.

Kennedy, Duncan, and Frank Michelman. "Are Property and Contract Efficient?" *Hofstra Law Review* 8(1980): 711–770.

Kennedy, Randall. "Persuasion and Distrust: A Comment on the Affirmative Action Debate." *Harvard Law Review* 99(1986): 1327–1346.

Killian, Lewis M. "White Southerners." In *Through Different Eyes: Black and White Perspectives on American Race Relations,* edited by Peter I. Rose, Stanley Rothman, and William J. Wilson, 89–113. New York: Oxford University Press, 1973.

Kilson, Martin. "The New Black Intellectuals." *Dissent* 16(1969): 304.

Kim, Sunny. "Gender-Related Persecution: A Legal Analysis of Gender Bias in Asylum Law." *American University Journal of Gender & Law* 2(1990): 107–128.

King, Martin Luther, Jr. "An Experiment in Love." In *A Testament of Hope: The Essential Writings of Martin Luther King, Jr.,* edited by James M. Washington, 16. New York: HarperCollins, 1986.

————. "I Have a Dream." In *A Testament of Hope: The Essential Writings of Martin Luther King, Jr.*, edited by James Washington, 219. New York: HarperCollins, 1986.

————. *The Martin Luther King, Jr. Companion: Quotations from the Speeches, Essays, and Books of Martin Luther King, Jr.* New York: St. Martin's Press, 1968.

————. *Where Do We Go from Here: Chaos or Community?* Boston: Beacon Press, 1968.

Kirp, David L. "Schools as Sorters: The Constitutional and Policy Implications of Student Classifications." *University of Pennsylvania Law Review* 121(1973): 705–797.

Kitwana, Bakari. *The Hip-Hop Generation: Young Blacks and the Crisis in African American Culture.* New York: Basic Civitas Books, 2002.

Klarman, Michael J. *From Jim Crow to Civil Rights: The Supreme Court and the Struggle for Racial Equality.* New York: Oxford University Press, 2004.

Kochman, Thomas. *Black and White Styles in Conflict.* Chicago: University of Chicago Press, 1982.

Konadu, Kwasi B. *A View from the East: Black Cultural Nationalism and Education in New York City.* Syracuse, NY: Syracuse University Press, 2009.

Kozol, Jonathan. "Overcoming Apartheid." *The Nation* (December 19, 2005).

Lack, Robert. "Letter to the Editors." *New York Times* (March 9, 1981).

Ladd, Everett C. *Negro Political Leadership in the South.* Ithaca, NY: Cornell University Press, 1966.

Ladner, Joyce A. *Tomorrow's Tomorrow: The Black Woman.* New York: Doubleday, 1971.

————. "Tomorrow's Tomorrow: The Black Woman." In *The Death of White Sociology,* edited by Joyce A. Ladner, 414, 420–421. New York: Random House, 1973.

Lasch, Christopher. "The Trouble with Black Power." *New York Review of Books* (February 29, 1968): 10.

Lauter, Paul. "The Short, Happy Life of the Adams-Morgan Community School Project." *Harvard Educational Review* 38(1968): 235–262.

Lawrence, Charles. "The Id, the Ego and Equal Protection: Reckoning with Unconscious Racism." *Stanford Law Review* 39(1987): 317.

Lecky, Robert S., and H. Elliot Wright, eds. *Black Manifesto: Religion, Racism, and Reparations.* New York: Sheed & Ward, 1969.

Levine, Naomi, and Richard Cohen. *Ocean Hill-Brownsville: Schools in Crisis.* New York: Popular Press, 1969.

Levine, Robert S. *Martin Delany, Frederick Douglass, and the Politics of Representative Identity.* Chapel Hill: University of North Carolina Press, 1997.

Lewin, Tamar. "Herbert Wechsler, Legal Giant, Is Dead at 90." *New York Times* (April 28, 2000).

Lieberman, Myron. *The Future of Public Education.* Chicago: University of Chicago Press, 1960.

Liebow, Elliot. *Tally's Corner: A Study of Negro Streetcorner Men.* Lanham, MD: Rowman & Littlefield, 1966.

Lincoln, Charles E. *The Black Muslims in America.* Boston: Beacon Press, 1961.

Lomax, Louis E. *The Negro Revolt.* New York: New American Library, 1962.

Loury, Glenn. *The Anatomy of Racial Inequality.* Cambridge, MA: Harvard University Press, 2002.

————. "How to Mend Affirmative Action." *The Public Interest* 127(Spring 1997): 33–43. Available at http://www.bu.edu/irsd/articles/howtomnd.htm.

Loveless, Tom. *The Tracking Wars: State Reform Meets School Policy.* Washington, DC: Brookings Institution Press, 1999.

Lukács, Georg. "Reification and the Consciousness of the Proletariat." In *History and Class Consciousness: Studies in Marxist Dialectics,* 83–222. Translated by Rodney Livingstone. London: The Merlin Press Ltd., 1971.

Lusky, Louis. "The Stereotype: The Hard Core of Racism." *Buffalo Law Review* 13(1964): 450–461.

Lythcott, Stephen. "The Case for Black Studies." *Antioch Review* 29(1969): 149–154.

MacKinnon, Catherine, Carol Gilligan, Ellen Du Bois, and Carrie J. Menkel-Meadow. "Feminist Discourse, Moral Values, and the Law—A Conversation." *Buffalo Law Review* 34(1985): 11–88.

Mailer, Norman. "Black Power: A Discussion." *Partisan Review* 35(Spring 1968): 195–218.

————. *The White Negro.* San Francisco: City Lights Books, 1957.

Malcolm X. *The Autobiography of Malcolm X.* Edited by Alex Haley. New York: Grove Press, 1965.

————. *By Any Means Necessary: Speeches, Interviews and a Letter.* Edited by George Breitman. New York: Pathfinder, 1970.

————. *Malcolm X Speaks: Selected Speeches and Statements.* Edited by George Breitman. New York: Grove Press, 1965.

Malcolm X and James Farmer. "Separation or Integration: A Debate." *Dialogue* (May 1962): 14. Reprinted in *Black Protest Thought in the Twentieth Century,* edited by August Meier and Elliot Rudwick. Indianapolis, IN: Bobbs-Merrill Co., 1971.

Mannheim, Karl. *Ideology and Utopia: An Introduction to the Sociology of Knowledge*. Translated by Louis Wirth and Edward Shils. New York: Harcourt, Brace & Co., 1936.

Marable, Manning. "Black Nationalism in the 1970s: Through the Prism of Race and Class." *Socialist Review* 10(March–June 1980): 57–110.

———. *Race, Reform and Rebellion: The Second Reconstruction in Black America, 1945–1982*. Biloxi: University Press of Mississippi, 1984.

———. *W. E. B. Du Bois: Black Radical Democrat*. Boston: Twayne, 1986.

Marable, Manning, and Leith Mullings, eds. *Let Nobody Turn Us Around: An African American Anthology—Voices of Resistance, Reform and Renewal*. 2nd ed. Lanham, MD: Rowman & Littlefield, 2009.

Marcuse, Herbert. *Reason and Revolution: Hegel and the Rise of Social Theory*. London: Routledge, 1955.

Marine, Gene. *The Black Panthers*. New York: New American Library, 1969.

Marsh, Charles. *The Beloved Community: How Faith Shapes Social Justice from the Civil Rights Movement to Today*. New York: Basic Books, 2005.

Marshall, Ray. "The Negro and Organized Labor." *The Journal of Negro Education* 32(1963): 375–389.

Martin, Tony. *Race First: The Ideological and Organizational Struggle of Marcus Garvey and the Universal Negro Improvement Association*. Westport, CT: Greenwood Press, 1976.

Marx, Gary T. "Two Cheers for the National Riot Commission." In *Black America*, edited by John F. Szwed, 78. New York: Basic Books, 1970.

Marx, Karl. "The Fetishism of the Commodity and Its Secret." In *Capital, Volume 1: A Critique of Political Economy*, 163–177. London: Penguin Books, 1992.

Massey, Douglas. *Categorically Unequal: The American Stratification System*. New York: Russell Sage, 2007.

Matsuda, Mari J. "Looking to the Bottom: Critical Legal Studies and Reparations." *Harvard Civil Rights–Civil Liberties Law Review* 22(1987): 323–399.

Mayer, Martin. "The Full and Sometimes Very Surprising Story of Ocean Hill, the Teachers' Union and the Teacher Strikes of 1968." *New York Times Magazine* (February 2, 1969): 18.

Maynard, Robert. "Black Nationalism and Community Schools." In *Community Control of Schools*, edited by Henry M. Levin, 100–111. Washington, DC: Brookings Institution Press, 1970.

McCartney, John T. *Black Power Ideologies: An Essay in African-American Political Thought*. Philadelphia: Temple University Press, 1992.

McCoy, Rhody A. "The Formation of a Community-Controlled School District."

In *Community Control of Schools,* edited by Henry M. Levin, 169–190. Washington, DC: Brookings Institution Press, 1970.

McEvoy, James, and Abraham H. Miller, eds. *Black Power and Student Rebellion.* Berkeley, CA: Wadsworth Publishing, 1969.

Meier, August. *Negro Thought in America, 1880–1915: Racial Ideologies in the Age of Booker T. Washington.* Ann Arbor: University of Michigan Press, 1963.

Meier, August, and Elliot Rudwick, eds. *Black Protest Thought in the Twentieth Century.* Indianapolis, IN: Bobbs-Merrill Co., 1971.

———. *CORE: A Study in the Civil Rights Movement, 1942–1968.* New York: Oxford University Press, 1973.

Meier, August, Elliott Rudwick, and John Bracey, Jr., eds. *Black Nationalism in America.* Indianapolis, IN: Bobbs-Merrill Co., 1970.

Memmi, Albert. *The Colonizer and the Colonized.* Translated by Howard Greenfield. New York: Orion Press, 1967.

Miller, Laura. "Head Start: A Moving Target." *Yale Law & Policy Review* 5(1987): 322–344.

Miller, Loren. "Farewell to Liberals." In *Black Protest Thought in the Twentieth Century,* edited by August Meier and Elliot Rudwick. Indianapolis, IN: Bobbs-Merrill Co., 1971.

Moore, Wendy Leo. *Reproducing Racism: White Space, Elite Law Schools, and Racial Inequality.* Lanham, MD: Rowman & Littlefield, 2008.

Morris, Aldon D. *The Origins of the Civil Rights Movement: Black Communities Organizing for Change.* New York: The Free Press, 1984.

Moses, Wilson J. *The Golden Age of Black Nationalism, 1850–1925.* New York: Oxford University Press, 1978.

Moynihan, Daniel Patrick. "Text of the Moynihan Memorandum on the Status of Negroes." *New York Times* (March 1, 1970).

Muhammad, Elijah. *Message to the Blackman in America.* Chicago: Muhammad Mosque of Islam No. 2, 1965.

Munford, Clarence J. *Race and Reparations: A Black Perspective for the 21st Century.* Trenton, NJ: Africa World Press, 1996.

Murray, Albert. "White Norms, Black Deviation." In *The Death of White Sociology,* edited by Joyce A Ladner, 96. New York: Random House, 1973.

Muse, Benjamin. *The American Negro Revolution: From Nonviolence to Black Power.* Bloomington: Indiana University Press, 1968.

———. *Virginia's Massive Resistance.* Bloomington: Indiana University Press, 1961.

Myrdal, Gunnar. *An American Dilemma: The Negro Problem and Modern Democracy.* New York: Harper & Bros., 1944.

Newby, Idus A. *Jim Crow's Defense: Anti-Negro Thought in America, 1900–1930*. Westport, CT: Greenwood Press, 1968.

Newton, Huey P. *To Die for the People: The Writings of Huey P. Newton*. New York: Random House, 1972.

———. *War against the Panthers: A Study of Repression in America*. Chicago: Black Classic Press, 1996.

Nisbet, Robert. *Community and Power*. New York: Oxford University Press, 1962.

Nnaemeka, Obioma, ed. *Female Circumcision and the Politics of Knowledge: African Women in Imperialist Discourses*. Westport, CT: Praeger, 2005.

Norrell, Robert J. *Up from History: The Life of Booker T. Washington*. Boston: Harvard University Press, 2009.

Northrup, Herbert. "Organized Labor and Negro Workers." *The Journal of Political Economy* 51(1943): 206–221.

Nussbaum, Martha. *Cultivating Humanity: A Classical Defense of Reform in Liberal Education*. Cambridge, MA: Harvard University Press, 1997.

———. *For Love of Country: Debating the Limits of Patriotism*. Boston: Beacon Press, 1996.

Oakes, Jeannie. *Keeping Track: How Schools Structure Inequality*. New Haven, CT: Yale University Press, 2005.

Oba, Abdulmumini A. "Female Circumcision as Female Genital Mutilation: Human Rights or Cultural Imperialism?" *Global Jurist* 8(2008): 1–38.

O'Dell, Jack. "A Special Variety of Colonialism." *Freedomways* 7(Winter 1967): 7–14.

Ogbar, Jeffrey C. *Black Power: Radical Politics and African American Identity*. Baltimore: Johns Hopkins University Press, 2004.

Onwuachi, P. Chike. "Identity and Black Power." *Negro Digest* 16(March 1967): 31–37.

Orfield, Gary, and Chungmei Lee. "*Brown* at 50: King's Dream or *Plessy's* Nightmare?" Cambridge, MA: Civil Rights Project, Harvard University, 2004.

Orfield, Gary, David J. Losen, Johanna Wald, and Christopher B. Swanson, eds. *Losing Our Future: How Minority Youth Are Being Left Behind in the Graduation Rate Crisis*. Washington, DC: Urban Institute, 2004.

Pacion, Stanley. "Still Soul on Ice." *Dissent* 15(1969): 310, 313–315.

Page, Scott. *The Difference: How the Power of Diversity Creates Better Groups, Firms, Schools, and Societies,* New ed. Princeton, NJ: Princeton University Press, 2008.

Park, Robert. *Race and Culture*. Glencoe, IL: The Free Press, 1950.

Patterson, Orlando. "Race, Gender, and Liberal Fallacies." *New York Times* (October 20, 1991): 2.

Payne, Charles M. *I've Got the Light of Freedom: The Organizing Tradition and the Mississippi Freedom Struggle.* Berkeley: University of California Press, 2007.

Peeks, Edward. *The Long Struggle for Black Power.* New York: Charles Scribner's Sons, 1971.

Peller, Gary. "The Classical Theory of Law." *Cornell Law Review* 73(1988): 300–309.

———. "Creation, Evolution and the New South." *Tikkun* 2(November–December 1987): 72–76.

———. "The Metaphysics of American Law." *California Law Review* 73(1985): 1151–1290.

———. "Neutral Principles in the 1950s." *University of Michigan Journal of Law Reform* 21(1988): 561–622.

———. "Reason and the Mob: The Politics of Representation." *Tikkun* 2(July–August 1987): 28–31.

———. "A Subversive Strand of the Warren Court." *Washington & Lee Law Review* 59(2002): 1141.

Pinkney, Alphonso. *Black Americans.* Englewood Cliffs, NJ: Prentice Hall, 1969.

———. *Red, Black, and Green: Black Nationalism in the United States.* New York: Cambridge University Press, 1976.

Poinsett, Alex. "Where Are the Revolutionaries?" *Ebony* (February, 1976): 84–92.

Ponton, Mungo M. *The Life and Times of Henry M. Turner.* New York: Negro Universities Press, 1970.

Posner, Richard. "The *Defunis* Case and the Constitutionality of Preferential Treatment of Racial Minorities." *Supreme Court Review* (1974). Reprinted in *Affirmative Action and the Constitution,* Vol. 1, edited by Gabriel Chin, 249–280. New York: Garland, 1998.

Post, Robert. "Introduction: After *Bakke.*" In *Race and Representation: Affirmative Action,* edited by Robert Post and Michael Rogin, 13–28. New York: Zone Books, 1998.

Poussaint, Alvin F., "The Negro American: His Self-Image and Integration." *Journal of the National Medical Association* 58(1966): 419.

Powledge, Fred. *Black Power, White Resistance: Notes on the New Civil War.* Cleveland: World Publishing Co., 1967.

Quinn, Olive W. "The Transmission of Racial Attitudes Among White Southerners." *Social Forces* 33(October, 1954): 41–47.

Redkey, Edwin S. *Black Exodus.* New Haven, CT: Yale University Press, 1969.

Reed, Adolph, Jr. "All for One and None for All." *The Nation* (January 28, 1991): 86–92.

Reissman, Frank. *The Culturally Deprived Child*. New York: Harper, 1962.

Relyea, Harold C. "Black Power as an Urban Ideology." *Education Digest* 35(February 1970): 46–49.

Report of the National Advisory Commission on Civil Disorders. New York: Bantam, 1968.

Rist, Ray C. *The Invisible Children: School Integration in American Society*. Cambridge, MA: Harvard University Press, 1978.

Robinson, Armstead L., Craig C. Foster, and Donald H. Ogilvie. *Black Studies in the University*. New Haven, CT: Yale University Press, 1969.

Robinson, Dean E. *Black Nationalism in American Politics and Thought*. New York: Cambridge University Press, 2001.

Robinson, Randall. *The Debt: What America Owes to Blacks*. New York: Dutton, 2000.

Rojas, Fabio. *From Black Power to Black Studies: How a Radical Social Movement Became an Academic Discipline*. Baltimore: Johns Hopkins University Press, 2007.

Rosenfeld, Michael. *Affirmative Action and Justice*. New Haven, CT: Yale University Press, 1991.

Ross, Andrew. *No Respect: Intellectuals and Popular Culture*. New York: Routledge, 1989.

Rothschild, Mary A. *A Case of Black and White: Northern Volunteers and Southern Freedom Summers, 1964–1965*. Westport, CT: Greenwood Press, 1982.

Rudman, Laurie A., Richard D. Ashmore, and Melvin L. Gary. "'Unlearning' Automatic Biases: The Malleability of Implicit Prejudice and Stereotypes." *Journal of Personality & Social Psychology* 81(2001): 856–868.

Rustin, Bayard. "'Black Power' and Coalition Politics." In *Commentary* (September 1966): 35.

———. "Separate Is Not Equal." In *Black Protest Thought in the Twentieth Century*, edited by August Meier and Elliot Rudwick, 622. Indianapolis, IN: Bobbs-Merrill Co., 1971.

Sabbagh, Daniel. *Equality and Transparency: A Strategic Perspective on Affirmative Action in American Law*. New York: Palgrave Macmillan, 2007.

Salend, Spencer J. *Creating Inclusive Classrooms: Effecting and Reflective Practices*. 4th ed. Upper Saddle River, NJ: Merrill, 2001.

Sales, William W. *From Civil Rights to Black Liberation: Malcolm X and the Organization of Afro-American Unity*. Boston: South End Press, 1994.

Sartre, Jean-Paul. *Existentialism Is a Humanism*. Translated by Carol Macomber. New Haven, CT: Yale University Press, 2007.

Scheer, Robert, ed. *Eldridge Cleaver, Post-Prison Writings and Speeches*. New York: Random House, 1969.

Schiff, Martin. "Reverse Discrimination Re-Defined as Equal Protection: The Orwellian Nightmare in the Enforcement of Civil Rights Laws." *Harvard Journal of Law and Public Policy* 8(1985): 627–686.

Scott, Nathan A., Jr. "The New *Trahison Des Clercs*: Reflections on the Present Crisis in Humanistic Studies." *Virginia Quarterly Review* 62(Summer 1986): 402–421.

Scott, Robert L., and Wayne Brockriede, eds. *The Rhetoric of Black Power*. New York: Harper & Row, 1969.

Self, Robert. *American Babylon: Race and the Struggle for Postwar Oakland.* Princeton, NJ: Princeton University Press, 2003.

Sen, Amartya. *Identity and Violence: The Illusion of Destiny.* New York: W. W. Norton & Co., 2006.

Shapiro, Thomas M. *The Hidden Cost of Being African-American: How Wealth Perpetuates Inequality.* New York: Oxford University Press, 2005.

Sheatsley, Paul B. "White Attitudes toward the Negro." In *The Negro American,* edited by Talcott Parsons and Kenneth B. Clark, 303–324. Boston: Houghton Mifflin, 1966.

Shelby, Tommy. *We Who Are Dark: The Philosophical Foundations of Black Solidarity.* Cambridge, MA: Verso, 2005.

Sherrill, Robert. "Birth of a (Black) Nation." *Esquire* (January 1969): 70.

Shibutani, Tamotsu, and Kian M. Kwan. *Ethnic Stratification: A Comparative Approach.* New York: Macmillan, 1965.

Silberman, Charles E. *Crisis in Black and White.* New York: Random House, 1964.

———. *Crisis in the Classroom: The Remaking of American Education.* New York: Random House, 1970.

Simpson, George, and J. Milton Yinger. *Racial and Cultural Minorities: An Analysis of Prejudice and Discrimination.* 5th ed. New York: Plenum, 1985.

Singer, Joseph. "Legal Realism Now." *California Law Review* 76(1988): 465–544.

Sitkoff, Harvard. *The Struggle for Black Equality, 1954–1980.* New York: Hill & Wang, 1981.

Slack, Alison T. "Female Circumcision: A Critical Appraisal." *Human Rights Quarterly* 10(1988): 439–486.

Smock, Raymond W. *Booker T. Washington: Black Leadership in the Age of Jim Crow.* Chicago: Ivan R. Dee, 2009.

Sobran, Joseph. "Book Review: *Plural but Equal: Blacks and Minorities in America's Plural Society.*" *National Review* (September 11, 1987): 64.

Sokol, Jason. *There Goes My Everything: White Southerners in the Age of Civil Rights, 1945–1975.* New York: Knopf, 2006.

Sowell, Thomas. *Black Education: Myths and Tragedies.* New York: David McKay
Co., 1972.
———. *Civil Rights: Rhetoric or Reality.* New York: Harper Perennial, 1984.
———. *Race and Culture: A World View.* New York: Basic Books, 1994.
Stampp, Kenneth M. *The Peculiar Institution: Slavery in the Antebellum South.*
New York: Vintage, 1956.
Stangor, Charles, ed. *Stereotypes and Prejudice: Essential Readings.* Levittown,
PA: Psychology Press, 2001.
Staples, Robert. *Introduction to Black Sociology.* New York: McGraw-Hill,
1976.
———. "What Is Black Sociology? Toward a Sociology of Black Liberation."
In *The Death of White Sociology,* edited by Joyce A. Ladner, 163–168. New
York: Random House, 1973.
Steele, Shelby. *The Content of Our Character: A New Vision of Race in America.*
New York: St. Martin's Press, 1990.
Stephan, Walter G., and James A. Banks. *Reducing Prejudice and Stereotyping in
Schools.* New York: Teachers College Press, 1999.
Stone, Chuck. "The National Conference on Black Power." In *The Black Power
Revolt,* edited by Floyd B. Barbour, 189. Boston: Sargent, 1968.
Stoper, Emily. *The Student Non-Violent Coordinating Committee: The Growth of
Radicalism in a Civil Rights Organization.* New York: Carlson, 1989.
Strauss, David. "Discriminatory Intent and the Taming of *Brown.*" *University of
Chicago Law Review* 56(1989): 935–1015.
Strout, Cushing, and David I. Grossvogel, eds. *Divided We Stand: Reflections on
the Crisis at Cornell.* New York: Doubleday, 1970.
Sugrue, Thomas J. *Sweet Land of Liberty: The Forgotten Struggle for Civil Rights
in the North.* New York: Random House, 2008.
Sullivan, Patricia. *Lift Every Voice: The NAACP and the Making of the Civil Rights
Movement.* New York: New Press, 2009.
Tabb, William K. *The Political Economy of the Black Ghetto.* New York: W. W.
Norton & Co., 1970.
———. "Race Relations Models and Social Change." *Social Problems* 18(1971):
431–444.
Taylor, Edward, David Gillborn, and Gloria Ladson-Billings, eds. *Foundations of
Critical Race Theory in Education.* New York: Routledge, 2009.
Taylor, Ula Y. "Read[ing] Men and Nations: Women in the Black Radical Tradi-
tion." *Souls: A Critical Journal of Black Politics, Culture and Society* 1(Fall
1999): 72–80.
Terrill, Robert. *Malcolm X: Inventing Radical Judgment.* Lansing: Michigan
State University Press, 2004.

Theoharis, Jeanne, and Komozi Woodard. *Freedom North: Black Freedom Struggles Outside the South, 1940–1980*. New York: Palgrave Macmillan, 2003.

Thernstrom, Stephan, and Abigail Thernstrom. *America in Black and White: One Nation, Indivisible*. Cambridge, MA: Harvard University Press, 1998.

Thomas, Kendall. "'Ain't Nothin' Like the Real Thing': Black Masculinity, Gay Sexuality and the Jargon of Authenticity." In *Traps: African American Men on Gender and Sexuality*, edited by Rudolph P. Byrd and Beverly Guy-Sheftall, 327–341. Bloomington: Indiana University Press, 2001.

Troy, Tevi. *Intellectuals and the American Presidency: Philosophers, Jesters, or Technicians?* Lanham, MD: Rowman & Littlefield, 2002.

Turner, James. "Black Nationalism: The Inevitable Response." *Black World* (January 1971): 4–8.

———. "Black Students and Their Changing Perspective." *Ebony* (August 1969): 135.

Tushnet, Mark V. *The NAACP's Legal Strategy against Segregated Education, 1925–1950*. 2nd ed. Chapel Hill: University of North Carolina Press, 2005.

Ullman, Victor. *Martin R. Delany: The Beginnings of Black Nationalism*. Boston: Beacon Press, 1971.

Unger, Roberto Mangabeira. *The Critical Legal Studies Movement*. Cambridge, MA: Harvard University Press, 1983.

———. *Law in Modern Society: Toward a Criticism of Social Theory*. New York: The Free Press, 1976.

U.S. Bureau of Justice Statistics. "Jail Incarceration Rates by Race and Ethnicity, 2000–2009." Available at http://bjs.ojp.usdoj.gov/content/pub/pdf/pim09st.pdf (accessed on April 18, 2010).

Valdes, Francisco, Jerome Culp, and Angela P. Harris, eds. *Crossroads, Directions, and a New Critical Race Theory*. Philadelphia: Temple University Press, 2002.

Van Alstyne, William. "Rites of Passage: Race, the Supreme Court, and the Constitution." *University of Chicago Law Review* 46(1979): 775–810.

Van Ausdale, Debra, and Joe R. Feagin. *The First R: How Children Learn Race and Racism*. Lanham, MD: Rowman & Littlefield, 2001.

Van DeBurg, William L., ed. *Modern Black Nationalism: From Marcus Garvey to Louis Farrakhan*. New York: NYU Press, 1997.

———. *New Day in Babylon: The Black Power Movement and American Culture, 1965–1975*. Chicago: University of Chicago Press, 1992.

Vincent, Theodore. *Black Power and the Garvey Movement*. Berkeley, CA: Ramparts Press, 1971.

Wagstaff, Thomas. *Black Power: The Radical Response to White America*. Glencoe, IL: Glencoe Press, 1969.

Walker, Clarence E. *We Can't Go Home Again: An Argument about Afrocentrism.* London: Oxford University Press, 2000.

Wallenstein, Peter. "Black Southerners and Nonblack Universities: The Process of Desegregating Southern Higher Education, 1935–1965." In *Higher Education and the Civil Rights Movement: White Supremacy, Black Southerners, and College Campuses,* edited by Peter Wallenstein, 17–59. Gainesville: University Press of Florida, 2007.

Walzer, Michael. *Spheres of Justice.* New York: Basic Books, 1983.

Washington, Booker T. *The Future of the American Negro.* Boston: Small, Maynard & Co., 1899.

———. *Up from Slavery.* New York: Doubleday, Page & Co., 1901.

Wasserstrom, Richard A. "Racism, Sexism and Preferential Treatment: An Approach to the Topics." *UCLA Law Review* 24(1977): 581–622.

Watkins, S. Craig. *Hip Hop Matters: Politics, Pop Culture, and the Struggle for the Soul of a Movement.* Boston: Beacon, 2006.

Webb, Clive, ed. *Massive Resistance: Southern Opposition to the Second Reconstruction.* New York: Oxford University Press, 2005.

Wechsler, Herbert. "Killers of the Dream." *Progressive* (December, 1966), 12.

———. "Toward Neutral Principles of Constitutional Law." *Harvard Law Review* 73(1959): 1–35.

Weisbrot, Robert. *Freedom Bound: A History of America's Civil Rights Movement.* New York: W. W. Norton & Co., 1990.

Welner, Kevin, and Carol C. Burris. "Alternative Approaches to the Politics of Detracking." *Theory into Practice* 45(2006): 90–99.

West, Cornel. *Prophesy Deliverance! An Afro-American Revolutionary Christianity.* Louisville, KY: Westminster John Knox Press, 2002.

———. *Race Matters.* New York: Basic Books, 1993.

White, John. *Black Leadership in America, 1895–1968.* London: Longman, 1985.

White, Walter. "Segregation: A Symposium." *The Crisis* 41(March 1934): 80–81.

Whitman, Alden. "Obituary: Earl Warren, 83, Who Led High Court in Time of Vast Social Change, Is Dead." *New York Times,* July 10, 1974.

Whitten, Norman E., and John F. Szwed, eds. *Afro-American Anthropology: Contemporary Perspectives.* New York: The Free Press, 1970.

Wilkins, Roy. "Whither Black Power?" *The Crisis* 73(1966): 353–354.

Wilkinson, J. Harvie, III. *From Brown to Bakke: The Supreme Court and School Integration: 1954–1978.* Oxford: Oxford University Press, 1979.

Williams, Dana, and Sandra Shannon, eds. *August Wilson and Black Aesthetics.* New York: Palgrave Macmillan, 2004.

Williams, Hettie V. *We Shall Overcome to We Shall Overrun: The Collapse of the Civil Rights Movement and the Black Power Revolt (1962–1968)*. Lanham, MD: University Press of America, 2009.

Williams, Johnny E. *African American Religion and the Civil Rights Movement in Arkansas*. Jackson: University Press of Mississippi, 2003.

Williams, Juan. *Enough: The Phony Leaders, Dead-End Movements, and Culture of Failure That Are Undermining Black America, and What We Can Do About It*. New York: Crown, 2006.

———. *Eyes on the Prize: America's Civil Rights Years, 1954–1965*. New York: Penguin Books, 1987.

Williams, Patricia. "The Obliging Shell: An Informal Essay on Formal Equal Opportunity." *Michigan Law Review* 87(1989): 2128.

Williams, Robert F., Martin Luther King, Jr., and Truman Nelson. *Negroes with Guns*. New York: Marzani & Munsell, 1962.

Williams, Robert L. "The BITCH-100: A Culture Specific Test." Presented at the American Psychological Association Annual Convention, Honolulu, September 1972. Available at http://www.eric.ed.gov:80/PDFS/ED070799.pdf.

Wills, Richard W. *Martin Luther King, Jr., and the Image of God*. New York: Oxford University Press, 2009.

Wilson, Jeremiah Moses, ed. *Classical Black Nationalism: From the American Revolution to Marcus Garvey*. New York: NYU Press, 1996.

Wilson, William J. *The Declining Significance of Race: Blacks and Changing American Institutions*. Chicago: University of Chicago Press, 1978.

———. *Power, Racism, and Privilege: Race Relations in Theoretical and Sociohistorical Perspectives*. New York: Macmillan, 1973.

Winbush, Raymond A., ed. *Should America Pay? Slavery and the Raging Debate over Reparations*. New York: Amistad, 2003.

Wirth, Louis. "The Problem of Minority Groups." In *The Science of Man in the World Crisis*, edited by Ralph Linton, 347–372. New York: Columbia University Press, 1945.

Wolfe, Tom. *Radical Chic & Mau-Mauing the Flak Catchers*. New York: Farrar, Straus and Giroux, 1970.

Woodard, Komozi. *A Nation within a Nation: Amiri Baraka (Leroi Jones) & Black Power Politics*. Chapel Hill: University of North Carolina Press, 1999.

Woodward, C. Vann. *The Strange Career of Jim Crow*. New York: Oxford University Press, 1958.

Wright, Nathan. *Black Power and Urban Unrest: Creative Possibilities*. New York: Hawthorn Books, 1967.

Wright, Richard. *Black Power: A Record of Reactions in a Land of Pathos*. New York: Harper, 1954.

Young, Nigel. *An Infantile Disorder? The Crisis and Decline of the New Left.* London: Routledge & Kegan Paul, 1977.

Zigler, Edgar, and Jeanette Valentine, eds. *Project Head Start: A Legacy of the War on Poverty.* New York: The Free Press, 1979.

Zinn, Howard. *SNCC: The New Abolitionists.* Boston: Beacon Press, 1965.

Index

accommodationism, 54, 55, 56–57, 58, 59, 60, 61, 63, 170n

affirmative action, xiii, 2, 9, 45, 46, 51–52, 117; academic support and opposition to among academics, 153n; Black nationalist perspective of, 35, 37; legal debate, 72, 93–95, 115; social debate, xiii, 9–11, 17; and the Supreme Court, 154n

African American Studies, 30, 31, 39, 176n

Afro-centric, 14, 65, 100, 107, 121, 132, 172–173n, 176n, 184n

Albany campaign, 21

alienation, 25, 38, 44, 134, 148

American Communist Party, 192–193n

apartheid (American), xii, 4, 10, 11, 14, 22, 55, 57, 71, 75, 92, 109, 130

assimilation, xi, 19, 29, 31, 33, 51, 53, 56, 59–60, 62, 67, 114, 118, 131, 159n

"Back to Africa" program, 48, 56, 171n

Balkin, Jack, 71–72

Baraka, Amiri, 20

Benda, Julien, 139

"benign neglect," ix, xiv, 152n

bias, 4, 5–6, 8, 9, 13, 32; and public education, 16, 17, 18, 29, 119; in sociological research, 33

The Bell Curve: Intelligence and Class Structure in American Life (Herrnstein and Murray), 117

"Beloved Community," 43

Bennett, Lerone, 32

"BITCH" test (Black Intelligence Test of Cultural Homogeneity), 174n

Black bourgeoisie, 39, 107, 180n, 185n

Black churches, 24, 44, 107, 181n

Black Muslims, 20, 48, 60, 166n. *See also* Nation of Islam

Black nationalism, x, 19; and accommodationism, 56, 57; and affirmative action, 35; and the Black middle class, 60–61, 65; clash with integrationism, 51–70; and colonialism, 37–39, 58; community control over schools, 31; critique of integrationism, 23–32; and essentialism, 134; ideology, 20; influence within integrationist practice, 45–47; and integration, 49; and integrationism, 22, 23–24, 49, 67, 129; left-wing, 47–49; and legal

231

education, 35–36; marginalization of, 62; mass appeal of, 54; and militancy, 57, 65; and neo-colonialism, 38, 59; overlap with integrationism, 49–50; and patriarchy, 48; and racial justice, 46, 62; rejection of, 51–52, 63–70; as reverse racism, 51, 63, 67, 68, 69; right-wing, 47–49; and school integration, 26–32, 117–118; and social relations, 25; and sociology, 33; as traditionalism, 57; white embrace of, 68; white liberal reaction to, 66; and white radicals, 68–69; and white supremacy, 22–23, 63, 65
Black Panthers, x, 20, 41, 47, 48, 53, 62, 65, 113, 118, 132
Black Power, 20–23, 27, 36, 37, 43, 44, 49, 59, 64; Conference, 21; denouncers of, 52–53; integrationist critique of, 22–23; and Martin Luther King, Jr., 43; as reverse racism, 22, 51; slogan, 20–22, 52, 53
Black sexuality, 33–34, 66–67, 142, 147
Black student underachievement, 116–118
Brandeis, Louis, 80
Brennan, William J., 87
Brest, Paul, 93, 94, 97
Brown v. Board of Education, ix, xiv, 10, 12, 71–90; as cultural symbol, 97–98; and functionalism,76–77; and integrationism, 72; and judicial activism, 79–84, 86; legal controversy of, 77–78; and race consciousness, 98; Southern enforcement of, 108, 126
Browne, Robert S., 19, 27, 31, 118

capitalism, Black, 49
Carmichael, Stokely, 20, 21, 26, 27, 31, 38, 41, 47, 113, 118
centralism, 16, 17, 24
Christianity, 43

City of Richmond v. Croson, 152n, 154n, 198n
civil rights, 2, 21; linear evolution of, 1; nationalist view of, 45
Civil Rights Act, 21
civil rights movement, 42, 43, 44, 57, 86; polarization within, 21
Clark, Kenneth, 22, 118
class, ix, x, xii, xiv, 10, 16, 20, 26, 27, 28, 29, 31, 33, 38, 39, 45, 49, 52–54, 60–66, 70, 103–105, 110, 116–118, 126, 139–140, 143, 147
class rationalization, 33
Cleaver, Eldridge, x, 20, 33–34, 65
collectivism, xiii, 26, 42–43, 131
colonialism, 37–39, 58; academic, 33
colorblindness, 9, 45, 72, 88; contemporary triumph of, 90; rejection of, 97, 114
community control, 20, 24, 39; over police 39, 94; over schools 27, 30–31,175
confrontationalism, 59
Congress of Racial Equality (CORE), 20, 58, 61, 64; exclusion of whites from, 64; and nationalist drift, 61
Cornell University, 176n
Cosmopolitan, xi, 47
counter-majoritarianism, 79
Crenshaw, Kimberlé, 151n, 157n, 158n, 174n, 200n
Creole, 47, 183n
The Crisis (NAACP publication), 22, 56
Critical Legal Studies, 151n, 199n
Critical Race Theory, 151n
Cruse, Harold, x, 20, 27, 30, 31, 39, 55, 64, 132; on Black nationalism, 61–62, 64–65; on colonialism, 37
Cuffe, Paul, 164n
Cultural Deprivation Theory, 116, 118; and school integration, 117
cultural heritage, 2, 19, 26, 37, 48, 51
cultural imperialism, 99–103

About the Author

Gary Peller is a professor of law at Georgetown University. He teaches and writes in the areas of constitutional law, contracts, torts, and legal history.